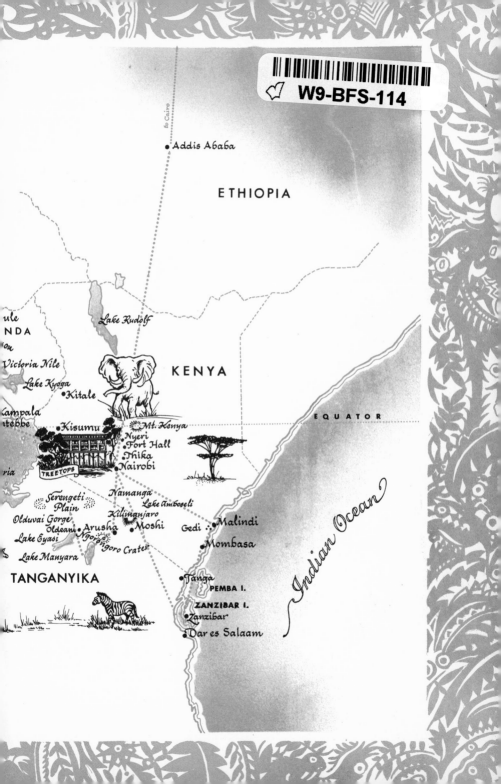

W9-BFS-114

to Cairo

●Addis Ababa

ETHIOPIA

ule
NDA
on
Victoria Nile
Lake Kyoga
Kampala
ntebbe
ria

●Kisumu

Lake Rudolf

KENYA

●Kitale

☼ Mt. Kenya
●Nyeri
Fort Hall
●Thika
●Nairobi

EQUATOR

TREETOPS

Serengeti
Plain
Olduvai Gorge
Oldeani●
Lake Eyasi
Lake Manyara

Namanga
●Lake Amboseli
Kilimanjaro
●Arusha ●Moshi
N'goro
goro Crater

Gedi ⦂. ●Malindi

●Mombasa

TANGANYIKA

Indian Ocean

●Tanga
PEMBA I.

ZANZIBAR I.
●Zanzibar

●Dar es Salaam

BOOKS BY ILKA CHASE

Elephants Arrive at Half-Past Five

The Carthaginian Rose

Three Men on the Left Hand

The Island Players

New York 22

Free Admission

I Love Miss Tilli Bean

In Bed We Cry

Past Imperfect

Always in Vogue (with Edna Woolman Chase)

Elephants Arrive at Half-Past Five

ILKA CHASE

Elephants Arrive
at
Half-Past Five

PHOTOGRAPHS BY NORTON BROWN

Doubleday & Company, Inc.
GARDEN CITY, NEW YORK
1963

To the animals of Africa, to animals everywhere,
who evoke compassion and delight and who restore to us
the old lost priceless sense of wonder.

Contents

Elephants Arrive at Half-Past Five

New York—Paris—Rome

THE CURIOSITY EVOKED by hearsay is potent, and from time immemorial travelers' tales have sped other travelers on their way. Listeners, gull or skeptic, doubtless hung upon the words of members of Paleolithic tribes who ventured across the river and beyond the hill and recounted the marvels of outer space.

Fired by their stories, the listeners set forth in their turn to see the world that lay beyond their familiar forest glade.

Hearing of wonders was tantalizing enough but with the advent of the printing press the fat was in the fire.

Generations yet unborn were destined to read of distant lands and to follow the four winds around the globe; to see for themselves what others had lauded. Sometimes to agree, sometimes to disagree. Violently.

I suppose anyone who has ever written a travel book has had the experience of being accosted by a reader with blood in his eye and a lawsuit in his voice. "*You* wrote that such and such a place was romantic. *You* said that there the food was good and the natives hospitable. Well, *we* didn't find it so!" The implication is crystalline: "Give us back our money."

Yet even if one has felt that way oneself, the next travel book dissipates the sentiment. "*This* one," we say, "sounds like our kind." My husband's and my trip to Africa was inspired by reading and by our love for animals. Since others may also find pleasure in them, I append in the back of this one a list of the books that whetted our appetites.

Having absorbed them, we were about to burst. "We've read enough," we cried. "Let's go!" Go? To Africa? What had we said? Like stout Cortez and his little band, we gazed at each other with a wild surmise but there are a few questions in this world to which, once posed, an affirmative answer is mandatory and that was one of them.

The decision made, the old familiar pattern began to emerge: financial juggling and visits to the offices of the American Express Company to set the wheels rolling. We were to find that an African journey required a good bit of time for the mysterious performance known as processing.

In my last travel book, *The Carthaginian Rose,* I inserted Traveler's Tips which readers have told me they found useful. They are repeated in the back of this book and I shall add here and there anything we learned from experience on our African junket that may prove helpful to others. One thing does occur to me:

Traveler's Tip No. 1. When sighting Africa, especially if safari-minded, give your travel agency enough leeway to plan properly so that your reservations at lodges or campsites may be confirmed. They are smaller and more primitive than conventional hotels and accommodations are limited. If you intend to shoot you will want to be sure to have lined up a good professional hunter who will act as your guide.

Unlike the venturesome Stuart Cloetes who are continually circling the globe and who prefer to arrive blind, so to speak, in new countries, Norton and I are all for informing ourselves, to as great an extent as is practical, on the history and people of the lands we are going to visit. Even with good will, we're not likely to be saturated with knowledge since we don't have the time to devote to study. We're too busy earning the money to go.

It did seem, however, that when visiting Africa a few words

of Swahili might not come amiss, despite the assurances of those who had never been there that everybody in East Africa speaks English. I was willing to believe that many Africans would speak better English than I would Swahili but it seemed reasonable to suppose we might occasionally run into untutored characters with whom we would want to communicate.

With this in mind, I called Berlitz. Did they have a course in Swahili and what did it cost? Well sir, they had a dandy and it could be mine for only $983. Murmuring that there had doubtless been some misapprehension, I only wanted to take lessons, not bring over a private tutor from Africa and pay his expenses, I hung up. It seemed more prudent to expend the money on the trip and hope to communicate by winsome charm and pantomime once we got there.

I did buy some language records for pronunciation and inflection, and although I didn't have much time to absorb them they were helpful. I also got a *Teach Yourself Swahili* book. The first couple of lessons are child's play. "I'll be chattering in a week," you think, but then the M and N classes begin, and tenses and places and, unlike German and French, there is nothing to relate to. . . . I grew more monosyllabic with every page.

What I could grasp was basic stuff: knives and baskets and the bad snake and the old man and his wives in the village. There were also a good many references to the spear of the cook and to the food he prepared, which, for the most part, was not good. That last bit was prophetic.

I have mentioned books read. There remained the problem of one to be written. Once an author comes up with a travel book, his, and quite possibly his readers', goose is cooked. Never again does he take a trip simply for the the trip's sake. Those carefree days are gone. Now everything becomes material or—that odious word—copy. Also, one hopes, tax-deductible. However, it is not quite so slick and opportunistic as it sounds. What happens, I think, is that if you enjoy travel you are eager to tell everybody about your great adventure. The writer quite genuinely wishes the reader were there, since, if he is reading the book, the chances are he is the sort of person who would enjoy the experience too.

I sensed an African book coming on and I was prepared. I had a supply of stiff-covered composition books, the kind children use in school, in which to keep my notes. Eying them one evening, my doctor husband asked what I had in mind. He asked in the tone of one who knows he isn't going to put much stock in the answer.

"They're my notebooks," I explained. "I have others too, little ones that fit into my pockets, and I'll write as we go along."

He looked at me incredulously. "In a Land Rover?"

"Why not?"

He sighed. Sometimes our relationship is like that of George and Gracie of blessed memory; but the obtuseness which, in Miss Allen, seemed so endearing on radio and television can, in reality, become quite trying to one's own particular George Burns.

"Sweetie," the man explained, "writing in a car is bad enough. In a *Land Rover* in the *bush* the going is rough. You'll never make head or tail of your notes." He refrained from adding what he knew to be true: that frequently notes taken at my own desk appear a day later to be so many hieroglyphics set down by an alien hand.

His information depressed me. About mechanical objects he's never wrong. He knows exactly how they're going to behave and how I'm going to react.

"But if a Land Rover's *that* rough, what shall I do? I'll be lost if I can't write."

"Not at all," he said crisply. "Do what you should have been doing long since. Get a tape recorder."

I suspect that to the uninitiated my "no" might have sounded a bit shrill but we were on familiar ground. I love that man but he is prone to gadgetitis. He, of course, claims there isn't a word of truth in the accusation, that it is simply his respect for the machine as an achievement of the human brain which I am not equipped to appreciate. He is quite right. All I say is, *he's* susceptible. Just let an object have gears or wheels, pistons or washers, and into his eyes comes the look of one besotted gazing at his love.

I was especially tender on the subject of the tape recorder because some years previously I had, at his instigation and against my better judgment, invested in a costly sort of super Dictaphone. It was to do the work of three secretaries. The only hitch was, it required three secretaries to understand it plus a graduate from M.I.T. to teach me to cope with it.

We were just recovering from that flare-up when a rich and grateful patient, thinking to please the physician who had so efficiently released him from misery, saw fit to bestow upon me a super de luxe Wollensak. Into it I was not only to dictate deathless prose but whole symphonies were to be recorded and played back for our delectation months after the great orchestra had disbanded. I wrestled for a while with this result of man's uncanny skill and then it too went into limbo to mellow, side by side, with the costly Audiograph. I do not say that these machines are not masterpieces of engineering. I simply say that they are not for me.

Nevertheless, the grain of sand had been imbedded in the oyster. The suggestion irritated but it stuck. If Norton was right about the jouncing, bouncing Land Rover, I was going to be in a bad way. Gradually my resistance began to disintegrate but I do not come of Quaker stock for nothing. Even their thrall, my husband, agreed that the two we had were too heavy to carry to Africa but if a new one was indicated let it be a bargain. I priced a couple and shivered, and then one day in a shopwindow I spotted a small, obviously lightweight recording instrument. I went in and asked how much. Thirty-five dollars. That sounded attractive but would it work? I called the good doctor. "If you like the looks of it, get it," he said. "What can you lose?" "Thirty-five dollars," I said. He laughed and left me. As I heard the receiver click into place I felt a little resentful. Why does he always let me make my own decisions?

There were other tape recorders in the shop and as he saw me eying them the proprietor hastened to extoll their charms and

the advantages they had over the little old thing that had lured
me in in the first place and that he had hymned with enthusiasm.
"Well, this one for instance," I said. "I suppose it *is* better than
that one. It looks more professional somehow. How much?"

"One hundred and thirty-six dollars."

"Isn't that rather high?"

"You get what you pay for," the man said. I got it and it was to
prove invaluable.

Our other pre-African purchases involved a journey to Abercrombie & Fitch. We assumed that in Nairobi there *would* be
stores catering to those going on safari, we weren't the only people since Dr. Livingstone who had had the urge to see Africa,
but the emporium of the Messrs. Abercrombie & Fitch is special
and the man doesn't breathe who can resist it. Norton goes there
under any pretext and, with Africa looming, he had a golden
alibi. Our basic requirements were boots and he was able to look
at me with a triumphant "I told you so" expression when the
salesman said that Mrs. Ernest Hemingway had just been in and
bought two pairs. Obviously all we professionals went there. For
the benefit of the uninitiated, safari boots are not actually boots.
They are more of a shoe made of a sort of rough reversed calf,
sandy in color; they come just above the anklebone and have
thick crepe rubber soles.

"What you want in the clothes line," Stuart Cloete, who has
spent years of his life in Africa, had said, "are neutral and earth
colors, something that blends with the landscape and won't attract the animals' attention. Olive drabs, browns, blue jeans—anything like that is fine."

I do not know if he has deeply considered whether or not animals are color-blind; there are advocates of both views, but even
if they cannot tell cerise from Kelly green, muted tones are best
in the bush, for the dust of East Africa is formidable, sifting into
eyes and teeth and hair, penetrating and permeating every crease
and pocket, and this even after what had been and continued to
be an unusually rainy season.

Traveler's Tip No. 2 Women! If going on safari, be sure to take scarves to wrap your head in.

Traveler's Tip No. 3 Camel's-hair brushes are invaluable for cleaning camera lenses. When not actually clicking, keep your cameras covered.

Basic clothing requirements attended to—we also bought slacks, shirts, and bush jackets—we turned our attention to cameras.

On our other trips, though heavily laden with photographic equipment, we had not taken movies. If you are going to be photographing the Parthenon, or Angkor Wat, well, they have been there a long time. The chances of their skittering about are slender but, with animals, movement is of the essence. We debated whether or not to buy a movie camera and then, one day, manna fell from heaven. About a ton of it, that was the trouble. Our friend John Rawlings, the celebrated photographer, fired by the thought of all that animation on the hoof that we would be seeing, lent Norton his own movie camera with telescopic lens. My husband accepted it with gratitude but it was so heavy that when we got to Paris, although feeling a bit sheepish, he decided to leave it behind.

Our date of departure was Monday, June 4, 1962. I had questioned a number of people about East African weather at that time of year and got a different answer from each of them, although the Americans to whom we spoke were firm in their conviction that the heat would be excessive.

"My God," they said, "Africa in June and July and *Egypt too?* You'll die."

My countrymen, I have noticed, usually do think that any foreign country one is going to in the summertime, with the possible exception of Scandinavia, is going to be almost unendurable because of heat. They should realize that very few places in the world—excluding perhaps the Gulf of Aden—are as bad as the eastern seaboard and the central plains of the United States in July and August. Once inured to the home climate, the American traveler may set blithely on his way; he has no place to go but up.

We ourselves were ready to take off but as our departure date drew near a wave of mounting uncertainty began to lap around us. Weeks before I had taken our passports to the American Express Company, who were to send them on to Washington for visas. Other times they had been returned to us long before we were due to leave. This time there seemed to be a hitch. About ten days before the fourth of June I began calling the office, and each time I was assured that there wasn't a thing in the world to worry about, they'd be there with time to spare. It became increasingly obvious that there was a schism between our idea of what was time to spare and that of American Express.

On the Friday before the Monday we were due to leave, I swept into the Fifth Avenue offices of the august company. "Well," I demanded, "how about it? Where are they, our passports?" It turned out that they were still in the Ethiopian Embassy in Washington. This triggered something of an explosion. "The *Ethiopian* Embassy, for God's sake! *That* little niggling country! I don't care if we *never* get there. We only thought it might be interesting to stop off since we have to be flying over it anyway to get to Cairo from Nairobi but to be held *up* by it! Do something, why don't you? Send a messenger to Washington to pick up the passports and bring them back here."

The gentleman assured me there was no need. "This is only Friday, Mrs. Brown, they're sure to be here in the morning mail on Monday."

"Are they being sent special delivery?"

"They don't have to be, there's the whole weekend in between. They'll be here, you'll see."

"I see," I said, "that there is no guaranty that they will be. They should have been here *days* ago. I would point out that the Air France plane leaves at 7 P.M. Monday evening."

"I know, I know," he said soothingly, "you go and have a nice weekend and don't worry."

Don't worry! And all the packing and all the farewells, not to mention that gone, anticlimatic feeling if we couldn't take off as planned. And supposing the passports didn't get back till Tuesday or Wednesday and we couldn't get places on the plane? A nice weekend!

Monday morning dawned clear and lovely, but I found small comfort in the June beauty. At nine-thirty I was on the phone. Well, no, the passports weren't actually there yet but then neither was the mail. On Monday delivery was usually a little late, ten or ten-thirty.

From the hairdressers I phoned at ten-thirty. No, but of course I had to realize that they had been sent by certified mail and that always took a little longer. Longer! Why not shorter? Naturally, the gentleman with whom I was dealing had not mentioned that fact to me on Friday. Not that he was entirely to blame, I suppose. Worse than a woman scorned is a woman trapped at home when she longs to be abroad.

At noon I called the doctor. "We've horsed around with this long enough," he said, "you'd better see if you can get hold of Howard Clark." Mr. Clark is the president of American Express and a delightful and able man. He is also a prolific one. Between them, via assorted marriages, he and his wife have nine children and Mr. Clark was in Connecticut at the graduation of one of them and was not expected in the office all day. His secretary, however, was able in her own right. "Don't give up hope," she said, "I'll put our trouble shooter onto it at once. The man is uncanny, what he can do, but it will probably be a little after two before I get back to you."

"The plane leaves at seven," I said faintly.

"Hold hard," she said.

At two forty-five she called. Mountains were moving, the trouble shooter was at the controls with rifles leveled. A car was coming to pick us up, we were to proceed to Rockefeller Center to the passport office. In Washington temporary emergency ones were being issued and the mails were being traced for our original ones, which would be forwarded to us in Paris. "If we ever get there," I thought.

Once in the passport office, it developed that I had to have more photographs. The doctor's were all right, but although I had three old ones they were all different. I had to have two alike. Leaving my husband holding the hand and taking the pulse of the young lady in charge of the teletype over which would come the Go signal from Washington, and whom, despite her professionalism, we had infected with something of our malaise, I fled to the lower depths to be photographed. "How long does it take to develop those libels?" I asked. "Forty-five minutes," the man said, "same for everybody. Good or bad, forty-five minutes." I glanced at my wrist watch. That would make it about four-fifteen. I went back up to the passport office. Nothing yet. We sat and waited, looking enviously at all the other people, each and every one of whom went out happily clutching an authentic, official, permanent passport. At four-fifteen I went back to the photographer. The art work was ready. I winced as I looked at it. There I was in horrid triplicate but at least I was legal.

I went back upstairs. Our young lady was coming out of the cubbyhole which housed our fate. "Nothing yet," she said brightly, "but I just know it's going to be all right." Norton and I smiled wanly. Belief in the supernatural has always seemed to us indicative more of credulity than of faith and we saw little reason to change our attitude.

At ten minutes to five she went to look at the teletype and darted out again. "Word has come through, you can go, you can go!" Speedy signing, numbers stamped, funny little sleazy passports thrust into our hands. We pirouetted from the window, reared, and were off. That was the last rapid action for the next two hours. It was now five o'clock, it was now the rush hour. The rush hour means there is no movement. On this beautiful June evening the Long Island Expressway was choked with cars bumper to bumper and it was only Monday, not even Friday. Swearing, groaning, our palms wet, we *crept* to Idlewild. But we made it. We checked in, we even had time for a much-needed drink before the flight was called. We drank to the trouble shooter and to the American Express Company. They had badly fumbled the ball, it was true, but they had retrieved it in the last minute of play and run ninety-nine yards for a touchdown and victory. We could afford a little magnanimity.

On the Air France plane, waiting for dinner to be served, we were given presents, including a good illustrated pamphlet on cooking and tidbits of perfume. The hostess also passed out the evening papers. In the *World-Telegram* was a column by Mr. Robert Ruark from which one might easily have concluded that the gutters of Nairobi were running blood. Norton and I looked at each other. "Well," he said, "you could write a piece about New York too and describe some of the goings on in Harlem and Central Park and it wouldn't make very reassuring reading. Let's not panic yet. We'll be seeing Stuart again in Paris and we hope Robert Ardrey in Rome. I'll be interested in their impressions." Robert Ardrey's *African Genesis,* which we had found scholarly in content and sprightly in style, was one of the books that had spurred us on, and when I learned that the Ardreys were living in Rome, I had written saying I hoped we might have the pleasure of meeting them there when we stopped off on our way to Nairobi.

Following Norton's sensible advice not to panic over a newspaper column, we ate an excellent dinner, drank delicious wine, and settled down for what remained of the six-and-a-half-hour flight.

Although East Africa was to be the highlight of our trip, as we would be landing in Paris anyway, we had decided to stop over for a few days. It is hard for me to imagine going to Europe and *not* stopping in Paris.

Flying over France, the countryside was lush and beautiful and as we neared the capital the little square stucco houses with their red tile roofs reminded me as always of a child's toy village.

At that early hour—6:40 A.M.—customs was non-existent. In fact, a rather grumpy, sleepy-eyed inspector waved us impatiently through the wicket with a "Come on, come on, what are we doing here?" expression that we found comical and a relief. We had nothing to declare but were charmed to save time.

We were staying with our friends the Geoffrey Parsons' and

arrived at the well-loved old house on the Quai d'Orléans to find everything normal: the elevator not working and Thérèse, the concierge, explaining that it was *most* unusual but this time the trouble was caused by those new people in the top-floor duplex. Ripping out the old boiserie and the bookshelves, workmen riding up and down all day with buckets and boards and plaster, it was an outrage but what could one expect?

For the student of French, after *"Passez-moi le pain, s'il vous plaît,"* and possibly *"Mais le vin, voyons!"* the most important phrase to master is *"L'ascenseur ne marche pas."* The French, a great race who have provided us with, among other scientific marvels, the dream airplane, the Caravelle, seem incapable of mastering either the elevator or the telephone system. Furthermore, a curious psychic net spreads across the land. The elevators are sensitive, with antennae pointing to stations and airports and harbors. They *know* when travelers will be arriving with luggage at the addresses where they are installed and *that* is the day they go on strike. *That* is the day they do not march. It is the hapless traveler who marches. In our case up five flights of stairs to the Parsons' apartment where, at that uncivilized hour, our hostess met us at the door in her dressing gown, coffee cup in hand.

Her welcome was warm if sleepy and we sat down to a feast of gossip and an excellent breakfast. As a matter of fact we placed particular emphasis on food during these four days and found out we had been wise to do so.

When going to East Africa it is advisable to cushion the culinary department at either end by good eating in Europe or possibly Hong Kong, for the food of Africa is one long dreary insult to the palate. Concentrate on the animals and birds and majesty of the countryside and think of something else at dinnertime.

One of our most delicious French meals we ate at the Coq Hardi at Bougival, where we participated in a photographic session with the Olivar de Araujos of Buenos Aires. Olivar was the proud owner of a new movie camera and posed us against the gold and bright blue ceramic roosters adorning the terraces and under an exquisite tree, its delicate lime-green leaves filtering sunshine, the negondo argenté.

By the time we sat down to luncheon the doctor had succumbed to the charm of the movie camera, an 8-millimeter affair, extremely simple, so he and Oliver claimed, to operate. Furthermore, it was light in weight. Compared to it, the sumptuous equipment of generous John Rawlings began to seem even more cumbersome. I could see my dear one's sales resistance crumbling. Like so many of us, the doctor is strong on thrift and economy until he sees something he wants. Then, obviously, there are all sorts of sound and practical reasons why it will be much cheaper, in the long run, to get it. Not cheaper than not getting it, but cheaper than yearning for it. That puts too much wear and tear on the nervous system.

In the end, it was Billie, Olivar's wife and a woman of fantastic generosity, who solved the problem. "Olivar, you know what we are going to do?" she cried. Inwardly Olivar may have winced but he has not lived with her all these years for nothing. "I know," he said. He even managed a smile. "Norton, you will take this camera. It is a bon voyage present from Billie and me. You are leaving tomorrow. I am staying and can easily get another."

"Olivar! We couldn't possibly, this is *far* too expensive a gift . . . we wouldn't dream . . . it's out of the question . . ." Three guesses how that argument turned out. Norton was enchanted but schizophrenic. It added that much more to our luggage.

Packing for Italy, we had one of those little domestic scenes to which travelers are prone. The doctor, I fancy, is not the only man who detests a lot of suitcases. Personally, I think he has a slight obsession about them. "When I board a plane I want my hands to be free," he cries, "free"—for all the world like some desperate East Berliner struggling to escape the wall.

"But, darling," I say, "we're traveling for two months," or three, or whatever it may be, "we've *got* to have clothes. I don't mind. I'll carry all the hand luggage. You just cope with checking the heavy pieces." In the end we compromised. "Compress, compress," had been his cry, but he finally did agree to take off with three suitcases instead of the two he had been advocating or the one he had obviously dreamed of.

With our considerably lightened load we set out for Orly and encountered a Vision. We were in one of those small downstairs waiting rooms from which one proceeds directly to the plane when she appeared, a statuesque Englishwoman with a brown face and dyed yellow hair. She was draped in a white lace sari, wearing white sandals, and carrying a beige topcoat, dressing case, recorder, and a large cellophane bag of artificial roses. Thus burdened, she was at a disadvantage when it came to hanging onto the sari, the upper part of which, swathed over a vague kind of camisole, kept slipping from her shoulder, conveying an effect of *déshabille* quite startling in an airport waiting room. She was being seen off by a young Indian who kissed her hand and bowed low when he left her. After he had gone she lighted a cigarette and sat smoking with her eyes closed, one hand to her brow, in a sort of yoga trance. We were enchanted. Who can match the English in eccentrics?

We had been eager to spend a few days in Rome, not only for its own sake but also because part of my family was there—the Bill Murrays and their two little girls. I was married to his father years ago when Bill was a child and I have always been devoted to him and, since his own marriage, to his wife and children. Thanks to the Air France trajectory—Paris, Rome, Cairo, Nairobi —matters had worked out very well.

We found the Murrays handsomely ensconced in a comfortable apartment with two maids. Doris said that life in Italy was expensive, that it cost them just about what it did in New York, but they had infinitely more space and service for the same price.

They welcomed us with a large cocktail party where our hope of meeting Robert Ardrey came true. His attractive wife, who did the animal illustrations for *African Genesis,* was with him, speaking in a British accent so precise as to seem foreign. She told me she was born in South Africa.

They were both at that moment advocates of a diet that caused the doctor, after they had left us and were mingling with other guests, to tap his forehead significantly but they were passionate about it. It was, it seems, the brain child of a man called Simeon, who claims to reproduce in the body, male as well as female, the conditions of pregnancy, except, I gather, no baby results. The theory was not clear to me but apparently you live on your own fat and thus reduce, although fundamentally I don't suppose it differs much from any other diet: you want to lose weight, you eat less.

With their backgrounds, the Ardreys were knowledgeable about Africa and articulate in their tale telling, notably so in a story of an encounter with a cobra. Like most first-time travelers to that vast continent, we were timid about the slitheries. "There are snakes, we presume?" we said tentatively. "Indeed yes." It seemed to me Mrs. Ardrey replied with undue relish but she had a tale to tell. One night she and Robert were dining in a very good hotel in the Congo but, with the exception of the proprietor and his wife, their state was solitary. It was during the Emergency. In Ireland they used to have the Trouble, in Africa the Emergency. The dining room was on the ground floor and they were in animated discussion when, looking up, what should they see oiling his way toward them but a great hissing cobra. The African waiters fled. The Ardreys apparently maintained their poise and the proprietor his presence of mind. He called for boiling water, which the boys brought in pails, gingerly setting them down just inside the door and ducking back into the kitchen.

The proprietor threw the water on the cobra to stun it and, as it made its ugly and agonized way along the wall, other boys leaned in from the outside and drove spears through its body. I make no bones of the fact that had I been present I would have been terrified and revolted, yet surely there must have been a more humane and equally effective way of destroying it. I am for winning the battle but torture of the enemy has always seemed to me repugnant. Of enemy animals, that is. My theory sometimes wavers where humans are involved. Some people obviously were born to be boiled in oil.

We spent four happy days with my "children," sight-seeing

and eating, and left Rome on a Tuesday evening around midnight.

While waiting at the airport for the Air France plane that would fly us to Nairobi, we studied one of our fellow passengers on a bench across the way. She was young, very black, wearing a scarf over her head, a khaki jacket, and a blue and white checked shirt. Her mouth hung open, her round eyes with their glistening china whites stared straight ahead, and on her widely spread knees she held a sleeping baby. Was she, we asked ourselves, ready for Uhuru? Ready or not, she would be getting it and, as the uninvolved, it behooved us to hold our peace and adopt a philosophic attitude of wait and see.

CHAPTER TWO

Nairobi — Treetops

THROUGH THE NIGHT HOURS we flew across the Mediterranean, skirting Greece and Crete, raising the northern coast of
Africa just before dawn. Looking sleepily from the window down
upon the dark earth below, I could discern the winding track of
the Nile. The Nile! The river that was old when mankind was
young. Pharaohs. Pyramids. Cleopatra. Serpent of. Elizabeth
Taylor. It was a pregnant moment. We started losing altitude and
shortly afterward set down at the Cairo airport.

As we had an hour before taking off on the last lap for Nairobi,
we walked through the warm humid darkness to the restaurant
in the hope of refreshment; coffee, and tea for me, or perhaps
fresh cold lemonade—that would be delicious. It would be but it
didn't exist. The restaurant was dingy and the tablecloths grimy.
The doctor, having barely closed an eye, was in a foul mood.
"This place is dirty," he said. I was feeling a bit short myself.
"You're not in an operating room," I said. "You can't expect anti-
sepsis. We'll doubtless see a lot of dirt before we're finished. You
might as well resign yourself." I felt realistic, sophisticated, and
smug but I think one must brace oneself for the Arab countries.
Mr. Clean is not their hero.

The Egyptian waiters who caught my eye afforded me considerable interest. They wore fezzes and lank, soiled café-au-lait-
colored robes—galabias—and looked like characters out of the
third road company of an old Schubert musical. One that had

been touring a long time and was tired. They gave no service. The only money we had with us was lire, which they took in their fingers, turning them over like monkeys, staring at them with distaste and handing them back. Around us at other tables passengers were getting waited on—with what were they paying? "We're fools," I said. "We should just have ordered and given them the lire when it came time to pay. They can get them changed here at the airport." Whether they could or not, they weren't for doing it and we regained the plane still thirsty and had to wait for breakfast to be served. The doctor was in favor of changing our itinerary on the spot and skipping Egypt on our return from East Africa. I clucked sympathetically but felt that by invoking the Taft-Hartley Act and allowing a cooling-off period he might be lured back to the site of the first civilization.

At about 11 A.M., nine hours out of Rome including the layover in Cairo, we landed in Nairobi. Right away it was exciting. The airport has a patio filled with strong, vivid tropical plants, photographs of big game, and zebra skins and spears on the walls. The effect is deliberate, I know, but it is also authentic.

As always on arrival in a new country, one's first impressions are inevitably formed on the ride from the airport. Our first impression of Africa was one of awe and a wonderful feeling of having come to the right place. That part of Kenya is a high flat plateau, the altitude of Nairobi is 5400 feet, and on either side the plains stretch away for miles. We felt a bit self-conscious at first about calling them the bush—it sounded theatrical. I rather favored veldt, but as everybody else refers to those vast open areas as bush we got around to it without too much difficulty. Bush grass is tawny in color and the flat-topped thorn trees are dark delicate silhouettes against the sky. Africa really looks exactly as it does in the movies and as it did in the *National Geographics* that were a classic feature of the dentist's waiting room in my childhood. I don't know what's got into dentists lately. Sophistication, I think, but something is missing. *Holiday* and *Vogue* and *Time* and *The New Yorker* . . . what kind of material is that to distract you from the ordeal ahead? I preferred the

Geographics, bursting with bush and naked natives, animals and waterfalls.

Nearing the city, one passes along Queen Elizabeth Way, a dual highway, the lanes separated by long beds of bright flowers. Although there are broad avenues, a few of them tree-lined, Nairobi itself is not a beautiful city. It has still, to some extent, the raw atmosphere of a frontier town: flat modern UN-like buildings, a few of them quite handsome, rising above rusty corrugated iron roofs.

We drew up in front of the New Stanley Hotel or, to be precise, in front of the Thorn Tree, a sidewalk café which is part of the hotel and through which one passes to reach the entrance. The Thorn Tree is nearly always crowded: with coffee and beer drinkers in the morning, cocktail drinkers before meals, and tea drinkers at every hour. They have cafeteria service too and we were told that the annual intake is very tidy indeed. It is amusing to sit there and watch the Land Rovers loading and unloading as travelers set forth on and return from safari.

Our rooms—and as we were in and out of the city so much we had several—were clean and comfortable with nice little balconies. While perhaps not as luxurious as the brochure implies, the New Stanley is efficiently run and Mr. Jack Block, the owner of the chain to which it belongs, is an experienced and accommodating hotelier.

Everybody who goes to Kenya eventually finds his way there and by this time the staff has become a little blasé. Before we left home we had been told by Peggy Harvey—the lady of cookbook fame—that Mary Hemingway would be in Nairobi at the same time we were. "She's a friend of mine," Peggy said. "Be sure and look her up." The Hemingway trail was getting hot. First Abercrombie & Fitch, then Peggy. In the course of our stay I did one day inquire if Mrs. Ernest Hemingway was in the hotel. The girl looked blank. "Mrs. Ernest Hemingway?" I sensed from her voice that she was innocent of the world of literature. "It's quite a famous name," I said hopefully. "I thought surely in Africa . . ." The girl shook her head. "Never heard of her." To our regret we did not meet Mrs. Hemingway in Africa—the pleasure came six months later in New York at a dinner party of Mrs. Harvey's.

Our first luncheon at the New Stanley was grim. The dining room is singularly gloomy and the meal was an introduction to what we were to experience throughout our stay in East Africa.

I do not condemn the British for their political and administrative shortcomings—at times they have been grossly unjust, show me the nation that hasn't—but by and large the evil they have done has been counterbalanced by the great good that has accrued to many countries under their colonization. What I cannot forgive is the fact that, generation after generation, they have gone clattering up and down the curve of the world imposing their fearful eating habits on the hapless natives of Africa and Asia who, in turn, perpetrate them on today's defenseless visitor. Brussels sprouts, the joint, and shape are now as indigenous to those exotic lands as they are to Birmingham and Liverpool.

In London and at the better inns around the English countryside there has been a great and sophisticated advance in eating habits in recent years. It has not reached the Commonwealth. In a land teeming with game and fowl, every sandwich made up for you by the hotels and lodges to take on a day's journey is composed of pork or ham. The odd thing is we never saw a pig the entire time we were there. They must have secret herds. Cans are *not* secret. *Everything* is tinned. And, as we were to discover, it is not necessary. Soil and climate are highly suited to agriculture, marvelous gardens and plantations do exist, but on a wholesale scale they have simply not got into the habit of eating fresh food.

What is curious about the New Stanley, since it must come from the same kitchen, is that while the dining-room food is so discouraging that of the grill is good. Some dishes indeed are delicious. The doctor especially enjoyed the oysters. We also found a very palatable South African wine for which we were grateful as imported French vintages are expensive. While we were enjoying it, however, friends told us a rather bloodcurdling tale of the system employed to produce it. The natives who work in the vineyards and bottling plants are apparently paid slave wages but given all the wine they can swallow so that they are in a perpetual state of semi-drunkenness. They do not revolt against their lot because of their befuddlement and addiction to the product. I cannot say whether or not this is true but it is the story that is making the rounds. Every time Norton and I took a swallow, we experienced a sense of guilt and used the coward's way out in self-extenuation. "There are only two of us, what we drink won't make any difference and we won't be here very long." We were ashamed but the wine was good and out in the bush we settled for chianti and salved our consciences.

Wearied by our journey, after our depressing luncheon we decided to nap a bit before setting out on our first adventure. Resting one's first day in a new country is always difficult but advisable when possible. About four o'clock we went down to meet Koske, who was to be our driver and guide on our various safaris. Koske, small, black, and intelligent, we fell in love with immediately. The car was something else again. We had been bragging happily at home about the rugged life upon which we were embarking. "Quite primitive really," we had said with a deprecating little laugh. "You have to love animals and adventure . . . be willing to take the rough with the smooth. Norton says those Land Rovers are *something*." Our friends had looked at us respectfully.

When one of the bellboys came up to us in the lobby and said, "Your car is waiting, Doctor," we hurried out. Koske introduced himself and pointed to our conveyance. Our jaws dropped. There at the curb, spick, span, and inviting, but not to us, was a dear little pale blue Chevrolet sedan. "Oh, Norton," I moaned, "no!" The blue baby from Detroit was a bitter comedown. The rugged life, the bush, the bouncing! Norton drew himself together and swallowed his own obvious disappointment. Koske was looking so pleased, it seemed only humane. "Well now, this is fine," the doctor said. "Looks very comfortable, but frankly we were expecting . . . I mean to say, in the bush, this is going to be effective?"

Koske's white teeth flashed. "Oh no, sir. When we start on safari day after tomorrow, Land Rover." He looked even more pleased. Our happy smiles equaled his own. "But this afternoon, to National Park just down the road."

That is one of the African fantasies. The Nairobi National Park, a forty-square-mile game reserve, *is* just down the road, about a ten-minute drive from the heart of town. You roll along a paved highway—the tarmac, as the British have it—turn off at a big rustic gate, pay ten shillings to the ranger at the ticket window, and enter wonderland.

On this great plain the same kind of animals whom, all one's life, one has seen in zoos and circuses and on cracker boxes roam free. There are no bars, no ditches or dikes or electrified wire; no whips or wooden chairs. It is the animals who are at home, humans are the intruders.

The first we saw were the antelope family, hundreds and hundreds of them, the most common creature—if one may use "common" in connection with so much grace and agility—in Africa. The Grant's gazelle has a lovely silvery sheen but our favorites were the gazelles of Mr. Thomson, small ginger-colored beasts with white bellies and a black line running from shoulder to rump, the males with very slender horns. Their brief black tails flick tirelessly back and forth like windshield wipers and they stare inquiringly and then scamper off, white scuts flashing in derision. Sometimes they spring through the tawny grass as though on pogo sticks. This is called stotting.

Other abundant citizens were the wildebeests or gnus, hymned by Flanders and Swann, fancied by crossword puzzle fans. We were to see thousands of them. They seem to be a cross between a moose, minus the great antlers, and a finely drawn buffalo, and they have cornsilk beards running from under their chins to their chests. They are gentle beasts who gaze at you with a puzzled but benign expression.

The wart hogs we found to be the comedians of the animal kingdom. Wart hogs should sue for libel. It is a terrible name and they are fine fellows with long square faces, small curling tusks, dark grayish hides, and thin tails, standing straight up with a pompon on the end, that move through the grass like the periscope of a swiftly knifing submarine. They are devoted family men and it is rare to see one by himself; the little woman and the kiddies are usually close at hand.

There were herds of playful zebra who butted each other gently and peered over each other's shoulders in the most engaging fashion. Nature has supplied a wonderfully protective camouflage for the babies, whose stripes blend with those of the mothers and others in the herd so that unless one is quite close and peering keenly they are invisible.

We were to do a good deal of peering in the course of our safaris, for while we have always felt we have reasonably good eyesight, we were to find that, compared to our driver, we were stone blind. Other people are contented with 20-20 vision. Koske had binoculars in his skull.

He would gaze for miles across the bush, which to us was as empty as the first morning of creation, and remark, "There's a Grant's gazelle" or "There's a hartebeest." For minutes we could see nothing, then, gradually, as we became a little more educated and began to know what we were looking for, we too could laboriously discern what had been obvious to him at a casual glance.

Our first giraffe, reward of the long peer, was lovely. There is something princess-like about giraffes, even the males. In movement mellifluous, the setting of their ears and horns makes them look as though they were wearing small diadems. They have sweeping maidenly lines and their aristocratic necks and loping walk remind me of the faery figures of a medieval tapestry. The giraffe as much as the unicorn is legendary, I sense a kinship between them. When they bend down their necks to drink they must also splay out their legs in order to get low enough to reach the water, and they do so with a curiously awkward, comical grace.

Easier to spot than the dappled giraffe are the baboons. Indeed one cannot escape them. The baboons are companionable thugs who hop onto the hoods of cars demanding handouts. We had no food to give them but in any event one is cautioned to treat them with aloof courtesy as their bonhomie is not guaranteed. One chap who seemed to find us *muy simpático* was lacking a paw, lost probably in battle over some ravishing damsel.

There are only three rules in the game reserves but they are stringent and stringently adhered to. The first, of course, is no guns. The other two are no noise (horn honking is taboo) and no getting out of cars.

Thanks to these wise precautions, the animals, especially in the Nairobi National Park where cars are a commonplace, have become very tame. It is perhaps disillusioning—few bared fangs or ripping claws—but you cannot have it both ways. Photography is encouraged and enthusiasts become quite dexterous in their gyrations as they lean from the windows, practically held by their feet, in order to get special shots without opening car doors and stepping to the ground.

The doctor is expert with a camera, so he was distressed and annoyed when he saw the results and felt that his first day's work was not up to his usual standard. I was a little disappointed myself but I was also touched. He is notably self-contained and I realized how excited he must have been. It is an exciting experience. There is something strange and marvelous about seeing so many kinds of animals living freely and peacefully together. Until, of course, the stomachs of the carnivores begin to rumble.

Any slaughter is brutal but in this respect animals are superior to man. They kill to eat. They do not devise obscene tortures or destroy for political aggrandizement. The period of terror of the animal being hunted is usually brief, his death swift and quickly forgotten by the herd.

The afternoon was wearing on and we were beginning to think that perhaps we would not witness the climax that day when we became aware of many cars converging on the same spot "*Simba?*" we asked excitedly, whipping out one of our three or four Swahili words. Koske nodded. "We go." He turned off the track and we went bumping across the bush to the spot where the cars were gathering, a small ravine choked with bushes and stunted trees. Maneuvering skillfully, he nosed a way to a vantage point and our delighted gaze fell upon the Prize. There, on a small hillock, lay a languorous lioness vastly indifferent to the press of cars around her. She blinked her eyes and occasionally gave a regal swish of her tail to the muted rapture of her camera-clicking votaries.

If you are hungry or in peril, shooting a magnificent creature is one thing, but simply to walk up to an animal who is doing you no harm and put a bullet into it is to me incomprehensible.

It is true that game must sometimes be shot in order to insure enough food to keep the herds intact but it should be done either by experienced zoologists or wardens who know which are the strongest and best animals to continue the strain or by hunters under their direction. Not by ignorant, trigger-happy nincompoops, calling themselves sportsmen, trying to prop up their sagging egos or compensate for impotence.

We watched our proud beauty for a long time, for even though we were to see many others our first free lioness was a memorable treat. We turned from her reluctantly only as darkness began to fall. We returned to the hotel and, having established Contacts in the hours since our arrival, decided on early bed so as to be rested for our first full African day.

While the New Stanley of course has electricity, the majority of the clientele is not of literary bent, feeling, understandably enough, that they don't have to go all the way to Africa to read a book. Probably for that reason, bedside lighting is sketchy. But for the benefit of those who must read regardless of their surroundings, I insert:

Traveler's Tip No. 4. Take a powerful flashlight with you, preferably one that will sit on a table. It will be handy for reading in bed or when writing and you'll need it in the bush anyway. Some of the camps have electricity but it is for the most part a courtesy term.

Traveler's Tip No. 5. Take matches. They are hard to come by in Europe, they are almost non-existent in Africa. You *can* buy them but they are never where you are and it's a nuisance.

When he heard we were going to Nairobi, our friend Leonard Astley-Bell of the Shell Oil Company had written a colleague in that city to be sure to look us up, and bright and early the next morning he did. The telephone bell pealed at eight o'clock. "Cooksey here," said a brisk British voice, "I've received Astley-Bell's letter. Can I be of help?" Though feeling sour at having been awakened, it turned out he could be. We had sent safari gear, books, heavy shoes, etc., by air freight before we left New York and Norton had to get out to the airport to collect them.

Traveler's Tip No. 6. When flying, ship heavy paraphernalia by air freight. It is expensive but much less so than the excess luggage charges of passenger planes.

"I'll be delighted to drive Dr. Brown to the airport," said Cooksey. Norton dressed and went downstairs. I had just stepped into the shower when the phone rang again. "Cooksey here," said our boy scout. "Where is Dr. Brown?" Dripping and mad, I felt like shouting, "Down there in the lobby, you fool," but restrained myself. He was, after all, being helpful and did get Norton out and back in jig time.

Shortly after noon we were picked up and driven to luncheon by Jack Hilton, a tall lean man with graying hair who has lived in Africa some thirty-five years and who is the deputy game warden of the Kenya National Parks. He is an interesting man, vastly experienced in his work, and he and his wife live in a small cozy house in Muthaiga, a pretty suburb about three miles out of Nairobi.

"There is some corner of a foreign land . . ." In the heart of that vast exotic continent, the Hiltons' house was England in microcosm. Cretonnes, Staffordshire, family photos, and two affectionate Persian cats, a mother and her one-eyed son. The theory that cats are aloof is largely myth. Those two slobbered over us, rubbing against our legs, purring and jumping into our laps at luncheon.

Mrs. Hilton—Pam—was concerned about her roses and Dr. Brown was in his element giving advice. He is a great rose man and willing to impart his lore. Of course not all rose growers have his advantages, which include human blood filched from the hospital blood bank once it starts to deteriorate and is no longer useful for transfusions. Human blood is just great as fertilizer.

Even though not so fortunate as Dr. Brown, other chaps too have been organically minded. Omar Khayyám for one, and nearly a thousand years ago. "I sometimes think that never blows so red the rose as where some buried Caesar bled." Right you were, Omar.

The Hiltons' luncheon went a long way toward retrieving their country's reputation for disastrous cooking. It was our first home-cooked meal since leaving the Parsons' in Paris and it was delicious.

Jack Hilton spoke feelingly of animals in the reserves under his protection. To us, their numbers, especially in the case of antelope, zebra, and wildebeest, seemed legion but he and other game wardens we were to meet had a personal acquaintance-ship with, and indeed intimate knowledge of, many of the wild creatures.

We had been talking about animals for a while when he suddenly said, "Oh, by the way, when you get to Amboseli, I wonder if you'll be good enough to inquire about Gladys? She's not been well lately and as I won't be able to get there for a bit I'll appreciate any news you can give me."

"Any friend of yours," we said, "is a friend of ours. Who is Gladys and where will we find her?"

"She's a rhino," he said, "a dear. I know you'll like her. Moses, the head ranger, will be able to tell you about her." We promised to look up Gladys.

Jack Hilton told us that new laws were being enacted whereby, when animal population explosion threatens the survival of the herds, Africans may shoot the animals provided they report the carcasses to the authorities, who will pay them a bonus if the death can be proved authentic—a much more satisfactory, not to mention humane, method than poaching.*

They are also trying to educate the Africans not to kill giraffes

---

* Since writing this I have learned from C. A. Spinage's *Animals of East Africa* that Gladys has been killed by poachers.

for their tails, with which they make fly swatters. To us this seems cruel and wasteful but it is hard for the African to see why the white man is lauded for shooting wild game for the heads when he is excoriated for killing for the tails. Nor can he understand why he is liable to a year in jail for poaching while Europeans are encouraged to hunt. The lame justification is that the white man pays for a hunting license and that the nice money stays in Africa. But if killing a giraffe for its tail and wasting the hide and meat seems, to say the least, an extravagance, the giraffes may have the icy comfort of reflecting that rhinoceroses are killed because of a conviction, prevalent in Asia and Africa, that their horn, which is not horn but matted hair, when ground up is a potent aphrodisiac.

There is still great uncertainty about the fate of the game if all the white wardens should be obliged to leave. The consensus seems to be that the Africans will quickly exterminate it through deliberate slaughter and neglect. On the other hand, some of the politicians are beginning to realize its enormous value as a tourist attraction.

In these troubled times of transition few people think of going to Africa to live and to establish businesses or farms, and certainly one does not go for art or architecture, historic tradition, or a beguiling way of life. Though parts of the country have great natural beauty, the primary tourist lure is the game, whether to destroy or to admire. Since tourist money is vital to the emerging nations, many of which achieve Uhuru in a state of bankruptcy, if the tribes themselves can profit from their unique heritage there is hope. The Amboseli reserve, for example, an area which in times of drought used to be overrun by Masai cattle competing with wild game for the water holes and doing incalculable damage, has now been made the Masai's responsibility. As they will receive entrance fees and ground rentals they may develop a genuine interest in game preservation.

It is my own forlorn hope that they will appreciate the fact that space and freedom and the stillness of the plains are, themselves, a lure to city-weary people almost as great as the animals and that they will not try to induce too many travelers to come at the same time.

Some of the British predict—and there is evidence that their predictions are already being substantiated—that the Africans will be obliged to ask the white man back, especially technicians and professional men. The difficulty is that they will now be obliged to pay the white men's salaries, whereas in the old days this expense was borne by the European colonizers.

As far as the game wardens of East Africa are concerned, those we met were secure through 1962 and they were reasonably optimistic about 1963. Further than that they would not speculate.

Leaving the pleasant Hiltons, we drove back to the city and went to Ahamed's for safari shopping. Ahamed's is a large Indian-owned one-story department store near the New Stanley Hotel. We made assorted purchases, including two knockabout hats, the kind that are meant to be faded by sun, wilted by rain, and in which I hoped to win a nomination for Belle of the Bush.

Sitting upon the shelves of the Messrs. Ahamed were several solar topis. We gazed at them wistfully but before our eyes they were gathering figurative as well as literal dust. The solar topi in Africa is as old hat as "White Hunter" and "Bwana." Today one says "Professional Hunter" and "You." Rarely, very rarely, "Sir." *Sic transit romantia.*

In any event the topis' presence in that part of the country was something of an anachronism. They are intended for a hot climate and don't let anyone tell you that it's hot on the equator. I think that fable was disseminated by schoolteachers in Maine in January longing for tropic warmth but in June and July, at altitudes varying from 5400 to 9000 feet, you will not find it. At dawn and evening you are barely comfortable in a thick sweater and woolen slacks.

That particular evening, however, we were somewhat more elaborate, for we had been invited by Diana and Bill Howard-Williams to dine and go to the theater. Diana is in public relations. She has red hair, a tiptilted nose, and a brief upper lip.

She is amused by Americans. "You are always saying, 'What's your problem?' Only Americans say that." Bill is a member of Parliament and completely indistinguishable from Winston Churchill. Any producer casting a play about the great statesman has only to engage Mr. Howard-Williams and he is nine tenths of the way home. The resemblance is uncanny. So much so that, although he dearly loves a cigar, Bill told us that when standing for re-election he discards it. The opposition makes too much hay jeering at him, saying he's too big for his britches, thinks in fact that he *is* Churchill. We found him an outspoken, entertaining person, a most eloquent member of Her Majesty's loyal opposition. He has lived in Africa for forty-five years, but, as he observed, "I go home for an occasional war, of course."

Speaking of Kenya, he said there are about seventy doctors in the whole country, of whom thirty to forty are Africans, but there is not one African surgeon and seven dentists service a population of over seven million.

We dined Chez Joseph, a restaurant that is doing its best to raise the culinary standards of Nairobi, and listened with interest and some astonishment to our host holding forth on the Mau Mau. He did not approve of the activities during the Emergency of 1953, '54 and '55. "But," said he, "they were fighting a powerful opponent, the British government. They used what weapons they had." In view of the horrors they perpetrated, I thought this very broad-minded.

The Hiltons, who also lived through that alarming period, had also been objective about it. "Of course we never went any place without a revolver," Jack told us. "We carried one even in the bathroom, wore one with our dinner jackets, and slept with it under our pillows. The only trouble was, sometimes we'd go off in the morning and forget it. At night, when we went to bed again, we'd find that our African houseboys had laid it neatly under the pillow on top of our folded pajamas." The houseboys must have thought the bwanas daffy, but they were willing to co-operate.

The play the Howard-Williams' took us to see was *The Irregu-*

lar Verb To Love by Hugh and Margaret Williams. No relations. It was an entertaining comedy that had recently completed a long run in London and the Donavan Maule Theatre Club, with a cast half professional, half amateur, gave it a lively production.

The club is highly regarded because, while Nairobi is a capital city, it is young. Theater, opera, music, museums, other than the Coryndon, which is natural history, are still to come. With few exceptions the stores impressed me as being small-town rather than cosmopolitan but there are specialty shops offering objects and accessories made from hides and fur which are well designed and often quite elegant. Often quite expensive too.

True to British tradition, Nairobi is more a man's town than a woman's, and many a traveling lady will be depressed by the hairdressers. I tried four separate beauty shops and none of them was any good. Manicurists are virtually non-existent. The idea of automatically having them at the hairdressers', a custom followed around the world, has not yet taken hold in Nairobi. When, before I knew about this, I innocently said I would like a manicure too, the proprietors studied me with interest. Lions and giraffes they were accustomed to; I was an exotic specimen. Any woman who does find a manicurist cherishes her with the regard a New Yorker reserves for a gifted cook and she must be summoned specially from some hidden retreat and you have to have excellent references before she will deign to touch your little finger.

In other integration respects East Africa is ahead of America. Black Africans lunch, dine, and take tea at the New Stanley with white men and in groups of their own. At the Outspan Hotel in Nyeri we saw six or eight Africans sitting with a couple of white friends. In Kampale, Uganda, more than one white girl was dancing with a colored man.

One evening we saw two or three Africans in dinner jackets. They were handsome and exceptionally well groomed. I could not help speculating as to whether, when the white man with his black tie moved out, the black man with his white tie would move in.

The integration process is not rapid and it is not without pain. Various little tactful gambits are employed. One proprietor of a small hotel told us that he rented rooms to Africans but tried to arrange matters so that white clients were not asked to share a bath.

In political life, Africans and Europeans mingle freely. Mr. Tom Mboya, probably the most influential figure in the Kenya government, has a white British woman secretary and even those English who do not like him or his policies respect him. "He is a well-educated man," they say—he went to Ruskin College at Oxford—"and he is able." The lack of educated leaders is one of Africa's great handicaps.

It has always seemed to me that class rather than color is the true barrier to integration. In the American South for so many generations the colored people have been servants that it is extremely difficult for Southerners to accept them socially. So far integration has worked best among artists, especially theatrical artists, who are great respecters of talent; and in the professions too there is beginning to be recognition and acceptance of ability.

The next morning, after our evening with the Howard-Williams', we left the New Stanley on our first sortie. We were not actually on safari but we were going to spend a night at Treetops, one of the high spots of an East African tour.

For once, feminine intuition functioned to effect. As we would be in and out of Nairobi several times and obviously would not need in the bush the clothes we required in town, the idea of toting them with us induced melancholy. The doctor, the free-handed one, succumbed to the glums at the very thought. Suddenly inspiration struck me. "We'll simply ask the hotel to hold them for us," I said. "After all, we're in Africa, safaris are mother's milk. They probably kept stuff for Speke and Grant." We did ask them and they said cheerfully that they would be happy to keep our clothes in store. Just please list each article. Dresses and suits could stay on hangers, all we would have to pack in suitcases were our shoes and accessories. The difficulty was, we seemed to be remarkably well shod and to possess any number of cherished oddments. Also, since we had to take at least a couple of suitcases with us, we required cartons to hold the overflow, and cartons the world over are hard to come by.

Traveler's Tip No. 7. Carry hangers with you, either inflatable ones or the lightweight folding kind. They are a convenience in city hotels, necessity at the lodges in the game preserves.

A good many hours were consumed packing and unpacking and pursuing, with the staff, the carton treasure hunt. The room boys at the hotel were sometimes efficient but always sharp. They would come to us to announce that tomorrow was their day off and please could they have their tip? The first time this happened, since we had only been there a day or two, we assumed it was the custom of the country and, though it seemed odd, we did tip, inquiring whether, since he was our regular room boy, we would not be seeing him again. He grinned his assurance as he skedaddled through the door and, needless to say, we have spotted neither hide nor hair of him from that day to this.

I imagine they come to the hotels, serve for brief periods, and after collecting a little money, decamp. All the English who worked with African labor told us the same thing. Their saving instinct is nil. Although we ourselves found that it can rain copiously in their country, to the Africans that rainy day is apparently never coming.

They had another trait that we found curious too, but although this one confused us it entertained us as well. *Crowds* of Africans can assemble in your room within minutes and without your being sure of what is happening until you try to make your way through them to door or window.

First the room boy who makes the beds will appear, then the specialist in mosquito-netting canopies, then the one who fills the water carafes, then a friend comes to him with a message from the housekeeper, after which the bathroom boy arrives with a helper. If you are in the middle of the carton routine a little brigade of three or four looms in the doorway, each one bearing a box much too small for your needs, and a passing waiter sticks his head in to see if you require anything. Norton and I used to shout to each other, "Close the doors, they're coming through the windows." We decided that they were impelled by childhood environment. They live in closely set Rondavels in villages or in huts surrounded by thorn hedges to keep the cattle from straying and from being preyed upon by wild animals. It is a very communal existence and they are probably used to flowing together and coagulating into groups. The traffic jam was emphasized in the lodges and camps because there we also had Koske, our driver, and part of the time our own cook, Wamuti, as well as the camp cooks who came to see how we were progressing and, I do not doubt, to mock the efforts of the imported talent. Actually, we never minded much. I simply gave up dressing or undressing and sank to the bed until they drifted away.

We left Nairobi en route to the Outspan Hotel and Treetops about ten in the morning. This time none of that sissy stuff in the Chevrolet. We were in our doughty Land Rover. Koske was at the wheel, with luggage beside him. Norton and I sat in the seat behind him—my tape recorder on my knee, microphone cocked for penetrating observations, and behind us was piled the luggage, a modest amount as this time we would not be gone more than a couple of nights. We felt acclimatized and professional although we could not match an American whom we had seen setting out the day before with his party for a month's shooting safari under canvas. Their equipment and packing arrangements were formidable and everybody at the Thorn Tree Café in front of the hotel, whether they had ever been on safari or not, watched with a critical eye as the gear was lashed into two huge Land Rovers. As it happened, the American and ourselves had mutual friends at home. His professional training working in high gear, my doctor noticed a bandaged finger and, introducing himself, asked what had happened. The gentleman laughed sheepishly. "It sounds silly but I was bitten by a tame lion in Rome on my way here." Perhaps things are picking up in the Colosseum?

There is a difference in safari methods which was brought

home to us only when we actually got to Africa. In the beginning, being totally inexperienced, we had assumed that we too were canvas bound—that we would have a professional hunter or guide and camp out, under canvas, traveling by Land Rover. That dream came true in spots. We lacked the professional hunter but we had the guide. Without canvas, we still rode the Land Rover. When the suspicion that the arrangements we had originally requested had not been made began to seep through to us in New York, we were bitter. While the man with whom we were dealing was at fault in not telling us in the beginning that his office did not work with Ker & Downey, one of the best-known and most reputable East African safari organizations, the East African Tourist Bureau served us admirably and matters turned out for the best. A canvas outing is extremely costly.

While I imagine one may settle for less time, Ker & Downey quote for and are chiefly interested in safaris of a month's duration, and the simplest of these runs to $3500 per person. This comprises a professional hunter and one client shooting. It also includes gunbearer, skinner, and servants, camping equipment and provisions, with the exception of liquor. License fees are extra. If you do not wish to shoot but to go on a photographic safari as we did, the difference in cost is slight since you will still need the hunter or guide who, in the interests of caution, will be armed, and you need the sleeping, cooking, and toilet tents and servants to rig them. You obviously need the food and sustenance. The only saving comes in the gunbearer's and skinner's wages and in the hunting-license fees.

If not shooting, you will be allowed to pitch your tent on the campsites within the reserves. If you are shooting you are not allowed to enter them at all since protection of game is their reason for being.

Our method of travel was a compromise and despite our initial disappointment we found it immensely rewarding. Freed of the expense, to some extent the inconvenience, and the possible though virtually negligible risk of trouble inherent in a safari under canvas, the lodges are a happy solution.

They, however, came a little later. Treetops was a different and unique experience. One drives from Nairobi to Nyeri and the Outspan Hotel in the Aberdare Mountains. That part of Africa, Kikuyu country and ex-stronghold of the Mau Mau, is rolling and fertile, rich in beautifully tended coffee and sisal plantations. I had never seen sisal before and thought at first that they were huge pineapple plants, for the sharp leaves springing directly from the earth look just like pineapple tops. They are a grayer green, however, and from the thick bottom growth a tall thin sapling springs into the air, skinny little branches shooting from it, tufted at the ends like the tails of wart hogs. Sisal is used for rope, hemp, gunny sacking.

We passed villages picturesque to look at but primitive in the extreme. The prettiest one clustered on a slope, the rondavels, with their conical thatched roofs, set like checkers on the green hillside. These huts have one door, usually no windows, no chimneys, and no electricity or sanitation of any kind. Before the Mau Mau the houses used to be more isolated but with the Emergency the government ordered closer building for mutual protection. If there was any general store or post office we did not recognize it and concluded that the inhabitants probably corresponded via tom-toms and smoke signals.

The people walking along the road looked poor but not miserable. The old men seemed the most desolate but I think it was partly their clothes: long shabby khaki coats, British Army surplus. When they wore African garments they had more dignity and gaiety.

We saw an outstanding young woman with a smooth lovely café-au-lait face, her hair drawn back into an expertly coiled bun, wearing a pink robe draped over one shoulder. She had true elegance. Given a little experience and the wherewithal, she would have been elegant on Fifth Avenue or the Rue de la Paix. Like many African women, her carriage was magnificent. They carry great water pots on their heads and walk like queens. Sometimes the hewers of wood do less well, for they are also the bearers of wood, carrying it in great slings on their backs bent

East African landscape with thorn trees

Baboon in the Nairobi National Park—Great-great-grandpapa giving his descendants a long hard look

Result of the long peer—giraffe in the Nairobi National Park

Masai couple

Monsieur and
Madame Ostrich

Photograph by G. A. Mason Smith

Treetops, where our first elephant arrived at half-past five

Five forty-five at Treetops

Masai tribesmen at Amboseli—sight-seeing party in Land Rover

Amboseli rhinos—chin on rump of chum

Zebra in Amboseli

Big success at Manyara
with my Masai necklaces
bought in Arusha

Amboseli lions at
noontime

Michael Grzimek's grave

The doctor at
the gate of the
Ngorongoro Reserve

Olduvai Gorge—birthplace of the human race

Ilka and Dr. Lewis Leakey—the low monument beside him is the
site where he and Mrs. Leakey found the skull of Zinjanthropus

A noble head in
the Serengeti

Saddle-billed stork

Young relatives of
noble head—youthful pride
on the rock

over by the weight, the slings supported by straps passing over their foreheads. The strength of African women is extraordinary and large men are not in the least shamed when loads which they find hard to hoist are laughingly loaded onto the backs of trucks by their womenfolk. In a complex world one aspect of life in Africa is refreshingly simple. As far as we could discern there was no line, sharp or subtle, dividing men's and women's work. It's all on the girls' side.

Less than an hour out of Nairobi, Koske drew up at a roadside inn, a Blue Post hotel. Although his English was good, this time he elected to say nothing, merely bowing us out of the Land Rover and pointing. We followed his finger and, rounding the corner of a small inn, came upon a charming garden path leading to a gushing waterfall. We duly admired it, took pictures, had a cup of coffee, and returned to our jeep. That's one thing about travel in foreign lands: the tourist does as bid and usually to his advantage.

On our way to the Outspan we had our first encounter with the African giggles. Along the road walked an ancient crone. Her wizened breasts were naked and she had a humorous wrinkled old face. Norton wanted to photograph her. She seemed agreeable and I think would have posed for nothing but he made the mistake of offering her a coin. Her little eyes lighted with greed and she instantly demanded more. He shook his head no but she insisted yes, giggling with amusement. No and yes and no and yes. I do not know how long this game would have continued, for just then a young man came along (I decided he was her grandson) and she grabbed hold of him and swung behind him, tossing her skimpy cloak over her head and giggling uncontrollably.

The Africans were shy about having their pictures taken, at least they were coy, unless offered sufficient *pesa;* then frequently they would pose for several exposures. As a rule they did not smile; picture taking is a serious business. I think it is myself and can never understand the press photographers' insistence on "a nice big smile." Why all the teeth? What is so gay? Sometimes, however, even if offered money—although they would not run away—they would throw their cloaks over their heads so as to become invisible. It is quite possible that they still think a spirit lurks in the box. It is also quite possible that they think, "Why *should* I be photographed?" I tried to decide how I would feel if a foreigner were to come up to me on Madison Avenue and ask to take my picture. I'm afraid, with my old theatrical and television training, I would be charmed.

Stopping along the road for camera work, it was lunchtime when we reached Nyeri. The Outspan is a large, well-run hotel and we had a large, old-fashioned, comfortable room opening onto a brilliant stretch of lawn bordered by bright flower beds, the Aberdare Mountains rising in the background. Outspan is a South African word for the place where, at the end of the day's journey, the traveler unharnesses or outspans the oxen and camps for the night. Mr. Eric Sherbrooke Walker, who owns both the Outspan and Treetops, has described them with loving enthusiasm in his book, *Treetops*. I found it easy, pleasant reading, especially after having been there, but I think perhaps the cook was out of sorts during our visit as the food did not match the owner's glowing description of it.

Treetops was already well established when Princess Elizabeth and Prince Philip were in Africa in 1952 but, for most people, its reknown dates from the night of their visit when the Princess' father died in London and she became the Queen of England. In his book Mr. Walker describes the occasion with discretion and respect for the young sovereign. According to him, the public impression that Elizabeth was notified of the King's death while she was at Treetops is erroneous. She learned of it the next morning on her return to the royal lodge at Sagana, a cottage in the forest given to the couple as a wedding present by the people of Kenya.

The tree home in which the visitor stays today is not the one visited by the Princess. That was burned by the Mau Mau in 1954. The new one, completed in 1957, is larger and has been built on the other side of the water hole in a much better position for picture taking in the afternoon, the time travelers usually arrive. On our own visit, we left the Outspan immediately after luncheon, wearing woolen slacks and sweaters (the altitude is around 6000 feet and the air is nippy), taking with us only a small overnight bag with toilet articles but still laden down with binoculars and cameras.

Traveler's Tip No. 8. Take binoculars, the best you can afford. They will add immeasurably to your pleasure in game watching.

Traveler's Tip No. 9. Even if equipped with enough color film to rival the NBC peacock, you will want black and white for late shots.

Our company was divided in two big safari cars or English jeeps. In ours, we were eight guests and the warden of Aberdare National Park, a delightful young man named Bill Woodley. We also had with us an older man, Alan Scott, a professional hunter, who carried a rifle in case the need to cope should arise.

It was a lovely drive through farmland rich in corn and red beans and tobacco, the earth as red as the earth of Georgia. We saw many beehives hanging from the trees but they are shaped differently from ours, being cylindrical and somewhat resembling giant Tootsie Rolls. The honey from them is dark and strong and delicious.

We drove for about half an hour and when we reached the edge of the reserve the jeep stopped and Bill Woodley got out. He chatted for a few minutes with a very spruce-looking African in an immaculate green uniform with a foreign-legion cap who stood rigidly at attention responding to the flood of Swahili with an occasional *ndio, ndio,* meaning yes, or so be it.

Mr. Woodley hopped back into the jeep and we drove on. Since I was sitting next to him I asked who the natty character was. "He was a terrorist general of the Mau Mau during the Emergency," he replied. "Very able chap."

My eyebrows rose through my safari hat. "You mean those obscene monstrous rites and everything?"

"Indeed yes."

"Well . . . er . . . has he seen the light? Is he now on our side, domesticated and all that?"

"Quite," said Woodley cheerfully. "Merely enforce strict discipline and show them you trust them. That's the key. Works very well."

Mr. Woodley is experienced and should know, but I felt he showed a benign faith in human nature not shared by me. And indeed I have heard before and since that one of the most baffling of African characteristics, virulent during the Mau Mau Emergency, is their capacity to turn against those who have been kind to them and are fond of them and whom, in turn, they admire and trust. I think it probable, however, that most of those who betrayed their white friends or employers did so because they were being terrorized by their own people. The number of Africans killed by the Mau Mau in proportion to whites whom they murdered was enormous.

"Africans don't really understand kindness and fair dealing." Many Europeans said it. Our own stay was too brief, our experience too limited, for us to be able to judge for ourselves but perhaps, at present, in that part of the world, colored and white are operating on different wave lengths. Kindness is not natural to the heart but stems from sophistication and experience. Kind children, for example, are rare.

I was thinking of these things as we drove deeper into the Treetops property.

About two hundred yards from our destination the jeeps stopped and everyone got out. We were asked to move quietly and not to talk. Mr. Scott took his gun from its case and started on ahead of us. It was exciting and a little theatrical but we were in the domain of wild animals and caution is advisable. At intervals along the path there are ladders against the trees up which one is supposed to bolt, and primitive shelters of thatch and branches behind which one is advised to dodge, if importuned by elephant or rhino, who from time to time stray across the trail.

It seems Princess Elizabeth was confronted at reasonably close quarters by an elephant whom she passed with a regal aplomb worthy of her great-great-grandmother.

Unmolested, we started walking, a German-Swiss couple, an English couple, two other Americans, and ourselves. I kept thinking hazily of Katherine Anne Porter's *Ship of Fools*.

The house or inn is a square hut built in the branches of flowering Cape chestnuts, its verandas supported on thirty-nine high pilings or poles. We clambered up a ladderlike staircase which, once we were all aboard, was hauled up and secured.

Treetops can accommodate twenty-four people including servants and host and hostess. Our hostess of the day was a charming young Frenchwoman. She told me she alternates with others and shepherds parties twice a week. The hotel is two-storied with a flat roof for viewing purposes and comprises a central dining room-lounge, a minute kitchen, a small bar, cubicle-like rooms with camp beds and warm blankets, and adequate bathroom facilities. The water closets are especially silent so as not to frighten any elephants who might be standing underneath at the moment of flushing. There are rooms on both sides of the building and it is wise to specify one on the pond side, which is the more interesting.

On the verandas you sit in comfortable airplane seats given to Treetops by United Airways. We dropped our bag in our room and hurried out at once.

Directly below us in the foreground was the water hole, the determining factor in the location of the hotel. It is a large muddy pond thick with water-lily pads upon which perched a sleek white aigret who kept us company through the night. The ground around the pond is heavily sown with salt to attract the animals, and two large floodlights or "moons" attached to the balconies are lighted when it grows dark. Beyond the immediate clearing lies the forest.

Some people have said they found Treetops a little overcivilized, a little tame for their tastes, but I do not agree. Aside from the lighting, which is necessary, since many animals come after dark and one cannot count on the moon, there is no artifice. True, in the dry season they pump water into the hole so the animals may continue to drink there. This seems to me intelligent and

if it is also tame I am for it. The salt provided for them is vital
to their well-being. Other than that, nature is on her own. There
are no trained animals, no beaters herding them through the
glades onto the stage, and while there is always something, no
specific game is guaranteed. However, if a visitor does not see a
rhino, elephant, or buffalo, despite the dependable smaller
beasties, his night is on the house. Most people hope for elephants and frequently they get them but sometimes they do not.
We were hoping.

Very quietly the wild creatures started to appear: waterbuck,
wild boar, deer, bush buck, and the debonair wart hogs. They
wandered about drinking and licking the salt, quite oblivious of
their fascinated audience, who enthusiastically adhered to the
cardinal rule of silence. People speak only in whispers and the
game is not disturbed. The wild boar had a grand time wallowing
in the muddy water and rolling about on the dirt afterward. The
whole spectacle was strangely silent, the silence occasionally
shattered by the sharp chattering of baboons, who would stop as
abruptly as they started.

A troop of sixteen baboons presently appeared and gathered
close around the pilings, looking expectantly upward, but they
had to wait a bit for their reward. We were cautioned not to
leave camera lenses, handbags, or small possessions on the chairs
when we went inside as baboons are light-fingered parties who
step easily up onto the veranda railing and scoop up any goody
that catches their fancy.

Since Treetops is a British enterprise, it was not long before
tea was announced. It was served on the flat roof and was delicious, hot and strong, with thick slices of raisin cake. I know the
cake was good but not because I ate any large amount. I didn't
get the chance. As soon as they saw the cake appear, the chaps
who had been gazing up so expectantly came scrambling onto the
roof, hands outstretched. They brought their babies who, while
holding tight to Mummy, extended peremptory paws for their
own rations. Fresh pineapple, of which there was a large supply,
was particularly welcome.

I left the roof for a few minutes and when I started back up again I encountered, sitting on the stairs, a large baboon assiduously munching cake. I waited courteously until he had finished and felt grateful when the French hostess appeared in the doorway above me, spoke to him severely, and ordered him up again. He went with a shrug. There was no reason to expect he would bite me but baboons have businesslike teeth.

During tea we discussed the probability of elephants. The day before had been bonanza time: 150, *and* a leopard! Leopards are very rare; still, just to be in leopard environment was stimulating.

Tea and games over, I went back down to our places on the veranda, leaving Norton to wander and photograph. I was alone there with the exception of the German-Swiss couple a few seats away. It was growing colder but I had on a warm sweater and a blanket over my knees.

Traveler's Tip No. 10. Take woolen gloves to Treetops. Your hands can get very cold.

I was looking about, watching a deer and a few meandering wild boar, and admiring the spiral grooved horns of a waterbuck, when I happened to glance down toward my right. There, just below me, rounding the corner formed by the tall supports of the balcony came an elephant. He was alone and moving quietly. I whispered to my companions, "Look, look there." We watched him as he strolled in leisurely fashion toward the salt which he began scooping up in his trunk. Later he knelt and began rooting in the earth with his tusks. I glanced at my watch. It was half-past five.

For thirty years now the Walkers have been putting out salt so that the earth is saturated. Even when the daily supply has all been licked and sucked from the surface a rich store remains. As Alan Scott said to us, "The salt is the mustard, the minerals in the earth are the meat."

We gazed at our single elephant with wonder and fond pride and then, a few minutes later, the miracle happened. On they came in their numbers: ears spread, long trunks swinging, the great primeval shapes loomed through the trees. On and on they came until we counted ninety in all. They advance on silent feet but they snuffle and snort and grunt and unexpectedly bellow. To a tyro in jungle life their roar is exactly what he anticipates from a lion.

There were old bulls and cows and irresistible babies. They milled about, drinking at the water hole, sniffing the salt with the sensitive tips of their trunks. In the press one would expect the babies to be stepped on but it never happened. It can happen, I believe, if something terrifies a herd and it stampedes but that night was relatively peaceable. If a baby strayed a little it could always find its mother again. The evening was a lesson in humility. I cannot tell one elephant from another, but a baby elephant can. Furthermore, he is adept at getting his supper, standing under the maternal belly, his small trunk upraised to the source of supply.

From time to time a bull would give halfhearted chase to a waterbuck, who skipped a few paces away and went on with his salt rooting.

Mindful of the jokes about elephantine gestation, we asked Bill Woodley how long the period actually was. Mr. Woodley knows. "Twenty-two months," he said, "and the lactation period is also twenty-two. This means elephants can breed about once every four years, although sometimes it is longer than that." They reach puberty when they are between twelve and fifteen and their life span is between fifty and seventy years, sixty being about the average.

Shortly before dinner was served at eight o'clock, the elephants wandered off into the forest glades and the rhinos appeared. We counted seven in the course of the night.

When it gets dark at Treetops and the house lights are turned on a black curtain is dropped over the door so the brilliance will not alarm the animals. The big flood lamps fastened to the balconies come up slowly, simulating moonrise, and the beasts accept them as nature's own.

After cocktails everybody sits at one long table with an ingenious device down the middle, a sort of trolley track along which slide the various dishes. Each person helps himself, avoiding boardinghouse reach. I wish I could say that the food was better but it is acceptable and the gourmet touch is scarcely what one goes there for. As Mr. Walker states in his book, with admirable candor, "Our black cooks are never cooks by profession but are all ex-N.C.O.s from the King's African Rifles or the Kenya police who have been trained in the Outspan kitchens. The reason for this is that it is easier to teach a brave man to be a cook than it is to teach a cook to be a brave man. The Treetops servants . . . have to be fairly hardy souls, unafraid of humans, wild game or hard work."

At ten o'clock nine or ten elephants returned to the pool but one of the rhinos, possibly because she had her baby with her, charged them angrily and the great creatures lumbered off. We went to bed finally as we were to be up at six-thirty. Tea is served at seven and then everyone departs for the Outspan and a big breakfast. I woke from time to time during the night and looked out the window to see the rhinos and one or two more audacious elephants quietly working at the salt or drinking in the pool. In the morning the rhinos had disappeared and seventeen elephants had congregated. It was necessary to chase them away since we would be descending the ladder in their midst. Wondering how this was done, I discovered it to be simple in the extreme. One of the African boys takes a can of pebbles and shakes it loudly. This so unnerves the stalwart beasts that they make off into the forest, ears flopping, absurd tails wagging in alarm.

Coming out from Nyeri we had an adventure. As I was down the ladder ahead of him, Norton said to me, "You go along in the first car, I'll come in the second." At night I wouldn't have done this but on a fine bright morning I felt independent. We were rolling down the road in the jeep when we saw looming ahead of us a rhinoceros. He kept coming and we kept going. Our black driver seemed to feel he was another car which would pull over and let us pass. The rhino's attitude was different. Their eyesight, I believe, is poor and the shape bearing down on him was distinctly antipathetic. A few yards away, he suddenly charged. Bill Woodley, sitting beside the driver, had said nothing, expecting, no doubt, that the man would turn off the road of his own volition. When he didn't, Mr. Woodley shouted at him and spun the steering wheel. The jeep swerved abruptly down a small embankment and the rhino charged past, narrowly missing the passenger seated above the wheel in the back seat. It was quite palpitating.

When we told Norton about it later, he looked relieved that we were all right, but since we were, he obviously wished he had been there too.

Having heard a good deal about the Mount Kenya Safari Club, owned by a small syndicate of which William Holden, the movie actor, is a member, and as it was not too far from where we were, we decided on a visit. En route, we crossed the equator. Climactic note: at approximately 6000 feet at noon of a June day, the weather was cold and cloudy.

We were not members of the Mount Kenya Club on arrival but ten minutes and twenty shillings later we were elected. The small payment makes one an overnight member with bed, board, bar, and pool privileges.

The club is magnificently located with a sweeping view across a wide valley of farms and forests to the soaring snow-capped heights of Mount Kenya. There are bright, meticulously cared-for lawns, beautiful flowers, swimming pool, a large main house, and several cottages. A Santa Barbara atmosphere prevails. I should say that the club is luxurious and comfortable rather than tasteful. The bar is dizzy with zebra hides and indifferent carvings. The drinks are good. The buffet looked tempting but could have served for a Hollywood banquet scene. In the East African tradition, all the food was papier-mâché.

We recrossed the equator, spent the night at the Outspan, and on Sunday returned to Nairobi to consolidate our luggage and pick up reinforcements: one *mpishi* (cook), Wamuti by name. The roughing it was about to begin.

CHAPTER THREE

Amboseli—Manyara

WE WERE HEADED for the Amboseli Game Reserve but would be spending two nights outside it at the Namanga River Inn and afterward would proceed to the Ngorongoro Crater. There, we had been advised, we would require our own cook. Wamuti accordingly entered our lives. He was a gentle, black young man speaking little English and cooking, when he did, with his left foot. He spent many hours of travel nodding in the front seat beside Koske, deep in slumber. We decided that the tourist agency had sent him along as a kind of sedentary pet to keep our little driver company.

As this was our first venture into true safari country, the surfaced roads would eventually end and in front of the New Stanley Koske was preparing, securing our luggage under a commodious tarpaulin. He was right to do so yet even then the dust sifted in.

One doesn't always have to wait for the reserves to see game. Casually, along the roadside, we encountered five black ostriches and countless gazelles. It was on this trip too that we began to notice the birds. We saw our first super starling, a creature of fantastic brilliance, its iridescent plumage sapphire blue and emerald green, flashing like a spray of jewels in the sunshine. We also saw the slender crested crane, its crest a feathery wheel atop its head. We had anticipated the animals but we were unprepared for the beauty and variety of the birds. Africa boasts two and a half times the number of species to be found in the United States. One day, after we had returned home, I was telling my friend Deppy Messinesi, a slender but staunch pillar of the fashion world who has been for many years on the staff of *Vogue,* about this wealth of Africa. "They have incredibly brilliant plumage," I said, "but there are some lovely monotone ones too, beige and white and gray and black. They have great elegance."

"Oh, I can just see them," she cried, "the Balenciaga birds."

The road to Treetops had lain through Kikuyu territory. We were now in the land of the Masai: mile after mile of spreading plains, for the Masai are great cattle owners. They have enormous herds, so the myth that the Africans have to poach because they are starved for protein seemed exploded. It was exploded still further when we learned that in parts of Africa poachers kill thousands of animals merely for their hides. The meat goes uneaten except by hyenas.

As far as the Masai are concerned, they are not likely, in the near future, to profit from the domesticated nourishment at hand because, although they drink the milk and drain the veins of the cattle for blood which they also drink and carry about in calabashes, they do not kill and eat the animals. They are used for money, bartered for wives. The more cows and steers, the more women. Women are desirable because they do the work and increase the yield of a man's farm and bear him sons. Very satisfactory system. No ulcers. Herds of goats are also used for barter but I believe you must offer more goats than cows in order to buy a wife.

If this custom, which is not exclusive with the Masai, did no harm, it might seem curious but acceptable, even if exasperating, to those whose ways are different but it does a great deal of harm.

As Dr. Bernhard Grzimek points out in his chapter in *Survival of the Free,* the magnificent book on wild life compiled and edited by Dr. Wolfgang Engelhart, the herds are not put to good use. In speaking of the destruction of the habitat of wild animals, Dr. Grzimek writes: "The tall Watusi tribesmen of Ruanda-

Urundi hardly hunt at all, and they certainly never kill a mountain gorilla. However, they keep vast herds of long-horned cattle, not to make use of them but merely out of pride of possession. During recent years they have driven more and more of these cattle, tens of thousands, into the Albert National Park of the former Belgian Congo, although they are forbidden to do this. The cattle have laid waste the comparatively small areas which are the home of the mountain gorilla, reducing the extent of the high lying bamboo forests so that the great anthropoid apes have less and less space in which to live. The Masai of the Serengeti Plain do very little hunting, but their densely packed herds of undernourished cattle destroy all the vegetation gradually turning the land into a desert. The Masai are constantly cutting down the few bushes and trees in order to build rough fences to keep their cattle together at night during their wanderings. However, those few trees had previously given shade and protection to the few sources of water which flow even during the dry season. One after another has now failed, so in the course of time the wild animals, which could supply far more meat per acre for the nourishment of human beings than the domestic cattle which are not native to Africa, are bound to disappear."

Misguided, destructive, tragically wasteful, the Masai are a handsome people, quite tall and straight with aquiline features. The warriors plaster their hair with red mud, and either everybody is a warrior or it is a popular fashion. They carry long slender spears and wrap themselves in earth-colored cotton cloaks. The cloaks or robes, called *lazos,* are worn by both sexes and the draping of them is haphazard—ladies' breasts are frequently exposed—but somehow when everything is chocolate brown it isn't so noticeable.

Men as well as women are frequently loaded with beads, long heavy earrings, and countless necklaces.

We were interested in how they got their ears to hang in loops almost to their shoulders. Koske explained that in early childhood the lobe is pierced and a small piece of wood inserted. Every few days this is removed and a larger piece put in its place. As

the pieces get bigger, so, naturally, does the hole until it is no
longer a hole but a big loop through which any number of orna-
ments may be strung. They also do it to a lesser degree in the
tops of their ears. Wamuti had one ear done that way, albeit on
a modest scale, but Koske himself had not.

In the course of the journey we came upon a deserted Masai
village and got out to explore. The huts, built by the women,
are shaped rather like large loaves of brown bread and are usually clustered inside a thorn stockade. The architecture is odd because, although the Masai are relatively tall, the houses are only
about five feet high. Curiosity impelled me inside one despite the
doctor's warning that I would emerge covered with fleas. I had to
stoop to enter and once inside remain bent at a right angle.

Made of wattle and mud, the huts are held up by a small interior forest of thin sawed-off saplings through which the inhab-
itant must worm his way if he wants to move about. The people
build fires inside the huts for cooking and warmth but as there
are no chimneys or windows the smoke finds its way out through
the entrance and cracks in the walls.

When the smoke and the fleas become excessive and particularly if the cattle require fresh pasturage, the Masai simply leave
their villages and move on. My exploration was interesting in a
way but on the whole, if I am going to be viewing abandoned
dwellings, I prefer the châteaux of the Loire.

We arrived at the Namanga River Inn shortly before six in the
evening. Beside the flower-bordered driveway was an enormous
round birdcage, almost as big as a rondavel, filled with brilliant
chirping parakeets—budgerigars to the English.

There were palm trees in front of the inn and the whole thing
looked so like a setting for *Rain* that one expected Sadie Thomp-
son and the Reverend Davidson to appear momentarily. It is
really impossible not to describe it as a stage set. As in the
manuscript of a play, right and left are from the point of view
of the audience. The whole front of the hotel is an open area
paved with flagstones sheltered by a high pitched roof of thatch.
On this terrace, which is at ground level, tables and large easy

chairs. Two steps stage center lead into the office. To the right a
stand with postcards. Off right is the bar, presided over by a
dingy little black man wearing a red fez, a long faded *kanzo* or
robe, and a red velvet vest. There is an enormous open fireplace
with a raised hearth and easy chairs around it. To the left of the
terrace a path leads off to a small group of log cabins which are
the bedrooms. At rise the stage is empty with the exception of
Mr. Gethin, the manager, who is in the office.

He is a large, red-faced man wearing khaki shorts, a short-
sleeved shirt, and a sweater vest. To our question as to whether
there were any newspapers available he replied gruffly, "Only
my own *Times*. I subscribe to it." This seemed a little unpromis-
ing so we did not press the issue and ask to borrow it. As we got
deeper into the play we learned that Mr. Gethin had owned the
hotel for thirteen years and that his father had started it before
him. When we first made our entrance, however, we were so
exhausted from a long drive in the Land Rover that Norton
ordered two double scotches from the bar and brought them to
our cottage to sustain us while we bathed and changed for dinner.

We became devoted to our outsize jeep but there is no question
that they take getting used to. At first the sensation is similar to
that experienced when riding a bucking horse after ten years'
absence from the saddle. It is also like being in a small boat in a
choppy sea, smashing down hard on the concrete waves. However, we were to find that in the bush, although we sometimes
proceeded at an exhilarating five miles an hour, we did proceed.
The Land Rover is Dependable. In sand, in swamps, across
streams, up slippery banks—it never failed. "Four-wheel drive,"
said the doctor. I did not understand the mechanism nor did I
have to. Mine was the simple, unquestioning faith of a little child
in a strong, infallible father.

Our one-room cottage was quite large, with twin beds and the
ubiquitous mosquito-netting canopies. We ourselves sought shelter under the canopies from assorted insects but they serve another purpose. Men who have lived their lives in Africa swear

by them as lion dispellers. "We know it sounds crazy," they say,
"but we have slept in the bush through the years and as long as
we have the netting over our cots we feel secure. For some reason
the lions never penetrate it." Of course, the system need fail only
once but faith is a potent force and apparently there is no dis-
suading your true believer.

In our cottage we had also had a bath almost as big as the bedroom. It was a bit *dégagé* since there were chinks between the
logs through which the sun and rain of Africa penetrated but,
while there was no tub or stall, there was a shower head pro-
truding from one wall and if you stood under it for a long, long
time the water finally ran very hot.

Another fringe benefit was the view. Our windows looked out
on a beautifully tended vegetable garden in which grew row
upon row of crisp green lettuce. Lettuce! We had had nothing
but brussels sprouts since we had been in Africa. "Look," I cried
to Norton, "lettuce. Maybe there'll be salad for dinner." The prospect was headier than the double scotches. It was also illusory.
There were any number of African waiters about and every
course was served by a different one but every course was dog-
gedly British and the lettuce leaves were used for garnishing,
not eating. Later, sitting around the fire in the bar drinking
coffee, I asked Mrs. Gethin why this was. She had a charming
gentle face and the old-fashioned adjective "womanly" suited her
well.

She smiled at my question. "I've thought of serving salads,"
she said, "but to tell you the truth, it is our American clients who
discourage us."

I could hardly believe my ears. "But how can that be?"

"Well, you see," she said, "they think fresh fruits and vegetables
are dangerous in Africa because they are convinced we use night
soil by way of fertilizer. I tend that garden myself and I assure
you we do not."

"You must put a sign over the buffet," Norton said. "'Americans, fear not! Our lettuce is unpolluted!'" I like to think the
Gethins did.

They told us that the Kenya leader, Jomo Kenyatta, was once scheduled to spend a night at the inn when electioneering in that part of the country but when he realized that he was in Masai territory he hurriedly pushed on. Mr. Kenyatta was not beloved by the Masai. There is a division of opinion about him, one faction maintaining that he actively led the Mau Mau in the horrors they perpetrated upon their enemies; the other side insisting that he merely condoned them—the choice would appear slender. But in any event Masai tribesmen had been among Mau Mau victims and Mr. Kenyatta felt that the climate was not beneficial.

The Gethins showed us a picture of a charming young giraffe whom they had had almost from the day he was born and whom they dearly loved. When he died on his first birthday, they were heartbroken. They had recently had some painting done and Mr. Gethin, who had seen him licking the paint, thought perhaps he might have died from lead poisoning. Their more conventional pets when we were there were two dachshunds and a female police dog named Trudy.

Displaying the several elephant tusks that adorned the terrace, Mr. Gethin showed us one with the end slightly grooved and worn flat like a chisel. He said that was because an elephant always favors one tusk over the other for ripping the bark off trees.

I can understand billiard balls and piano keys but the insensate passion for bibelots of carved ivory seems to me excessive and the idea of killing an elephant to use its feet as scrap baskets makes me physically ill.

The next morning we left the inn for our tour of Amboseli somewhat earlier than we had intended, owing to the British-African custom of "knocking you up with chai at seven."

Traveler's Tip No. 11. Carry your own "Do Not Disturb" signs with you. Some places do not have them and if there is no sign on the door, come hell or high water, you will be roused with morning tea, sometimes at six or six-thirty.

In one respect we did not regret being up betimes; the early mornings of Africa are very beautiful. The mist, like a silently rising curtain, reveals hills and trees of a marvelous shade of blue-green, both soft and vivid. In June and July the early mornings are cool and we were glad we had dressed warmly.

Africa, I should say, is the country of the great peel. At dawn you will want slacks and a heavy woolen sweater. As the morning progresses, the top layer may be removed but a light woolly of some sort is still welcome. At noon, when the sun rides high, a shirt or blouse is enough.

The entrance to the Amboseli reserve is only a few hundred yards down the road from the Namanga River Inn on the border between Kenya and Tanganyika. We passed many Masai on the way and a group of them were squatting on the ground at the border post where we stopped and Koske went in to present our credentials—or whatever it was he had to do. In the morning chill, the tribesmen, draped in their thin earth-colored cotton cloaks, looked damp and dejected.

The juxtaposition of the centuries in Africa is jolting. The Masai walk on hard-surfaced roads, they know automobiles, telephones, telegraphs, and radios. As of October 1962 the two-edged blessing of television loomed on the horizon—and they subsist on milk and blood, buy their wives, and dwell in huts in which they cannot stand upright.

It seems to me myopic to think that so vast a continent with its millions of human beings will not eventually match, possibly surpass, Europe, America, and Asia in civilization. By which I mean a mechanized, sanitary, convenient way of living. Possibly they will eventually match the rest of the world in culture too—the arts and sciences—but, judging from our stringently limited experience, I should say that the distance they must travel is far. The present era in Africa is the morning of a long, long day. There are certain very real hurdles to be surmounted before the advent of a political and social unity which we tend to think of complacently as a United States of Africa, something just like home.

As Mr. William Howard-Williams pungently observes in a small book of his collected speeches and reports:

"We recognize that Europe is basically made up of the Germanic, Latin and Slav races. Thousands of years of co-existence have not altogether blunted the antagonism these races used to feel towards each other. And Europe is, by comparison with Africa, an extremely small continent.

"In Africa, the differences between the many races are much deeper. Due to distances and lack of communications, until recently there has been no form of co-existence between them—but only, from time to time, warfare. . . . At the Berlin Conference in 1885 these facts were completely ignored as unimportant. Yet, by any standard, they should have been the first consideration in deciding frontiers which were to become international boundaries. . . . Take Kenya. Tribes belonging to all four racial groups (Bantu, Nilotics, Hamitics, Nilo-Hamitics) were arbitrarily thrown together and told they were, from then on, one nation. Of course they did not become one nation and it is unlikely that they ever will. Even to-day they cannot speak to each other as they do not have a common language . . . and now that so-called political emancipation is overtaking them, the political strife is along clearly defined tribal lines. . . . The concept of a coalition government taking in all racial groups is entirely alien to all of them. . . . Every country which was in this way 'created' at the Berlin Conference was under European rule. . . . This in the first place meant the African had no alternative but to accept the white man's ruling . . . in the second place the white man ruled which meant that no tribe belonging to another racial group was placed under the rule of a tribe or group of tribes belonging to an alien racial group.

"The situation is rapidly changing as independence or self rule comes to one African country after another. Under the white man's rule all the antagonisms and hatred had to be kept under control. Now that the white man is leaving there is no longer any reason why the tribes should not obey the exhortation they receive from the spirits of their forefathers, to right old wrongs and to slaughter the offensive alien tribes in their midst."

And he goes on to say that under a Belgian administration the world came to believe there was such a thing as a country called the Congo but that to the African living there it had never existed and the prospects that it ever will are slight.

Watching the Masai huddled beside the road as they listened to the radio and looked at the mechanical monster, the Land Rover, we spoke and wondered about these problems as we waited for Koske to come out of the border post. He showed up in a few minutes and we drove on to the entrance of the park.

Our first experience in Amboseli was with death. Under a small culvert across the track, we saw hundreds of catfish trapped in the mud as the water seeped away. They were thrashing madly in their efforts to breathe, and standing on the bank was a flock of marabou stork waiting for them to die. The marabou are ugly creatures with black backs and white vests, long beaks and naked red wrinkled heads and necks. They look like disagreeable miserly old men and we disliked them on sight.

On the other hand, to our surprise, we found the rhinos endearing. In a group, we were able to pick out Pixie, a celebrity whom we had heard about from Bill Woodley at Treetops. She was renowned for her lack of ears, having been born without them. And her mother—my, my, what a small world it is—was Gertie, a close friend of Gladys, the object of Jack Hilton's solicitude. Gladys was greatly improved, her armor plating all but glittered. Rhinos, left to their own devices, are playful creatures and there were several rolling about enjoying a warm sand bath. Two of them made up a game. After rolling over and over, they lumbered to their feet and one of them laid his chin across the rump of his chum. The chum would then start off at a reasonably good clip, swerving and turning unexpectedly, and the object was for the chin rester to stay in position, not to be thrown by any sudden switch in tactics. We watched them for quite a long time. To me it was more diverting than baseball. I could understand the theory better.

Rhinos, like elephants, are usually accompanied by tickbirds, of either white or neutral plumage. The birds go along for the ride, perched on the broad solid back. In return for seeing the world via this convenient and economical means of locomotion, they peck over the host territory, relieving it of bothersome insects. Occasionally we would see a solitary rhino separated from dear ones, and about these my own dear one felt a little wistful. "Must be lonely," he said, "off there by themselves with no one but those little birds to talk to."

We were learning and implementing a long-held conviction that all members of the animal kingdom, beasts and humans alike, with few exceptions, require companionship. The good zoos of the world are, in many respects, admirable, I have come reluctantly to the conclusion that they are even necessary, but I have always thought that they behave with unmitigated cruelty toward those animals who are kept in solitary cages through unending hours, year upon year upon year. The loneliness and boredom they undergo in their safe and relentlessly sanitary quarters are soul-destroying. Much as I despise the idea of animals in circuses, I think the St. Louis Zoo probably performs a humane act in training its monkey population to ride bicycles and cavort in general at daily matinees for the delight of the children. The attention of both segments of the population is engaged and they both have a merry time.

The Amboseli reserve, adjacent to Kilimanjaro and the snows thereof, covers an area of some twelve hundred square miles. From the gate we drove for an hour and a quarter to Ol Tukai lodge, a small group of cabins where travelers may put up overnight if not staying at Namanga River.

On the way, I had a moment of uneasiness which I kept to myself out of embarrassment and shame. A group of Masai appeared in their cloaks, carrying long spears. As we drew near they formed a roadblock and it became obvious we would not be able to pass through them without violence. As Koske slowed the Land Rover to a halt, I had a momentary chill in the pit of my stomach. Supposing the Natives were Hostile?

As matters turned out, they were young, curious, and friendly. Koske knew one or two of them and in a few minutes we started up a bit of commerce—the age-old bartering for beads—only this time it was the white man taking or, more accurately, *trying* to take beads from the natives. The Masai necklaces of colored beads are strung on wires, each necklace being larger than the one above it, so that they finally end with stiff, brilliantly colored bibs over their chests. In the case of the ladies, the effect is interesting, the bibs bobbing above sometimes quite extraordinary protuberances. In Arusha, Norton bought a postcard of one such damsel and Koske and Wamuti grinned when they saw it. She was evidently quite a celebrity. "Marilyn Monroe," they said knowingly.

I wanted very much to buy a necklace or two from one of the girls who looked at us with interest as she blew her nose delicately between thumb and forefinger. She at first appeared willing to sell but then began getting very coy about the price. She took off a necklace and let me handle it but then snatched it back, demanding more money. Ten shillings seemed steep and I lost interest. Norton, however, did give one of the young warriors a shilling and he posed with me, looking dignified and brave. As I have said, the Masai are a handsome people; the modeling of their heads is often fine and delicate, they have a bone-deep beauty.

For the first time we began seeing donkeys among the cattle and I noted with satisfaction that, unlike their hapless small relations in Europe, their burdens, if any, were trivial and they seemed well fed. It apparently has not yet occurred to the Africans to use them as beasts of burden. That is women's work.

At Ol Tukai lodge we met Moses, the African overseer, the one who knew Gladys, to whom Jack Hilton in Nairobi had given us a letter of introduction. We also met the camp pet, a large black ostrich. Ostriches are of comic aspect but one must be wary of them. A well-placed, venomously intended kick can kill a man.

At the lodge we picked up a ranger guide. Koske, although he knew the Amboseli territory, could not be certain where specific animals might be found. The ranger, having made his rounds at dawn, knew approximately where we were likely to locate a pride of lions. Fearing they might wander away, I was all for putting on a burst of speed but it was explained to me that plains animals move mostly in the early morning and at twilight. When the heat is intense they lie to under trees very sensibly—unlike Mr. Coward's mad dogs and Englishmen—not exerting themselves in the midday sun.

The African ranger got into the front seat beside Koske and we went grinding and bouncing over the plain. Amboseli has lush green stretches alternating with broad stripes of powdery and insistent dust but the animals were so beguiling that they diverted our attention from the grit lodging in our teeth and on the lenses of the camera. There was a charming group of zebras and four giraffes and we sighted a female bush buck, a small, pretty creature with wide-apart round ears. We also came upon an old elephant under a tree. We thought him misanthropic until we noticed four companions not far away. It was at this point, the elephant roost, that we reached a small crisis which turned out to be the first all-important step in a valuable lesson.

Traveler's Tip No. 12. If, in the heart of the bush, you must obey a call of nature, do it. Do not let false prudery hold you back.

Some women find this desperately embarrassing. I myself hesitated quite a while but to put oneself through this particular discomfort is nonsense. Drivers, wardens, rangers, black or white, are men, yes, they are also human beings and you are not the first woman they have piloted across the African bush. If you need to relieve yourself, say so. You must inevitably come to it in the end, so why suffer?

My husband made it easier for me. He simply said firmly, "Koske, please stop. Mrs. Brown wants to get out." Koske stopped and I hopped down behind the Land Rover. Incidentally, whoever named those plains and savannas the bush had small sense of fitness. For mile upon stretching mile there is often not a bush in sight. The vehicle serves as screen. Of course it can't screen you from all sides and in Amboseli I looked around to find I had an audience of five elephants. In our set that isn't standard procedure—but why travel if everything is going to be so homelike? I returned to animal watching with renewed zest.

Our search for lion continued. We were driving along the edge of the lake and eventually picked up the spoor. Despite a good deal of reading about animals, I have always been a little vague as to just what spoor is. Is it only one thing or are footmarks involved too? Well, yes, they are. According to Merriam-Webster, spoor is "a track, trace, or trail . . . of a wild animal." This includes the droppings, and you may be surprised how enticing it can be when you come upon the fresh residue of a former meal and realize that your quarry is close at hand. We followed along the sandy lake shore till we came to a large clump of tall coarse grass and there they were: five enchanting sleepy lions. One lay on his back like a giant kitten. Another beside him watched us indifferently, blinking in the sunshine. The color spectrum was a soft delight. The pale blue sky, the pale green water of the shallow lake, the sand, the yellow-green reeds, and the tawny, white and powdery gold tones of the animals blending in a mellow haze. From time to time three other heads parted the reeds as the lions stirred and played and withdrew again to curl up and sleep unseen. Norton took many pictures, including some of two white vultures who circled overhead.

Toward lunchtime we turned from the lake shore and the languid charmers and drove until we came to a clump of thorn trees. Koske drew into the shade and we got out and unpacked our picnic lunch, the inevitable hard-boiled eggs and ham and cheese sandwiches spiked by cans of warm beer and some really good tiny bananas and tangerines.

The afternoon was drawing to a close when we drove out of the park and Koske, leaning over the side of the jeep, pointed to a puff adder slithering across the road in front of us. He was, I am enchanted to say, the only snake we saw in Africa. They have them, we heard shivery stories from others besides Mrs. Ardrey, but we are proof that it is possible to spend two months in the country covering a good deal of territory and not to see one unless he is deliberately pointed out to you.

There are, of course, people who warm to snakes. There was Elsie Venner for one. Elsie, who always wore a necklace to hide the faint birthmark of a snake around her throat, who dressed in fabrics with wavy stripes, whose handwriting had an unsettling slanting quality, and whose suitor, trapped and fascinated, helpless as a bird, saw a coiled rattlesnake about to strike him unaccountably lower its head and writhe away. Turning, he beheld Elsie, her eyes as flat and cold as the rattler's, standing near him, her breath coming with a slight hiss.

It was a great book, *Elsie Venner*, a milestone of my childhood. Oddly enough, among my contemporaries I was unable to find anyone who remembered it or knew anything about it until a literary friend did some research for me. To my surprise it was written by Oliver Wendell Holmes and first published in 1861.

Besides Elsie and her curious aberration there are the curators of snakes in zoos who feel affectionately toward their charges. I remember one day being shown around the Bronx Zoo by a most attractive young man who, after we had admired animals and birds galore, finally said eagerly, "Let's go in here, the snake house." I thanked him but said I really didn't have the time. His face fell. "Oh, but please. Please come. They're *my* snakes, they're my job. I mean, that's what I *do* here at the zoo." I went in and studied snakes.

We spent a second night at Namanga and before leaving the next morning met a pleasant English couple named Vincent and their eleven-year-old son, Bryan. At Treetops there had been an interesting man at dinner, a Mr. Gregory who loved animals and knew every game reserve in Africa as well as his own coffee plantation. We got talking about coffee over the breakfast table at Namanga and the Vincents asked if we would like to visit a plantation sometime. We said indeed yes and mentioned our Mr. Gregory, who apparently had a fine one. "He has," said Mrs. Vincent. "It's the one I had in mind to take you to. He's my brother." The Vincents asked us to let them know when we returned to Nairobi but, much as we wanted to, we simply did not have the time and I regret it to this day.

The town of Arusha is about seventy-five miles from Namanga and the road is excellent, for it is the paved highway that goes all the way to Johannesburg. Though no metropolis, Arusha is an important center in that part of the country. It has a hotel, shops, a hospital, and an airport. It also has a branch of the East African touring service with an obliging gentleman, Mr. Roy Springer, in charge. I called Diana Howard-Williams in Nairobi from his office, imploring her to make an appointment for me at the hairdresser's the day we would return to town—owing to the dust of Africa, despite a scarf around my head I was getting desperate —and also to ask if she would let Mr. Tom Mboya, Kenya's celebrated labor leader, know when we would be there. We had a letter to Mr. Mboya and she and her husband had said that they knew him well and would see if they could get us an interview.

These vital matters attended to, I went shopping. Souvenir hunters have a thin time of it in that part of Africa but who wants to go home empty-handed? Any tourist worth the name can always find *some* little trinket for which, once she gets home, she will have no use whatever. I bought a few small animals carved from wood. There are millions of them in every shop and hotel and street market in Africa, and always the merchants swear they are hand-carved and always I was perfectly certain they were turned out by some giant cookie-cutter concession. They do not vary by a hair. They are not very good but they are what is there. The interesting carving is in the Congo.

Two of my purchases, however, I genuinely liked. One was a length of material bought from an Indian which someday, before it rots away, I hope to have made up into a summer dress. These lengths of cloth are the *lazos* that African women drape themselves in with real flair. Mr. Springer had warned us not to pay more than fifteen shillings and I was just beginning to pride myself on my non-existent haggling ability—if the merchant says ten shillings my tendency is to say, "Surely you mean fifteen"— when another piece caught my eye. It was printed with sisal plants, charming in color, with a running border and the legend "Tanganyika Uhuru 1962." Pretty, patriotic, and souvenirful all at once. I wanted three yards.

"Twenty-four shillings," said the merchant and he said it firmly.

"Oh, come," I said, "it isn't worth more than fifteen if that."
He shrugged. "Twenty-four shillings."

I paid. I am spunkless but also I am ignorant. It was pretty,
the fabric was of better quality than the first *lazos* he had shown
me, maybe it was *worth* twenty-four shillings. I hope so. I dislike
being cheated but I have never cared for those hard bargainers
who try to evade paying for value received.

The other enjoyable purchases I made from the same man who
sold me the carved animals: two Masai necklaces, gay in color
and fine conversation pieces. I got them for two or three shillings
apiece instead of the ten demanded by the ambitious young lady
on the road.

Norton, not to be outdone, announced that he too had shopping
plans. His were eminently sound. He went to a liquor store,
emerging with several bottles of necessities including Italian
chianti for perking up the flaccid results of the African cuisine.
We made the mistake of not taking a bottle along when we went
to lunch at the Safari Hotel. The hotel did have a bar, however,
as well as a frightful smell. Liquor may ease sorrow or boredom;
it does not blunt the olfactory nerves. One usually associates unpleasant odors with a lack of sanitation but this one was due to a
contrary cause. The top of the bar, instead of being zinc, was
copper and it was bright. I suspect the polish used to obtain this
desirable effect was the culprit, but if the Safari has noticed any
falling off of patronage, they now know to what it may be attributed.

A good many Hollywood photographs were proudly displayed
in the bar because John Wayne's *Hatari* company had stayed
there when on location in Africa shooting the picture. One of the
final scenes takes place in the lobby, which was reproduced exactly.

En route to Manyara from Arusha we passed four young boys
in wild array. Their black faces were painted in gay white patterns of dots and lines, they wore ostrich feathers behind their
ears, a bit of casual drapery festooned their bodies, and they
looked for all the world like American youngsters on Halloween.

Koske told us they were on their way to their circumcision rites and their painted faces and feathers were to celebrate their entry into manhood.

They weren't the only novelty of the trip. We also saw our first secretary bird and our first beobab tree. The former are comical chaps although formally attired. Just as penguins are always in white tie and tails, so secretary birds, while not exactly in striped pants, give just the same a sober, diplomatic effect: black trousers, black backs and long black tails, beige undertrappings. A fan-shaped crest encircles their heads from ear to ear and their initial movements into flight are lumbering.

For me, the beobab trees are the Arthur Rackham illustrations of childhood fairy tales, but for Norton they evoked Kipling. They have short, very thick gray trunks and at that season of the year— June and July—are stripped of leaves, their naked branches weaving wintry patterns against the hot blue sky. We were told that the pulp of their pods tastes like bicarbonate of soda but we didn't try it. Perhaps it is because there is more sky in Africa than elsewhere that one is constantly aware of the curious and exotic silhouettes of the trees, whether isolated on the stretching plain or looming in the early morning mists from the rain forests on the mountainsides.

Nearing Manyara, a small community with a game reserve, we crossed a wooden bridge over a shallow stream where three Masai men were bathing naked. Their bodies would have delighted an Egyptian sculptor—they had the lean flat look of Egyptian art rather than the rounded forms and muscular development of the Greeks. They were very dark, very beautiful, and admirably equipped.

We liked Manyara for several reasons, among them the fact that I was a riotous success. When we got out of the Land Rover to buy some fruit and the Africans saw I was wearing two Masai necklaces they became delirious with laughter. I was, very obviously, the joke of the month. They pointed at me, called to each other, and doubled up with glee. I was abashed but pleased. My theater training has run to comedy rather than drama yet even so this was the first time I had ever rolled them in the aisles with a sight gag. The witty line has been more my forte but a laugh is a laugh. I co-operated to the best of my ability and the mirthful spectators clustered around, giggling and touching me.

When Norton brought out his camera and, reversing their usual behavior, two young girls eagerly took positions on either side of me, they started a small stampede. *Everyone* wanted to be in the picture.

The gateway to the Manyara reserve where one pays admission is a tiny one-room museum worth a visit for the sake of the exquisite butterfly collection, a few stuffed birds of beautiful plumage, and birds' eggs of lovely color. Also, for them as likes 'em, snakes in alcohol.

The road to the reserve winds through thick jungle growth, the first authentic jungle we had seen, and it was wonderfully lush and dense, great shafts of sunlight slicing down through the dark luxuriant foliage. Manyara, like the Nairobi National Park, is also, in a sense, a shopwindow, for although a small area it is perfect and representative.

However, it has its problems. Its northern boundary adjoins a rapidly growing community, Mto-wa-Mbu, which the park administrators are well aware is the source of future headaches. They will undoubtedly have to construct a fence to keep the game from wandering into the cultivated areas and, when dealing with large determined animals such as rhino, buffalo, and elephants, you need a large, determined, and expensive fence. They are hopeful, though, of getting funds and along the southern boundary have already deterred would-be Columbuses with a barrier partly composed of old elevator cables.

Poaching is not a serious problem but it exists, the Wambugu tribe from the top of the Rift wall raiding for ivory and the fabled rhino horn. The tragedy is when they do not kill outright but only wound the animals, who withdraw into the reserve to die frequently lingering and painful deaths.

The undergrowth in Manyara is thick and the Land Rover proved invaluable, for tracks are sketchy and we were obliged to make our way through tall grass and heavy woodlands. At the museum gate we had picked up a young ranger, a winner. Under his jauntily set green beret his dark eyes sparkled, his beautiful white teeth flashed in a happy grin, and he had a quite irresistible personality, a cross between a deeper-hued Harry Belafonte and Maurice Chevalier forty years ago.

This charmer guided us to an elephant thicket. Koske drove to within about twenty yards of a family contentedly munching trees, and then to the haunt of a lone rhinoceros who regarded us with a combination of ill humor and contempt. At one moment he started trotting toward us with a gait that might have developed into a charge but in midstream he changed his mind, shrugged, and turned aside. We were in our jeep ready to skedaddle but Koske, we discovered, was a man who liked to stand his ground. If the customers grew a little apprehensive, it was good for them, gave them their money's worth.

There is a lake in Manyara, the home of flamingos, and I suppose I should be enthusiastic about them, many people are, but to me they are anticlimactic. I want them to be the deep improbable shade they are on cheap postcards from Florida and always they are a washed-out, insipid pink. More satisfying to me were the Manyara zebras and the exquisite baby gazelles. In the park we saw our first impala standing immobile in a frieze like creatures on an antique urn. There is something marvelously satisfying about wild animals in their native environment, life in its ultimate perfection. Even animals we think of as ugly—rhinos, hippopotami, crocodiles—are right, their forms appropriate to their needs, surroundings, and personalities.

It was getting dark when we drove out of the park and up the steep bluff, the Rift escarpment, to the Lake Manyara Hotel with its unsurpassed view, one of the most breath-taking in Africa, of bays, bluffs, jungle, lake, and the vast spaces of southern Masailand stretching to the horizon. A telescope stands on the terrace with a guest eternally peering through it at the wild game below. At the time of our arrival a large party of Indians were wandering about but they seemed to be there only for the day's excursion, returning to Arusha in the evening.

The hotel is composed of long low wings so that each room, even the bath, has the superlative outlook, and theoretically one may sit in the tub mooning at leisure upon the glory of nature. In practice, one is, like a Baptist, subject to total (also unpremeditated) immersion, for the large picture windows are set low in the wall and up and down the terrace, just beyond, stroll other guests also absorbing nature's splendor. Should they turn their heads, they have an equally uninterrrupted view of a fellow boarder in his own splendor, mother naked in the tub.

My dear one didn't complain too much about the ducking acrobatics, but he did mutter that perhaps, on our return stopover, it might be wise to settle for hotter water and less spectacle. We did too, faring better the second time round as the view was still fine but we were nearer the boiler room.

Dinner was the usual indifferent fare but there was a group of French tourists also spending the night at the hotel and afterward, in the lounge, as we sat around the fire with our coffee cups, they started singing, very softly, old French songs. One of the women, I think, must have been a professional, for she had a lovely full deep voice. I have always loved French folk songs and under the influence of the minor melodies and possibly the dinner wine a few tears splashed into my cup. I was sad and very happy.

In the morning when I went to the desk to mail my newspaper column home I was informed that the mail truck had already left. There would not be another until Saturday and this was only Wednesday. I was lucky, however, for my distress was quickly alleviated by one of the charming vocal Frenchmen of the night before. "Can I not mail the letter for you in Nairobi?" he asked. "We are driving there today and tonight flying back to Paris. Perhaps you would like me to mail it in Paris?" I assured him that Nairobi would do very well but I felt for him and his party. Manyara to Nairobi in a day is a grueling drive and to have an all-night flight facing one on arrival is exhausting merely to think about. French! They were Spartan.

At the Manyara Hotel we were subjected to the same pressure from the African servants that we had experienced at the New Stanley—the ever extended hand. I asked the receptionist, an Englishwoman, why this was. "Are they ill paid?" I said. "Are they gypped out of decent tips by safari people ever on the move? Why the eternal gimmes, ranging from strong hints to outright demands for money?"

The English lady was short about it. Provincial, perhaps, but of strong views. "Not at all," she said. "It's simple. They're greedy. Worse than the French."

"Oh, not the French!" I was remembering the lovely songs and the kind and just departed gent, my personal, private courier. "You can't compare them to the French!"

She sniffed. "They're worse. African servants rob each other. They're mean and grasping."

We left Manyara shortly after nine of a gloomy morning, fog enveloping us like a wet gray blanket. Grasping or not, the Africans we passed along the road worried me. They are all right later in the day when the sun has broken through but in the early morning they must be bitterly cold with nothing but those cotton cloaks. Some we passed, Wambugus, Koske said, were draped in what appeared to be red and white checked table-cloths. We concluded they were members of café society. Others seemed to favor turquoise-blue pants. There were several of them, bifurcated exclamation points slashing the fog. Stopping at a roadside pump for gas, Norton photographed an ageless figure seated on the roots of a great tree; an Indian woman, immobile, draped in a white sari gazing into the rolling mist.

Traveler's Tip No. 13. Doctor's contribution to men. For the chilly hours a chamois shirt is warmer than khaki yet, unlike nylon, it has pores. It is not *too* hot.

The drive from Manyara to Ngorongoro is about an hour. The road lies along a high ridge and through the mist we could discern rolling hillsides planted with beans and maize, and below us, on the left, ghost trees dripping pale green moss rising from the rain forests lining the ravine.

There is a touching monument on this ridge, the grave of Michael Grzimek, the German boy, son of Bernhard Grzimek, director of the Frankfurt Zoo, who was killed in an airplane accident while making a game count of the animals in the Serengeti Plain. A vulture flew into the tail of his plane and bent it, blocking the rudder cables. The machine crashed and young Grzimek was killed instantly. His grave, marked by an upright marble slab, overlooks the crater floor and the thousands of wild animals for whose sake he died. The inscription reads:

MICHAEL GRZIMEK

12.4.34 – 10.1.59

HE GAVE ALL HE POSSESSED

INCLUDING HIS LIFE

FOR THE WILD ANIMALS OF AFRICA

A few small pots of brightly colored artificial flowers are set in the ground at the foot of the tombstone.

His father's book, *Serengeti Shall Not Die*, the account of their joint venture in mapping the migrations of the great herds and assessing their numbers, is of compelling interest and a fitting tribute to a young man who was brave, intelligent and, if one may judge by his photographs, extraordinarily beautiful.

CHAPTER FOUR

Ngorongoro Crater— Olduvai Gorge—Serengeti

THE NGORONGORO CRATER is a land of fable and magical things happen there. It is the place where the lion trees grow. Lions lie along the branches, their paws dropping down like pendant fruit. Herds of wildebeest and zebra sweep across the plain and clouds of golden butterflies blow over carpets of fragrant white clover.

Usually one aspires to the heights, the mountains beckon. Here the contrary is true, one cannot wait to get from the top of the crater to the bottom where the animals roam.

We reached the campsite on the ridge about midmorning and found we were cozily lodged in a log cabin with a bedroom, a sitting room with an open fireplace, a little kitchen, and part of a bathroom; the tub part. Also pitcher and basin. The other amenity was in its own little log cabin with pointed thatch roof about fifty yards away with, when the fog lifted, an inspiring view over the valley on the opposite side from the crater.

Koske and Wamuti unpacked the Land Rover and we explored our small domain with interest, particularly noting the kitchen where, we hoped, the gifts of our cook would be made manifest. So far he hadn't so much as boiled water for us but this was Der Tag. So we assumed. We turned out to be wrong but that was later.

The pressing business being game viewing, we set off, winding down the mountainside from an altitude of 7800 feet to the crater floor 2500 feet below. Ngorongoro covers about one hundred and fifty square miles. It is an extinct volcano, the largest in the world, and the greatest natural zoo in the world, accommodating over 40,000 animals.

The descending slopes are covered densely with rain forests and the road, a narrow affair, is one-way, changing from up to down at certain hours of the day. It is bordered by grass and wild flowers and the drop is precipitous only in spots but it is occasionally in those spots that the vegetation lapses and one has a brusque and unsettling revelation of what could happen should the trusty Land Rover skid.

When we reached the bottom we looked up. Clouds curved over the shoulders of the mountains like cloaks of swansdown but the mist was rising and the ground was clear.

There are masses of wild flowers in the crater, grown high when we were there because of the exceptionally heavy rains, and there is a lake, the haunt of flamingos and countless other birds, and a natural salt lick. When wild animals have enough water and salt they may be said to be living in a split-level ranch-type château with cathedral living room, colored television, and wall-to-wall carpeting.

The first beasts we saw were an agile family of baboons and then the zebras. A little later we came upon a huge herd of wildebeest. Something, perhaps our car, startled them and they set off at a gallop, streaming across the plain like a far-flung banner. The sense of freedom and exhilaration was heart-lifting and we thought of the time when such a spectacle was a common occurrence, before man had entered full tilt into the despoilment of his heritage.

We saw our first elands in the crater but Koske told us they are the shyest of all game and they kept their distance. Norton, switching from close-up to telescopic lenses, reminded me of a magician—the hand was quicker than the eye.

We saw the lions in a thorn tree as we were on our way to

picnic in the shade. There were four of them but, although lions often take to the trees to avoid flies and the noonday heat, this particular quartet was ill. Two of them lay limply along the branches and two of them stood swaying slightly from side to side the way sick animals do.

We passed by them and went on to another grove where there were a couple of trucks, a group of Masai, and a nice young Englishman who was the game warden. He was making his luncheon tea over a spirit lamp set on the lowered tailgate of one of the trucks and looked a bit disheveled, having spent two nights in the crater helping the arboreal invalids.

It was a pleasure to hear him speak his native language. His voice was modulated, his phrasing accurate, and he was informative without being pedantic.

A few yards away, the Masai sat on the ground beside the other truck, which contained a dead wildebeest. Their *lazos* were drawn about them, their spears stuck upright in the earth within arm's reach.

The day before, the warden had shot a wildebeest deliberately and left it at the foot of the tree so the sick lions might eat but this one was dead by mistake owing to an overdose of sedation. He explained to us what had happened and how they go about injecting the animals.

Their current concern was branding animals for identification and also withdrawing a little blood for tests. They thought the illness of the lions was caused by a rinderpest epidemic and they were endeavoring to find out what animals were the carriers. This humane intent was not, however, the only reason for their zeal. Because of the epidemic no meat could be exported from East Africa and commercial interests were feeling the pinch.

The hypodermic sedative is shot into an animal with an air gun. In the cartridge are Epsom salts backed by a small disc of paper; behind that is a copper plug and, behind that, vinegar. When discharged from the gun, the needle enters the animal's flank, the vinegar hitting the salt causes it to fizz, and this forces the dose into the muscle. It sounds to me more elaborate than the nuclear bomb but many men understand it, although they admit it is a tricky business—the most experienced of them still being subject to error.

The reason is that to do an expert job one should be able to judge, with a fair degree of accuracy, the weight and approximate age of the animal to be injected, not an easy task when the subject is one of a milling herd of several hundred or even thousands.

During the temporary paralysis which the injection induces, the animal may be hoisted into a truck, branded, treated, caged, poor love, whatever is to be done.

Several men are required for the "shooting" because, while the ideal is to have the medicine take effect within eight minutes, do the job, and have the creature back on its feet in another eight, occasionally as much as twenty minutes go by before the drug becomes effective. During that time a wildebeest can cover a lot of ground and get lost in the herd so one fellow's job is to be the private eye tailing the victim. Once it falls, the men rush up to it and one of them takes hold of the head and pulls the tongue forward so the animal won't regurgitate. Should this happen, the contents of the stomach may be sucked down into the windpipe, resulting in strangulation.

As a paralyzed animal can still see, it has been found that a blindfold temporarily applied helps to lessen its panic. There must be a man to do that and one to do the branding or draw the blood and still another to time the procedure.

This system is an enormous improvement over the old method of driving after the herds in cars, exhausting and terrifying them, and then lassoing one of their members. That's the way Mr. Wayne did it in his movie, *Hatari*, but that isn't the way we professionals go about it.

Our English warden was realistic about shooting the wildebeest for the sick lions but he was genuinely distressed that a misjudgment on his part had resulted in the death of the one we saw in the truck.

He told us that one means employed in counting zebra is to

attach bright blue celluloid clips in their ears but that is not entirely satisfactory as the clips may fall out. Occasionally they find them in lions' spoor and they know what happened to *that* poor zebra.

Dr. Grzimek and his son Michael resorted to wide bright plastic collars when making their zebra count in the Serengeti.

We fell to talking of the Masai and we said it seemed a pity they could not be persuaded to live with a little more sanitation, with a broader range of diet. "One cannot go fast in these matters," the warden said. "Africa is a land of mistakes and delays and disappointments." Most lands are, I suppose, but with improvement available—provided, of course, one looks upon the white man's way as improvement—it seems too bad not to take advantage of it.

We mentioned the Peace Corps and the warden said he understood an American engineer was coming to the crater, he hoped he would. He spoke candidly of himself and other Englishmen in his position. Their salaries are paid half by the Tanganyikan government and half by the British. This is known as Commonwealth Aid. "Of course," he said, "the Tanganyikans want eventually to put their own men in jobs like mine." And he added with the objectivity we found characteristic of all the British we met in East Africa, "It's only natural."

We returned to the lion tree after luncheon. They were still there but the warden told us most of the lions had voluntarily left the crater because of the epidemic and the flies.

We saw, too, our first hyena. Their reputation is bad but, except when their jowls are smeared with blood, a spectacle for which we had a ringside view a few days later, hyenas are not unattractive. They have round ears and furry muzzles and the babies are quite charming. They live in holes like prairie dogs but it is true that they are lethal enemies.

Mr. Dodd, who runs the Ngorongoro Lodge, told us of a man who, against his advice, insisted on camping out with only a ground sheet and a sleeping bag. No tent and, I assume, no mosquito netting. A hyena attacked him, biting his foot and holding on with jaws like a steel clamp until, drawn by screams, the camp people came running. They shot the hyena but the foot was dangling by only a few shreds of flesh. They poured antibiotics into the man and rushed him to the Arusha hospital but there was no way of saving his leg. It had to be amputated just below the knee.

There were vultures in the crater but we had hopes for the lions as the birds were not yet circling their tree. Apparently there is still a good deal of scientific discussion as to whether vultures have extraordinary eyesight or an incredibly keen sense of smell or simply extrasensory perception. How do they know when an animal or person is going to die? An experiment was conducted in which a dead sheep was placed in a field. The vultures descended immediately to devour it but when another one was placed under cover and they could not see it they circled aimlessly. The eyes would seem to have it. On the other hand Mr. C. A. Spinage in his book *Animals of East Africa* holds out for a sense of smell suspecting that currents of hot air flowing upward may carry scent to the birds at great height.

Just as we had seen a herd of wildebeest galloping, in the late afternoon as we were heading homeward a long file of zebra went streaming past us. All those stripes on the gallop looked like a blurred modern photograph of cars streaking along a highway.

I said to the doctor, "I estimate one hundred and fifty. Know how?"

He is an obliging man who bites on cue. "How?"

"I counted the first twenty-five and calculated the rest."

"Oh," he said, "I assumed you counted the stripes and divided by twenty-seven." We had been told that that is the average number of stripes per zebra.

We waved farewell to the fleet of foot and to the flamingos in the lake and were about to regain the track for the return trip up the side of the volcano when Koske's binocular eyes sweeping the bush espied elephant. We turned off into grass taller than the Land Rover and made our way toward them. They were moving in quiet and leisurely fashion but actually our view was not too good, for Africa had got wind of Oscar Hammerstein and, though grass instead of corn, it was still as high as an elephant's eye and only their backs and the tops of their heads were visible above it.

The return to our log cottage was delightful. It was getting cold again and a fire was crackling in the hearth, a little jar of fresh flowers stood on the table, and tea was nearly ready. It was just like Sara Crewe.

After tea I worked up my diary, playing back the tape in the Webcor and typing busily. Norton sat by the fire smoking his pipe. "It's all right," he said, "this African life. Woman works, man relaxes." Not wishing to spoil him, I didn't tell him that his mechanical genius was indispensable. I never did grasp the principle of the reels and kept thinking that the recording went on on both sides instead of top and bottom of the same side and sometimes, in wild abandon, I erased my own voice by recording over it before I had got the notes down in the composition book. Modern inventions are wonderful but the wheel is still all right and so are paper and pencil.

My literary labors finished, I went through the kitchen to take a bath. The system is primitive but the water is hot. There is a tank out back under which a fire is lighted, and as the pipe coming from it through a hole in the wall is only about six inches long, the water flows into the tub at the boil.

Shortly before supper Mr. Dodd asked us to join him in the bar for a cocktail. A photograph of Michael Grzimek hung on the wall—needless to say, he and his father are revered in that part of the world—and although we had never seen him we had read and heard a good deal about him and looked at the youthful laughing face with a sense of personal loss. His is a difficult name and we asked Mr. Dodd how to pronounce it. It is pronounced as though it were spelled Jemik.

We had been anticipating that this evening we would be eating the product of our own *mpishi* Wamuti, but no. He stood about watching while one of the camp boys prepared dinner.

Canned soup, brussels sprouts, potatoes, and two little nubbins which I interpreted as unicorn's hoofs. That's why we didn't see any unicorns in the magical crater. They kill them for the hoofs for dinner.

The doctor had some harebrained theory that we were eating beef and persisted in believing that the sorry results were to be attributed to circumstances, raw materials, and the fact that, despite their reputation, Africans are inexperienced at the pot. He may be right on all three counts, I still maintain it's the fault of the settlers. Had the Cavalleros, settlers of New York's superb Colony Restaurant, settled the colonies of East Africa, instead of the British, there would be a different tale to tell and different food to eat. Like teacher, like pupil.

Having finished our bottle of chianti by the fire, I kissed it— it had such a civilized taste—and sleepy from the fresh air and all the wonders we had seen that day, we went to bed when the homemade lights went out at 10 P.M. We awakened in the morning to surreptitious mouselike sounds from the kitchen—the local *mpishi* at his sunrise chores—and sure enough, at six-thirty in he came, a colorful little figure in a long green robe and red fez bearing morning *chai*.

Six-thirty may seem betimes but at that we were laggards. The night before our room boy had given us to understand that Koske's orders for the next day's march were for 3 A.M. We gave startled cries and, unlike Gertrude Lawrence's famous Jennie, in twenty-seven languages we *could* say no. I delved into my little stack of Swahili grammar and phrase books and emerged with seven-thirty as a more probable hour.

The distance from Ngorongoro to Seronera Lodge in the Serengeti Plain is ninety-eight miles but seven-thirty was soon enough, and as the Dodds waved us on our way, Mr. Dodd called out, "Don't get the wind up if you're stopped by elephants. I left for Arusha about this time one day last week and what between the fog and the elephants I was a good hour late for my appointment. They stood in the road and wouldn't *move*."

September and October, he told us, are the most perfect

months for visiting the crater; the air is clear and sparkling, there is no fog, and presumably in high humor under these pleasant circumstances, elephants allow motorists the right of way. In *No Room in the Ark*, Mr. Alan Moorehead plumps for the month of January when the great migrations start out for Lake Victoria. We hope to return at both seasons.

The thick gray curtain was beginning to lift from the crater floor as we set out and the first clear light revealed our first hartebeest with his curious squiggly horns rising from his head in a wide V and projecting sharply backward at the tips. He was Mr. Jackson's hartebeest. I would rather have an animal named after me than a flower. Loving nearly all of them as I do, I wouldn't care which one, but those that are, so to speak, privately owned all seem to be of the antelope family.

Our first hartebeest cut us down to size. We were beginning to get a little smug about our ability to recognize animals on our own, without prompting from Koske as to what particular species we might be looking at. We had been too quickly susceptible to the tourists' snobbism: who can recognize a breed first? Antelope we considered we had pretty well pigeonholed but we became humbler as our knowledge increased: there was always a new variety.

Along the road we passed a Masai village awakening to the new day. Cattle were milling about among the fourteen or fifteen huts encircled by a thorn hedge and people and smoke were issuing from the doorways. Part of the herd had already started for the day's grazing, old men of the tribe and the *totos* (children) shepherding them along the hillside. Again I noted the happy lot of the donkies. They looked plump and contented, and since the Masai have few possessions their burdens are trivial, even the gourds in which the milk is stored being carried by the women.

A little farther on we saw a hyena finishing off a meal and five vultures circling, waiting for the remains. Far off on the horizon great clouds of smoke billowed into the sky, the Masai burning the grass. I do not subscribe to the scorched-earth policy myself.

Plow the vital elements back into the ground is my theory, but Norton said many American cattlemen do it too. It's supposed to eliminate the old matted grass and leave room for the fresh young shoots; maybe it does.

The track we were following dipped at last into the Olduvai Gorge and the weight of aeons began to press upon us. Here it is probable that the human race began. In his engrossing book, *African Genesis,* Robert Ardrey tells of the discovery by Mary Leakey and her husband, Dr. Louis Leakey, in 1959 of a fossil skull consisting of four hundred fragments, the remnants of the first maker of stone tools.

Dr. Leakey announced the find as the earliest known true man and named him Zinjanthropus. There are scientists, as well as Mr. Ardrey, who question the authenticity of the claim that he was the human ancestor, but ape or man or something in between the discovery was epochal and, according to fossil tests conducted at the University of California, he lived 1,750,000 years ago.

In his book Ardrey describes Dr. Leakey so vividly that when we knew we were going to his part of the world we hoped very much to have the opportunity of meeting him.

With that in view, I had written to Mr. Fairfield Osborn of the New York Zoological Society, whom I had met once or twice, to ask if he would forgive my imposing on slender acquaintance and if he would be kind enough to give us a letter of introduction to Dr. Leakey. I had his answer within a couple of days. "No, I won't," he said. His candor made me laugh but I could not take it amiss. He went on to explain that he'd given too many letters of introduction and he had to stop someplace. We, I gathered, were the ideal spot. Also, although he is too big a man for petty vengeance and in all probability he had completely forgotten the incident, if indeed he had ever been aware of it, it would have been no more than human had he wanted to get back at me a little.

I once received a letter from him asking for a contribution to the Bronx Zoo and I replied, "The chief thing I want to do about zoos is to abolish them." I had recently been to one, not his, and was immeasurably depressed by the sad, boring captivity in which the animals were held but as I was reading *Serengeti Shall Not Die* when I received Mr. Osborn's letter, I did send a modest contribution to the Wild Life Trust for Africa for the Michael Grzimek Memorial Fund.

Fortunately, as far as our hopes for Dr. Leakey were concerned, though spurned by Mr. Osborn, we had other sources.

Good Dr. Brown's scientific colleagues rallied and when we arrived in Nairobi we asked two or three people we met where we might find Dr. Leakey and present our letters. "Oh," they said, "he's not in town. Off digging somewhere. Skull nutty. But the letters wouldn't do you any good anyhow. He's terribly busy and never sees anyone." We felt let down but contained our disappointment as best we could and went about our business.

Still, because of him, and Zinjanthropus and Robert Ardrey, the Olduvai Gorge had a special aura and we regarded it with fascination. It is a gash in the earth twenty-five miles long, it has the configuration of the Grand Canyon on a much smaller scale and is paler in color, but in its layers of rock and stone and sand lies the record of the earth's occupants, animal and human, reaching back through the mists of ages to the formation of the planet.

Koske drove to the edge and we got out of the Land Rover and took pictures of each other silhouetted against the panorama of history and were filled with awe and the coffee Wamuti poured from our thermos bottle.

Later, driving along the rim of the canyon, we passed another Masai village. The effluvium issuing from it caused me to think of the Mesdames Chanel and Arden. If they are looking for an enlarged market for their perfumes, that village is fertile territory. All the airs of Africa did little to dilute the stench. We drove hurriedly on and presently came to a rough camp. As we stopped, a tall good-looking young African came up to us and we asked if there was any work in progress. "Yes," he said, "they're digging in one of the beds on the opposite side of the gorge. It's not very interesting but if you want to watch it's all right."

We decided that, interesting or not, we wanted to see it. Who could say? Maybe a skull to make Zinjanthropus look modern would be uncovered right before our eyes.

We accordingly went grinding and braking three hundred feet down to the bottom of the gorge and there, sure enough, on an opposite slope was a group of Africans with pickaxes leisurely hacking away at time's depository.

We watched them for a few minutes although in point of fact our informant at the camp had been right. As a spectator sport it was less rewarding than watching the excavators at work in New York digging holes for new office buildings and apartment houses through which modern skulls will stream. Norton snapped some pictures and we were about to climb back into our jeep when we saw a party of men coming toward us—several Africans and three white men, the tallest of whom, a vigorous figure dressed in a khaki coverall, his white hair blowing in the breeze, called out, "Good morning." My husband stared for a moment and then walked over to him. "Good morning, sir," he said. "My name is Norton Brown. Dr. Leakey, I presume?" "Yes, I'm Leakey, how do you do?" He held out his hand. Well! Tradition was purring along nicely.

It was indeed Dr. Leakey and he proved to be most cordial. We explained who we were and told him about our letters and he laughed and introduced us to his colleagues: young scientists and laborers who were working with him. "Want to see the spot where we found Zinjanthropus?" he asked. This is scarcely an invitation one declines, so as he hopped aboard his own Land Rover and took off at a gallop we followed in hot pursuit. Eager as we were, we couldn't have been in quite such a rush but Dr. Leakey was. Dealing with unimaginable aeons of time, one might expect him to be leisurely in his approach but he is a man in a hurry. There is so much—so much to find. Robert Ardrey describes him as "charging like a Spanish bull down the corridors of his museum [the Coryndon in Nairobi] or along the crimson gravel roads so like straight bloody cuts on the face of shining Kenya." The description is apt. He talks fast too; it is an effort to follow him yet one tries because words dropping from his lips are gems of knowledge and experience.

We got out at a spot on the barren sun-baked hillside where there is a low monument-marker, a sort of tombstone to the dawn-time creature. "Man of about eighteen," Dr. Leakey said. "That was the span of life in those days. Sometimes they might go up to twenty-eight, rarely beyond." The digging had uncovered two thousand stone and pebble tools and eight thousand animal bones. He broke off a fragment of stone, a sort of porous concentration of silt, a petrified form, and handed it to Norton, who treasures it. After all, how many possessions do you have that are 1,750,000 years old? Your fur coat only *seems* that old.

We ran to another site, somewhat lower, where Dr. Leakey had unearthed the hand, jawbone, and collarbone of a child and the foot of a woman, circa 1,800,000 years old.

Each stratum of earth and stone represents a time lapse of about one hundred thousand years. Dr. and Mrs. Leakey named their finding Zinjanthropus because Zinj is an old Arabic word for East African. Although Robert Ardrey writes of him with the greatest respect and enthusiasm, he does say that Dr. Leakey erred in defining the skull as that of true man and that the term Zinjanthropus was incorrect. When we mentioned to the eminent anthropologist that we had seen the Ardreys in Rome he was perfectly courteous although his own enthusiasm seemed under control.

After viewing a few more sights dating from time out of mind, Dr. Leakey asked us if we wouldn't like to come up to camp for a drink. It was now midmorning and hot so we accepted with pleasure. The camp stands on a rise of land with a cool breeze blowing through the central living quarters, an airy pavilion-like structure consisting of a roof of thatch and bamboo upheld by high poles.

A refrigerator stood silhouetted against the sky and, thanks to a kerosene engine, manufactured a plentiful supply of ice. There were long shelves filled with books, including an abridged Oxford English Dictionary, boxes and boxes of specimens, and strings of small white bones dangling from the rafters like garlic in a French kitchen. A haunch of beef was also dangling. The steer from which it had been separated was modern but we did see an ancient antelope skull and the jaw of a prehistoric rhino half again as large as that of his descendants currently roaming the African plain.

One of the stone axes and a chisel belonging to the eighteen-year-old Zinjanthropus lay on the table. It was a very strange feeling to hold it in one's hand and try to comprehend 1,750,000 years.

I have mentioned the rapidity of Dr. Leakey's speech. He drinks at the same clip but what he was swilling down bottles of, while we drank our leisurely beers, was lemon squash. He apparently dotes on the stuff. We met several other members of his staff including two young doctors, one a Dr. Hay from California, the other an Englishman, and then Mrs. Leakey joined us. The Leakeys must have a wonderful life. For thirty years, according to Robert Ardrey, they have worked together with passion on the most absorbing detective story ever unfolded: the origin of the human race.

When we mentioned our friend, Paul Fejos, who has since died but who was at that time director of the Wenner Gren Foundation, Dr. Leakey observed that he was going to the foundation's anthropological conference at Burg Wartenstein in Austria in July. Mrs. Leakey said she wished she were going too but the program she had on hand in the Olduvai Gorge was too demanding for her to get away. Woman's work is never done.

They told us how the African laborers, the ones we had been watching on the hillside, hack away at a site until they reach the level of interest. The Leakeys and their colleagues then take over, working literally with fine brushes and the most delicate dental instruments as, with infinite care, skill, knowledge, and luck, they expose the powdery fragments of bones aeons old.

Dr. Leakey said that enough material had already come to light in their excavations to keep him busy till the end of time. Sometimes, if a site does not seem to be developing according to expectations, they will switch to another, getting under way quickly before their money runs out. Financing their work is an eternal and pressing problem but if a place shows enough promise funds are probably forthcoming, although I believe that in Africa, unlike scientific expeditions in Asia, they have never had the money that the importance of the project justifies.

Every morning the camp's young doctors hold a clinic and between fifteen and twenty Masai flock there daily to be treated. A group of them were gathered under a big tree, laughing and chattering and discussing their symptoms. Norton inquired about their ailments. "Mostly eyes," Dr. Leakey said. "Without chimneys the smoke in their huts is frightful and their eyes are badly irritated. Then too they have a belief that they mustn't shoo away any flies that light on their faces because if they do their cattle will stray." Also, it seems they are susceptible to pneumonia, information that did not surprise me. Those highlands can be bitter cold and all the Africans we saw seemed underclad for the chilling mists of early morning.

Besides its human inhabitants the camp also boasted a large domestic menagerie: assorted puppies, Dalmatians, a monkey named Simon who explored the interior of our Land Rover in praiseworthy detail, and a baby wildebeest. They had found him when he was no more than a day or two old. His mother had been killed by a lion and the umbilical cord was still dangling. Although Norton took a picture of him and Dr. Leakey and me, it is not included in the photographs in this book because of a loss over which I am still grieving, still, with reason, kicking myself.

When we returned from Africa I wrote an article about our trip which appeared in *Vogue*. They wanted three or four photographs to illustrate it and asked me to send over several from which they might choose. After much consultation Norton and I selected eleven which we both considered to be among the very best he had taken, the pearls of the collection. I then entered a period of aberration. Valuing them as I did, the normal procedure would have been to call *Vogue*, say, "The article and slides are ready, please send a messenger." Any chump would have done so. Not I. I had them mailed. I did not even specify registered mail and they never arrived. It was some days before Allene Talmey, *Vogue's* feature editor, or I was aware of it, each assuming we had not heard from the other because of outside matters. When the hideous truth burst upon us, eruptions took place in every post office in town. Word sped right up to Mr. Christenberry, Postmaster of the city of New York. A dauntless woman, Miss Helen McLaughlin of the Claims Department in New York City's great Eighth Avenue terminal turned the mails inside out. Those couriers whom neither rain nor snow, nor heat, etc., still shudder when they remember the great upheaval. It was in vain. An advertisement offering a reward in the New York *Times* was in vain although it did elicit two responses: one from the *Herald Tribune* and one from the *Journal-American* asking if I did not want to advertise with them.

By the time this book appears it will be more than a year after the event, but I still mention it in the wild hope that in some lost and found department, down behind some counter of a post office, sandwiched behind some desk in an office of the Graybar Building, *Vogue's* headquarters, an envelope thick with dust containing what is so dear to us and not worth a Confederate nickel to anyone else in the world will come to light and that it will be sent back to me by a peerless reader. If one could be sentenced for such idiocy, atonement might bring relief but I am prosecutor, judge, and jury. There would appear to be no defense.

On that sunlit day in the Olduvai Gorge, however, unaware that he was married to Zinjanthropus' next of kin, Dr. Brown snapped away, anticipating long happy sessions back home when, reviewing the slides, we would be able to relive the pleasure we were experiencing at the moment.

Beside the wildebeest, there was another camp pet who caught my heart, a bush baby. Native to East Africa, especially the warm and humid coast, this is a tiny, furry, nocturnal creature, not a lemur, not a monkey, and not a minute kangaroo yet having some of the characteristics of all three. He has no pouch but he is not unlike a kangaroo in shape and his jumping range is incredible. He has enormous round eyes like a lemur, rounded upright ears, and the tail and little hands of a monkey. Your own hand is amply big enough to hold him. He also has teeth like needles and we were told that two bush babies of the same sex will often fight to the death. The one who gets in the last bite wins. The scientific name for this bundle of beguilement is *Galago senegalensis*. One of the young scientists had one as a pet. He let me hold him and I nearly never left camp. I wanted to spend the rest of my life with him. Later, back home in America, I owned a bush baby. I loved that little animal in a way that I have never loved anything or person before or since. I cannot explain the sympathy, the amusement, the affection and pity he roused in me. When we were out on parties I would think about him and long to get home to him, for he slept all day and was playful and gay through the night. He was my little love, my secret wealth, but the thought of his loneliness made my heart ache and I was trying hard to get him a mate.

After I had had him for two months and five days I found him dead on my writing table at three o'clock of an October morning. Someday I may write about him but I cannot do it now.

We left the camp in the Olduvai only because Dr. Leakey and his companions were obviously busy and we did not want to out-stay our welcome. We turned from them reluctantly and headed for the Serengeti Plain.

Driving along, Koske pointed out a phenomenon which mysti-fied him and me but which Dr. Brown understood. It was a huge gray sand dune which moves about five feet every year. Spooky to the uninitiated but merely nature's way to the scientist, and caused by the wind blowing ever in the same direction. The sand blown away is piled up again a little farther off. The phe-nomenon is named, with accuracy, Shifting Sands, and it is the home of hundreds of gray-brown birds, sand grouse.

We drove for a long time over a bumpy, virtually non-existent track, crossing mile after mile of what we assumed to be the Serengeti Plain, and we were getting disheartened, for sup-posedly this is the home of the largest concentration of wild game in the world and so far we had spotted exactly three Thomson's gazelles, one giraffe, and one ostrich. Actually, as we learned later, we were not in the plain proper but in a vast anteroom, an endless expanse of baked earth and short dry grass.

Observing all this emptiness, the eager do-gooder, the inexperienced animal-loving tourist (ourselves), exclaims, "Hooray, not so many people as we feared; paradise for the beasts." This, of course, is not true. Where human beings have not encroached upon territory that might be considered a sanctuary for wild life, it is not out of affection for them or a sense of responsibility about them or the recognition that they too have rights upon this earth, but only because there is no water. Where there is no water, animals cannot live any more than can people.

Yet in the enormous arid expanse there was a certain wry comfort. It was a relief to find that one of our fears—that tomorrow will bring Levittown to Africa—is, temporarily, unjustified.

Conceivably a water table may one day be discovered under the parched savannah of East Africa and from some source may come the money to make it of practical value but that is still day after tomorrow.

Both the British game wardens and the ambitious leaders of African states are concerned about the poor state of the roads leading into the game reserves and there is no question that they are bad. Personally, we got tired and our bones ached at the time; in retrospect we are glad about the tracks. Dust in dry weather, muddy in the rains, and full of holes at all seasons, they discourage tourists. Yet we are well aware of the need of tourist money to maintain the wild-life sanctuaries only, inevitably, the more tourists, the less sanctuary.

Practically speaking, although it did not apply to his collection since pictures are not harmed by people crowding to look at them, the viewpoint of the famous art collector, the terrible-tempered Mr. Barnes of Philadelphia, "*I* bought them with *my* money, others keep out," works admirably in the game reserves. Ideally speaking, a rich misanthrope should endow the sanctuaries and visitors should be allowed only in trickles, Africans leading the way. For one of the problems of the country is that so many young Africans have never seen the wild game and have no awareness or understanding of the unique treasure that is theirs.

Since bumping along in a Land Rover, grasping the rail screwed to the back of the front seat to keep from banging one's head against the roof or from flying out like Mary Poppins when the sliding panel was pushed back, allowing the doctor to stand on the seat for unobstructed photography, makes for quite an appetite, we finally stopped for lunch in the shade of a group of thorn trees. As people who look for many months of the year at the cement and concrete of New York, we found gazing up through the green lacy branches into the cloudless blue of the noontime sky marvelously refreshing.

Even the lunch seemed palatable. Tea as a rule was good and Kenya coffee is excellent. In fairness, there was little to complain of in the bread and tinned butter. Since we seldom eat desserts, except perhaps when offered a delectable airy soufflé—rarely at our own dinner table—we have no complaints in that department. It is the meat and vegetables that are tedious.

When picnicking in Africa, however, there is one enormous recompense, a fringe benefit so great that poor food pales into insignificance. Here at home when on a picnic we are satisfied if it is in a rural setting, if we have a magnificent view, or if the meadows are fragrant and the trees provide welcome shade. In Africa there is all sorts of scenery *plus* the animals. You look up from your supine ham sandwich, you peer over the rim of the teacup, and you are quite likely to see—only a couple of hundred yards away—three giraffes posing in a frieze between two thorn trees. This happened to us and it was pure delight.

Driving along after luncheon, we encountered our first cheetah. Chap by the name of Cassius, I should imagine, judging from his appearance, and we feared some poor little Thomson's gazelle was not long for this world. As Koske swerved toward him he got up and loped off, a handsome sight in his elegant polka dot coat. That time he went slowly, but cheetahs are the fastest animals on earth and, in brief spurts, can run as fast as sixty miles an hour. He and the rhino in Manyara were among the few lone animals we saw.

There were a good many foxes on the plain, which explained the scarcity of Thomson's gazelles. There are few tidbits a fox relishes more than a baby gazelle but as the foxes stay mainly in the dry savannah the little creatures are better off taking their chances in more fertile areas. To be sure, the lions fancy them too but the mortality risk is at least spread out among themselves, wildebeests, and zebras.

The more experienced we became in game watching, the more we realized how like fishing it is. There will be long empty stretches of nothingness and then suddenly the excitement of a strike: one spots an elephant or a rhino or a herd of zebra. The struggle to land the fish translates, in animal viewing, into the struggle to get close enough and at the right angle for a good shot with the camera. And just as in fishing you question other anglers, so do you inquire of the few other travelers you may meet where they have seen game. Perhaps under that rocky ledge will be a trout. Perhaps on that outcropping of rock will be lion; you head toward it.

It was on this segment of our safari that we saw our first topi. They are dandies, these lads, with heavily ridged lyre-shaped horns, brown socks, and rich purple patches on rump and foreleg.

Having crossed the eternal anteroom, we entered at last into the Serengeti Plain. We knew this because we passed a sign that said so. It also said, "Animals have the right of way." Imperceptibly the vegetation changed, the grass becoming longer and more lush. We bounced and jounced along, spotting hartebeests and zebras and the shy distant elands, and eventually the road calmed down and the last forty-five miles to Seronera Lodge were relatively smooth rolling.

The lodge is a group of six rondavels with the usual conical roofs of thatch. Though authentic in shape, they are built of plastered concrete blocks rather than mud. Our bathroom was housed in a lean-to: flush toilet and washbasin with cold running water. Hot water and tubs were in a nearby bathhouse.

We are great ones for "atmosphere" yet, much as we enjoyed Seronera, the atmospheric part seemed a trifle forced. If you are going to have bathrooms and Western furniture, they fit better into non-round houses. The master, unpacking his gear, looked about and sniffed. "Might as well build a Hawaiian village on the Bronx Parkway." He doesn't like anything phony. When it came to the little dining room, the lodge people themselves went square in a separate hut with a couple of tables and an electric refrigerator.

Our first evening we dined there on Wamuti's efforts. So that was why he had not cooked before! We respected his abstinence. If knowing one's limitations is the first step to success, our *mpishi* is going to be president.

Our mess hall was roofed with thatch and there were screens at the windows and along the top of the walls which did not come up to meet the ceiling. It's good we are so crazy about wild life because it was with us in abundance during the meal. What were either very large mice or very small rats scurried up and down the outside of the screens and, toward the end of dinner, more exploratory types found their way inside and kept running up and down the walls. A couple of bats came in for dessert.

I managed to keep a grip on the hysteria mounting inside me, but during the rest of our stay we dined in our own hut; it didn't seem quite such a rodent social center.

It actually was very comfortable, with two windows, twin iron cots with mosquito-netting canopies, and heavy wooden brackets bedecked with a flowered cretonne valance supporting a pole on which we hung our clothes. Three straight chairs, a couple of tables, and a stand with a lamp between the beds completed the furnishing. Price: 20 shillings or $2.80 per person per night.

We had been welcomed on our arrival by Lasse Allan, an extremely pretty Scandinavian woman who runs the lodge with her husband and who speaks, besides Swedish, perfect German, English, and what sounded to us like perfect Swahili.

Tired by our travels, I enjoyed the hot tea brought me by our room boy. It had been made by Wamuti but he didn't bring it. Jobs in Africa are as sharply defined as they are in the stage hands' union. Mr. George Meany would be pleased.

After tea, no longer able to endure the state of my hair, a fanciful and distasteful wig of mud, I retired to the tubs and the hot water. The water was mud color too but it was wet and hot.

Traveler's Tip No. 14. Ladies! Be sure to take a good shampoo and your own rinse if you use one.

In the midst of my laundry work the doctor knocked on the door and announced that he was off with the game warden to see a leopard. Did I want to come? Obviously I wanted to but there I was: trapped, wet, and naked. "But you go ahead," I shouted magnanimously over the gushing water. "Don't mind me, just get good pictures." Since wild horses wouldn't have held him back I thought I might as well wish him Godspeed gracefully. As it turned out, my graciousness cost nothing. He returned shortly, disconsolate. The leopard had departed for points unknown. Actually, Cassius, the cheetah of the plain, was as near as we got to a member of that family the whole time we were in Africa.

That evening the doctor was awash with little ploppets of information. Shortly after his abortive leopard sortie he came into our hut with the news that Joy and George Adamson of "Elsa" fame—*Born Free* and *Living Free*—were camped in the Serengeti. They had had to fly to Arusha because she had some trouble with an eye but were expected back the next day. We were cautioned not to mention Elsa. Joy Adamson, it seemed, was still so emotionally involved with the lioness that at the mention of her name she was likely to burst into tears. "She may bring up Elsa herself after about half an hour," our informants said. "But don't you be the first to do it. She is still devastated by the death."

The men in the camp nodded sagely and said it was too bad Joy Adamson had never had any children. Implying, I suppose, that those who have them need nothing else. Possibly this is true, although, practically speaking, I have never seen it work out that way and even were she the old woman in the shoe, though conceivably pressed for time, living as she did and once having acquired Elsa as a cub, it seems to me unlikely that Mrs. Adamson's love for and interest in the lioness would have been any less.

I myself do not relish childless couples making fools of themselves over some yapping snuffling little dog, chirping to it in baby talk—I do not relish talking baby talk to babies—but that is because silliness is unattractive, not because affection is.

The Serengeti men were a little resentful, I think, because so much publicity from the books had accrued to Mrs. Adamson. "George had a lot to do with training that lioness," they said, "and most of the pictures are his." Yet time and again Mrs. Adamson mentions Elsa's affection for George and how she used to sleep in his tent, one paw always in contact with him. As we were to discover later, he is indeed a lion man.

Nor is he alone. There is a good deal of stamina in those parts. Our first evening, while we were dining with the livestock, Jan Allan came into the mess hut looking handsome and dramatic in green jacket and green shorts topped by a red woolen serape edged with fringe and carrying a long flashlight. He told us that a few nights before his car had broken down twenty-three miles from camp, and he had had to walk all night through lion country in the dark with no protection other than the big flashlight. Personally, I should have been uneasy but I suppose courage is often a matter of no alternative. Probably Mrs. Allan, wondering what had happened to him, was worse off than he was.

He seemed rather disillusioned about Africans although he liked Chief Adam Sapi, the newly appointed African chairman of the Tanganyikan National Parks, but he said that when some of the other colored government men came to visit the plain, they said, "My God, how do you stand the bloody place?" and decamped as quickly as possible for the more urban delights of Dar es Salaam.

When we had finished coffee we said good night to Mr. Allan and went to bed at ten o'clock when the lights went out. We slept almost at once but in about an hour I awakened and the

sound I heard made me far from happy. Four or five feet from
my bed was a carton with liquor bottles—the chianti and more
potent fortifiers—and a paper bag of lemons. From this cache
issued a sound, a rustling sound and stealthy. It would stop for
a moment and then would come the soft crackle of paper and
then an ominous rustle as a Thing moved. I lay there quivering
with fear but I was too newly come to Africa to dream of getting
out of bed to investigate a strange sound in the darkness. I did
take the flashlight and point it in the direction of the carton but
could see nothing as the light merely reflected on the mosquito
netting without penetrating it. For a few moments, however, it
stopped the noise but when I turned it off the miniature reign of
terror started up again. I began thrashing about in bed and
knocking on the light stand in the hope of stilling what my in-
flamed imagination told me had to be a poisonous snake—and in
the hope of awakening Dr. Brown. My husband is a dear man
and affectionate but once he's asleep he is lost to me. He is Just
and his sleep is that of a little child. *Wars* could be fought in our
bedroom and his healthful slumber would continue unabated.
Also, I respect sleep and in a woeful world am reluctant to bring
those I love back to consciousness before a robust daylight hour
when one is better able to cope. But if I *inadvertently* awakened
him—that was something else again. To my relief, inadvertency
triumphed. The sounding of the last trump finally brought him
to. "What in God's name are you doing?"

I explained the problem. "Listen to it," I said. "Just listen." The
craven thing, of course, maintained guarded silence.

"You're bats," said the doctor.

"That may be, but you get up and get it out of here," and as I
heard him relapsing into a muted snore, "Honey, *please.*"

Reluctantly he began windmilling his way out of his mosquito-
netting canopy; reluctantly he got on his slippers and shuffled toward the carton. "Probably a mouse," he said.

"Not a scorpion maybe?" Since possibly just the word would
cause whatever it was to turn into one even if it wasn't I was too
terrified to say snake. "Put the carton outside. Darling, please." I

didn't win. Moving the carton in the dark was a nuisance. He fumbled about in it and found the bag of lemons. "If you heard a crackling, it's probably a beetle or something in the paper bag." He opened the door of our hut, set the bag on the doorstep outside, returned to bed, and within seconds was back in the land of nod. Within minutes the stealthy rustling started up again. This time dread galvanized me to action. If it was a nest of cobras, better to be shed of them. I disentangled myself from under my own canopy, went to the carton and, numbed by fear, dragged it across the floor to the door which I opened and through which I kicked the horrid cargo. I banged it to, locked it, and scampered back to bed. It was then that I became aware of the roaring.

The roaring didn't frighten me. It was awesome but I knew it was from the lions near the camp. They were big forthright beasts and since they had plenty of gazelles to feed on I did not feel they would be likely to come bounding through the windows to munch on us. I was drifting to sleep when on the far side of the room I heard the sinister rustling begin again in the thatch. By now I was very sleepy and very irritable. To hell with it.

In the morning I was able to ignore the terrifying trivia but I did say, "How about those lions?" to the doctor.

"What lions?"

I stared at him incredulously. "You mean to tell me you didn't hear that roaring?"

He had heard it but was reluctant to accept its magnitude. Not that he didn't want to, it was simply that the fact that we had heard, with our own ears, the roaring of free lions in the bush was too unlikely, too marvelous, to be true. "They were bullfrogs," he said.

"Bull frogs! In the middle of this vast arid plain? They were lions!"

"They were lions," he cried. "Let's go!"

On the way out the door we stumbled over the carton, garage of ghoulies and ghosties and long-legged beasties and things that go bump, hiss, and rustle in the night. We ransacked it, finding nothing but the bottles and six unoffending lemons in an otherwise empty bag.

At seven forty-five Koske rolled up in the Land Rover, Leon, a camp guide on the seat beside him, and we started off on one of the eventful days of our lives.

We were bumping over the track less than a mile out of camp when the two men together cried, "Look!" There, just ahead of us, was a pride of lions, some twelve or fourteen of them gazing enviously at their leader, a big-maned male lying in the grass tearing at a haunch of wildebeest. The pecking hierarchy in the lion kingdom is rigidly controlled; the Master brooks no competition. He looked at us, rose without haste but with the air of a man who resents being importuned at table, and with the bloody remnant dangling from his jaws moved a little farther away, lay down again, and continued his breakfast.

We turned off the track, following him into the tall grass. The pride straggled along too, but we felt their chances to be slim. He was the head of the house, he was a rich man, and there would be no crumbs from his table.

When he raised his head to fix his family at a respectful distance, we could see his muzzle and chest covered with blood. After we had watched and photographed for quite a while Koske turned the jeep and headed in the opposite direction. In a few minutes we saw a lioness alone on a hillside. She was off on our right and presently we became aware of a wildebeest moving leisurely toward her through the long grass on our left, her baby following docilely in her footsteps. From time to time he would lift his head to the sweeping African skies and sniff the sweet morning air. When the lioness caught their scent she started moving stealthily toward them. Tense, we watched and waited. It was dreadful. We didn't want it to happen but we knew it was going to and we wanted to see it. On they came, the wildebeest and her baby moving rhythmically, unsuspectingly, to their doom. Suddenly the mother stopped in her tracks and her head went up. The air and earth were filled with silence but, alarmed, she broke into a gallop. The baby started after her but the

lioness circled behind her, swift as lightning, and pounced. The
baby sank beneath the weight. It made no cry but the grass
waved violently. The lioness leaped and pounced again. This
time the small animal's neck was broken and it lay still. I was
blinded by tears, but Leon started to laugh. Furious, I turned on
him. "How *can* you laugh at pain and terror!" He went on laughing. Whether at me or at the slaughter I do not know. Norton
had continued filming through the brief drama but his own eyes
were wet.

The mother wildebeest's anguish was pitiable to see. As she
wheeled and came back toward her baby, the lioness feinted in
her direction. She retreated, then advanced again. Again the
lioness started toward her but more, it seemed, to fend her off
than to attack. Having killed her prey, that, for the time being,
sufficed. The wildebeest hesitated, started forward again, then
turned and galloped off over the hill to join the herd.

Now, we thought, the lioness will fall to. Not at all. She hauled
the carcass a few yards from where it had dropped and then
went off to call her cubs. We did not lose sight of her and we
know that she did not growl or roar but in some way she com-
municated because shortly they appeared. There were several of
assorted sizes and we did not know if they were all her own
because apparently pride life is familial, aunts and cousins looking after nieces and nephews, but in any event, the three smallest
cubs went up to the carcass, sniffed happily, and settled down
to breakfast, as contented as babies with bottles. The mother
strolled off and lay down under a tree. We circled the cubs slowly
in the car while Norton took pictures and they raised their heads
and watched us indifferently although one of them did give a
comical abrupt snarl like an outraged kitten.

We got back to the camp for coffee about eleven and everyone
told us we were lucky because one may sometimes stay for several weeks in the bush and not see an actual kill. Results, yes,
just as we had seen the breakfasting lion and were to see several
wildebeest and zebra carcasses but not the act itself. Since it
happens hundreds of times a day and there is nothing one can

do nor, indeed, should do to stop it, I suppose we *were* lucky, but it was a poignant moment.

During the rest of the day I wrote in my diary; we read and relaxed and fed the super starlings, who for all their brilliance are cozy types who take crumbs from your hand. We also cottoned up to the social weavers, more modest little specimens, gray-brown in color with something Dickensian and humble about them. They have charm, though, and live up to their name, being sociably inclined, coming to perch on your shoulder or your knee and peck daintily at your offering.

About four o'clock, as we were leaving for our afternoon's reconnoitering, Jan Allan came to the door and said the Adamsons were back from Arusha and had invited us for cocktails that evening and would we like to go? Would we ever not! Mr. Allan said he'd pick us up at seven.

We were stalking leopard but found that, where lion are, leopard often aren't. Still, ever hopeful, we were heading for a high outcropping of rock when a mother wart hog came galloping across the track, five babies streaming out behind her like the tail of a kite. Norton's camera, by now well trained, leapt to attention practically of its own volition, but too late. They vanished into the high grass.

Continuing on, we rounded another outcropping and there, sunning themselves on a great flat rock, were eight enchanting lions, yawning, stretching, and romping together. They were a charming and entertaining spectacle and we took any number of pictures. We were so near them we didn't need the glasses but I kept looking through them anyway, not wishing to miss a whisker, and at one moment, pointing them rather aimlessly at everything far and near, I was rewarded by the sight of two bee eaters, lovely little green and yellow birds perched on a long swaying blade of grass. It seems they always hunt in pairs. They sit there looking small and helpless and as though butter wouldn't melt in their mouths until some unsuspecting bee buzzes by and then—snap! Ex bee.

After a time a couple of lions came down from the rock and

into the grass very near us, where one of them proceeded to relieve himself. I watched him with the close interest I bring to bear on Thor, our Weimaraner, in these matters. I want to make sure he is in good health. He almost always is and so, I was happy to see, was the lion. This important function attended to, he gave a large, gratified yawn and started moseying off through the grass. I was standing on the seat of the Land Rover—we had pushed back the panel in the roof—looking over the plain through the binoculars, when not far away I saw our family of wart hogs. At the same instant one of the lions got their scent and started forward. "Oh, my God!" I said to Norton. "There's going to be another kill." Happily not this time. Wart hogs go like greased lightning. The lion followed in pursuit but only briefly and seemingly more for the deviltry of the chase than with any serious intention of dining. He looked already well padded.

We drove around for a couple of hours. The animals are, of course, the prime objective, but we were in a lovely parklike section of the plain and sometimes Koske stopped the car and we sat there looking our fill at the open groves of acacia trees and the tawny sea of grass bathed in the late afternoon sunlight. High purple clouds were mounting the sky and a storm was brewing but for the moment the whole world seemed still and peaceful. Norton said, "This is our great trip." I thought so too.

After a while it was time to return to our rondavel and freshen up for our cocktail party. Norton had a Bowie knife he rather fancied. "Think I'll just take this along," he said. "You never know."

A few minutes before seven, as Jan Allan stopped in front of our door in his Land Rover, the storm that had been threatening through the afternoon broke in fury. It seems it never rains in the Serengeti Plain in June. It is unheard of—but we foxed tradition. During our tenure there were several deluges.

Norton dropped his raincoat over my shoulders and we piled into the front seat beside Mr. Allan and started off. It proved to be quite a drive. Slithering and sliding, we advanced along a river of slime that in the afternoon had been a river of dust. Several times we skidded to a stop, the car turned at a ninety-degree angle across the track. If the dauntless Land Rover got bogged down the evening promised to be glum. The prospect grew glummer when our friend at the wheel observed, "we're just about at the spot where last year a lion dragged a European from his tent and killed him."

"Did he now?"

"Yes, poor chap, he really had it. Head was in the lion's mouth, you know." Ah well, different countries, different small talk.

The Land Rover was persuaded to point to our destination and we ground our way forward inch by slippery inch through rain falling in sheets. As a matter of fact the Adamsons were camped a mile and a half from the Seronera Lodge. As a matter of impression, it was fifteen. Finally, through rain picked out in slanting silver slivers by our headlights, we discerned a small but sturdy gleam—the Adamsons' camp. We had arrived. Jan Allan drew up in front of two tents set cheek by jowl lighted by kerosene lanterns and there were Joy and George Adamson advancing through the torrent to meet us with the cordiality and aplomb of good hosts greeting guests arriving, bone dry, in white tie and earrings, on a Fifth Avenue threshold.

"How do you do," Joy said. "It was nice of you to come in all this rain." I had forgotten that she is Austrian. She speaks with a strong accent and the machine-gun delivery of Dr. Leakey. George, who is English, speaks with an English accent and is not in such a rush. He is of middle height, with a neat beard, piercing wide-open blue eyes, and a well-functioning pipe. We scuttled the few yards through the rain into a tent brightly lighted by a kerosene lantern hanging on a pole on the right side of the entrance. The left-hand pole supported an unrolled green canvas toilet kit belonging to Mrs. Adamson. There was a small shelf at the bottom on which was propped a round silver picture frame containing a photograph of Elsa, the world-famous lioness.

One side of the tent, lifted and supported on poles, formed a sort of projecting roof so that we sat within a three-sided shelter. A camp cot stood against the back wall with a table in front of it around which were grouped three canvas-backed chairs. On the table was a plate of small open-faced sandwiches, bologna and cheese, and three gin bottles, one containing gin, one whisky, and one martinis. There was no ice—where would it come from? And the martinis were English—half gin and half bitters. Believe me, after that drive they were absolutely splendid.

Mrs. Adamson is a woman of average height in, I should say, her early fifties with a broad brow, wide-apart blue eyes, a turned-up nose, and a small mouth. She was wearing pants, a green blouse, and a gray sweater, her pale, closely waved hair tied back with a ribbon. "I am furious about the rain," she said to me, "I washed my hair especially for you." It was one of the nicest compliments I ever had.

We sat down, Norton and George Adamson on the cot behind the table facing out, I in a camp chair at one end of the table, Jan opposite me, and our hostess facing in, her back to the rain and the night.

Generous drinks were poured into our goblets and we were urged to help ourselves to the sandwich hors d'oeuvre. As we had been warned not to mention Elsa we acted as though we had never heard of the lovely creature but the strain of continence was relieved by Mrs. Adamson, who referred to her almost immediately. She did not speak so much of the animal herself as of the Elsa Appeal, a fund which she and her husband have established for short- and long-term projects dedicated to the preservation of African wild life, which in several sections of East Africa is marooned in the midst of cultivated areas. As the human population encroaches, they are doomed to extinction since, as Bernhard Grzimek points out, in the nature reserves man has every legal advantage over animals, which are only protected as long as the land is not required for agriculture or other purposes.

One of the most moving and successful examples of Elsa Appeal rescue work involved kob antelopes. There are only about five hundred remaining in the eastern plateaus and plains, most of them concentrated on farms. It isn't that the landowners are unsympathetic but in times of drought they are serious competition to the livestock in available grazing areas. It is a case of "Either they go or we destroy them." In just over a fortnight the Elsa team succeeded in capturing and transporting forty-four of them to a location where they won't conflict with domestic herds.

The Adamsons want very much to capture specimens of other rare and dying breeds and transport them to sanctuaries "where the government is stable, stable." They are deeply concerned with the fate of game in the politically immature and rocky governments of Africa. George thought that Australia would be a good land, and Canada too for certain breeds. Norton suggested Mexico; its topography and climate, he felt, would be ideal.

There are now three Elsa books: *Born Free, Living Free,* and the third one, *Forever Free,* finished the week before our arrival. Their author told us they are to be produced as a two-part picture with MGM and the Disney interests contending briskly for the rights.

She spoke of her projected lecture tour in England, starting in September, and said that she was scheduled to tour America in 1963. The books at the time of our visit had sold 1,700,000 copies in English-speaking countries alone, significant perhaps of the yearning people must have to get away from the world people are creating, of a longing, even if unconscious, to return to the natural world of earth and sea from which we emerged.

Thanks to royalties, the Adamsons are well off. If they chose, they could live with ease but when we were with them their worldly possessions consisted of their house in Isiolo, the capital of the arid Northern Frontier Province, the two tents, in one of which we sat that night, and the de luxe Land Rover parked a few yards away. Their money goes into the Elsa Appeal.

They were in the Serengeti Plain searching for their lioness' three cubs Jespah, Gopa, and Little Elsa, whom they had transported and released there after the death of their mother. Their chief concern was Jespah, one of the males, who had been shot at by natives and carried an arrowhead in his rump. They were making desperate efforts to find him and, if it seemed necessary, have Dr. Harthoorn, one of Africa's leading veterinarians, operate to remove the arrow.

To do this they had not only to find the lion but to obtain permission from the director of the park for the operation to be performed.

The Adamsons themselves, Billy Collins, Joy's publisher, and Noel Simon of the Wild Life Society had all petitioned the director time and again to grant this permission and always his answer was no. To a layman such a decision is incomprehensible but it was apparently based on the fact that he had once known of a horse who also had an arrowhead in its flank and after two years it had fallen out of its own accord. He said, too, that the Adamsons' searching for the cubs would disturb the wild life of the park.

As Joy Adamson states in *Forever Free*—which, of course, at that time I had not read—"We did not think it realistic to compare a domestic herbivore with an arrow in its rump to a carnivore, who, in order to eat, must hunt with unimpaired physical strength." The director sounds like one of those unfortunate men who, unencumbered by common sense and once having taken a stand, are stuck with it and even should they secretly undergo a change of heart are incapable of reversing themselves.

That the dangerous lion is the wounded lion—if he is in pain—would seem to be borne out by the story of the farmer Jan Allan had told us about on our way to the camp. The lion who had made the attack was shot the next morning and was found to have a septic wound in his shoulder, a very serious handicap in hunting. Hungry and finding an easy prey, he had killed to eat. Spooky note: it had been a hot night and the man had not put up his mosquito netting.

To us, in our ignorance, finding the cubs in that enormous area seemed a hopeless task but the Adamsons were determined and were perhaps rewarded, for five months later Norton received a letter from George in which he said:

"At last I have abandoned the search for Elsa's cubs. I believe that I found one of them, the lioness Little Elsa. One morning I had stopped in a little valley and was having a late breakfast. I heard a zebra snort and saw it trotting by, pausing and looking back. A lioness approached, I hid myself. She came past the car without looking and entered a small gully where I could see the tip of her tail flicking up and down (a sign of indecision). After a few moments she came out and again came past, closer this time but still not looking in my direction. She climbed a small tree with a leafy top where she was completely concealed in the foliage. Through my glasses I could just see her eyes watching me intently. I got up and showed myself and called. She continued to watch. I then drove the car up to the tree and slowly past. She climbed down and started to follow. I went on some way and turned back to find her up the tree again. As I drove past she once more followed and sat herself down thirty yards from where I stopped and regarded me calmly as I walked about. I saw her again six more times and on each occasion she came to meet me. On the last, she was in the company of another lioness, aged and having only one ear. That was the last I saw of her. I expect "One Ear" took her away. While I cannot be a hundred percent certain it was Little Elsa, her behaviour and appearance were very convincing. This was the beginning of October. I carried on the search until a few days ago [middle of November] but found no further trace. When I left there was an immense concentration of wildebeeste and zebra in the Lake Magadi area, probably 50 or 60 thousand animals, an awe-inspiring sight."

Joy Adamson is realistic in her love of animals and spoke quite frankly of the need for cropping the herds (killing excess numbers) so that the remaining ones will have sufficient grazing land. She hopes that the Africans can be taught to do this humanely and she too mentioned the efforts being made to get them to report the game they kill to the government for a reward and thus prevent cruel and senseless poaching.

As we sat sipping our drinks and talking or, more accurately, listening—as I say, Mrs. Adamson is loquacious—Jan Allan happened to glance outside the tent. In a momentary pause during which our hostess took a swallow of her drink, he said casually and somewhat in the manner of a person referring to a neighbor's recurrent cat, "George, there's one of those lions again." Our eyes followed his pointing finger. There, sure enough, standing in the teeming rain just beyond the open flap of the tent, was a large lion. He looked at us with interest and we looked at him. That is to say, the three men and I did. Mrs. Adamson didn't miss a beat, didn't even turn around but went right on talking. My throat felt rather dry and my dear one, I noticed, took a hurried sip of his cocktail. He told me later that under the table he removed his knife from its sheath. He was prepared to sell his life dearly.

"Oh yes," said George, sounding resigned, "they come around all the time. Last night there were four."

"What did you do?" I asked.

"What could I do? I shone my torch on them and banged on the table but they wouldn't leave; they were playing with my canteen." It seems he had a brand-new twenty-gallon water canteen which he had hung on a rope between two trees. "They thought it was a fine toy, batted it about like kittens."

"Didn't they damage it?"

"They completely ruined it but they didn't mean to. They were young," he added fondly.

We looked into the streaming night. The lion was still there and after a while he sat down. George was gazing at him admiringly with his bright blue eyes; Jan Allan pulled on his drink; Joy Adamson went on talking. They were respectively English, Scandinavian, and Austrian. Norton and I are Americans. Not liking to let down the side, we tried to appear as nonchalant as our companions, and actually it was not as scary as it may sound, the reason being, I suppose, that it seemed so improbable. The lion and our little group regarded each other amiably for some time and then, doubtless thinking, "What the hell, if they're not even going to offer me a drink . . ." our chum got up and strolled out of sight.

We asked our host if he slept on the cot on which we were sitting. "Of course," he said. "There's nothing to worry about, I have my netting." He believed it too. The next night, however, when we were dining at their house, Gordon Harvey—he was the Serengeti game warden—observed that he was trying to drum some sense into George but didn't seem to be having any luck. Joy Adamson did say that she used to sleep in a tent too but one morning she woke up and found a strange lion staring at her across the table so she began to think better of it and took to sleeping in the lionproof Land Rover.

When it came time to take our leave, Jan Allan said, "Wait a bit, he may be just outside. Wait till I shine my torch." He went out of the tent first, which I thought very gallant. "Yes," he called back, "he's here. Hold it till I get the door of the Land Rover open." He went over and opened the door and then called, "All right, Doctor, the lion's on my left. You come first, stand between me and your wife. Now, Mrs. Brown, you run." I was the arrow to its mark. Norton and Jan were pretty fleet too. We banged the door, waved good-by to our hosts, who seemed quite relaxed among the livestock, and started our slippery journey back to Seronera.

In the course of the evening Joy Adamson had told us that she tried to answer all her fan mail, a formidable task as the letters number in the thousands. "But it's awfully hard to do it by hand," she said. I asked if she had no secretary. "I've tried and tried to get one," was the reply, "but so few of them seem able to adapt to this life." The help situation is tough all over.

As we drew near the lodge a big herd of wildebeest and zebra galloping across the track were caught in our headlights. The rain glanced like spears off their shoulders and flanks and their eyes glittered. They had been frightened by lions and during the night I heard a roar that sounded very near. I got out of bed and went and looked out the window. The rain had stopped and when the moon broke from behind a cloud there was a lion strolling casually through the lodge between the rondavels. I expect lions roar in different keys and there is supposed to be, and indeed is, something wild and splendid in the sound but, in the interests of truth, I must report that the voices of those lions of Serengeti also resembled a prolonged basso profundo moo.

Although the next day was gray and cloudy we went out early and, having heard the nocturnal serenade under our windows, were not surprised to come almost immediately upon two big-maned adult lions lying near a freshly killed wildebeest. We paid a return visit an hour or two later and they were still there. Lions will seldom leave a kill before having devoured it completely even if this takes two or three days because they know that, if they do, they will return to a skeleton. The hyenas and vultures will have finished it off. The bush is wonderfully free of litter. The lion, or usually the lioness, makes the kill and the lion eats his fill. His family have what he doesn't want, hyenas and vultures scour off any remnants, and the bones are eventually demolished by ants. Traveling through many bodies, the nutriment returns to the plains where it fertilizes the grass on which the wildebeests and zebras and gazelles feed, who are then eaten by the lions and off we go again. This is known as the life cycle and it is an admirably conceived and economical process.

Besides the old guzzlers, we saw that day four charming young lions in the bush who moved away as we drove near them and Koske said they must be new to the Serengeti as the older inhabitants were acclimated to spectators in modest numbers.

Also, noticing vultures circling, we headed toward their center of interest and came upon a group of four or five hyenas and many vultures battling over the carcass of a zebra. They would rend the flesh and lift their dripping jaws to snarl at each other and we shivered and felt that we were indeed witnessing nature in the raw which, in the words of the old cigarette advertisement, is seldom mild.

We came upon three giraffes and big buffalo too. Buffalo look and are mean beasts and a wounded buffalo is a deadly adversary. They charge with their heads down and, as the top is solid bone, with the impact of their heavy bodies behind it, the result can be mortal. We did not get out of the Land Rover in their vicinity.

Driving leisurely about looking for birds, we got an extra dividend in the sausage tree. It is graceful in shape with giant sausage-shaped pods dangling from its branches.

We also went to visit the camp store, a dusty little two-room shack run by an Indian. He stocked grain and a few groceries and toilet articles. Far from home American industry was represented by tubes of Colgate toothpaste and shaving cream, and film of the Kodak Company was provided in abundance.

We bought a can of beets as, being a thin vegetable, they could substitute for salad. We had asked Wamuti to do this but after deep consultation with Koske he returned with the news that there were none to be had. When we showed him our can, he grinned triumphantly and explained our error. "That is beetroot. You do not ask for that. Just for beet. Beet*root* I know." We were humbled.

The afternoon remained damp and dreary and the tsetse fly annoying. With luck you're not bothered by the flies at all but they can be a pest, therefore *Traveler's Tip No. 15.* Take a stick or spray can of fly repellent. Since reading Rachel Carson make it a stick. We returned to camp and to tea with Lasse and Jan Allan and admired their pleasant small house and photographs of their two sons, who were at an English school outside Nairobi.

In a big wired enclosure they kept a baby otter as a pet. He was very tame and they were devoted to him but were making plans to send him away. He required water which they could only provide in a tiny pool and in any event pets in the Serengeti are not a good idea. The risk of their being destroyed by lions is too great.

When we got back to Nairobi I sent the Allans Gavin Maxwell's enchanting book about his two otters, *Ring of Bright Water,* which they had not read.

Later that same evening we went to dine with the Gordon Harveys. As it was a chilly rainy right I wore a sweater and skirt but Mrs. Harvey was abloom in flowered silk and I felt remiss.

On the other hand, since the fire was so far back in the fireplace that it gave out little warmth I also felt cozy.

When asked what I would like to drink I said gin and bitters but there is a soda water called bitters too so the drink was long and clear instead of being short and pink. It is at moments like this that one remembers George Bernard Shaw's remark to the effect that England and America are two countries separated by the same language.

The Adamsons arrived and I was relieved to see that George had survived another night inviolate under his mosquito netting but Joy Adamson's legs were badly bruised and I feared perhaps she had had an encounter with our sociably inclined pal after we left but she said no, she had been thrown forward in the Land Rover when they unexpectedly hit a bad place in the road.

We fell to talking about her projected lecture tour in England in September and she claimed to be scared to death, and a few minutes later, speaking of Elsa and her cubs, for whom she and George had been searching for seven months, she burst into tears. "I can't help it," she said. "I can't help it. How can I talk to people about her? They never let me forget her."

I thought of her lecture audiences. It was a foregone conclusion that owing to the popularity of her books she would be playing to packed houses and there was already the barrier of her accent to be overcome. Tears too would make her incomprehensible.

"Look, Mrs. Adamson," I said, "I hope you won't think me rude or heartless but may I tell you something? I do a great deal of speaking myself and I've been in the theater. Believe me, nothing is so calculated to lose you audience sympathy as too many tears. Move your listeners all you can but let them do the crying. With animals as your subject, they'll laugh and sob very easily. You have only to push the button."

"But I loved her so. How can I not cry?" The tears were pouring down her face.

"I tell you what you do," I said. "You think about Elsa all the time from now till September and sob your heart out. Then when

A gray and silver
waterbuck—Serengeti

Hyenas and vultures on
a zebra kill—Serengeti

The Jan Allans' otter
with lion cub chum

Photograph by Jan Allan

A lofty princess among the thorn trees

Wild Fido—wild dogs are
quite pretty and
very ferocious

Carved door of Zanzibar

Children in Zanzibar market

Indian temple in Mombasa

Ferry at Kilifi, scene of my humiliation with the tape recorder

Two damsels encountered on our
morning's drive around Malindi

Sign at entrance to Queen Elizabeth
National Park, Uganda

Two of them having it

Murchison Falls from above—the Nile cascading between the twenty-foot cleft in the rocks

Hippos in the Victoria Nile

Uganda kob

Water buffalo—
everybody face the camera, please

A crocodile smile and nary a tear

Ladies on parade—the only time we saw them balancing their loads with one hand

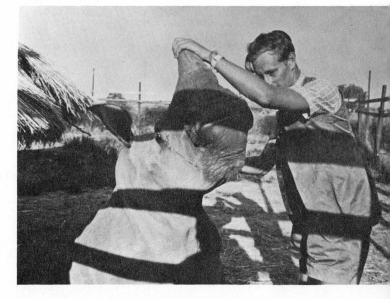

Roger, the Murchison Falls Park game warden, and his pet baby rhino

you get up in front of your audiences you'll be dry-eyed, strong, and in command of the situation."

Later on she wrote me a charming letter, saying the tour had been immensely successful—she had had audiences numbering as high as four thousand—and thanking me for my advice.

Gordon Harvey told us that the Tanganyikan government allows £45,000 a year for the national parks and the fiscal year expires the end of June. He and Allan and the others assumed that the allowance would be carried through 1962. Beyond that they had no idea. It is hoped that capable and dedicated men will be appreciated and asked to remain on the job and that the new independent African governments will be persuaded of the wisdom of preserving their magnificent heritage of wild animals and space.*

Although it had not been her intention to come to the United States until 1963, we had the pleasure of seeing Joy Adamson again on two or three occasions when she made an unexpected visit to New York in December of '62. She was doing the groundwork for a grueling fifteen-week lecture tour in the winter of 1963, raising money for the Elsa Appeal, and following a schedule of interviews, speeches, and television appearances in New York, Washington, and Philadelphia that was enough to kill one of the lions to whom she is so deeply devoted.

We were able to squeeze in an evening at the theater. She had not been in a theater in five years so, thinking she might enjoy an American musical, I got tickets for *No Strings*. Dining at the River Club, Norton and I drank a toast to the three of us being together again. "May you get your dearest wish in 1963," we added.

"Oh!" she said wistfully, "I want to find Jespah."

As she sat beside me in the theater charmingly dressed, in an elegant black coat, a veil with tiny bows over her well-coifed hair, I thought with amusement of the first night we had seen her

---

* Since writing the above this hope has been defeated. In March of 1963 the Allans were relieved of their job by the Tanganyikan ministers in Dar es Salaam. The Harveys too have left the Serengeti.

in the rain in the Serengeti with the lion outside the tent. She was thinking of animals too, but in a different context. After the performance, when I asked her if she had enjoyed it, she said politely that it was very nice and then burst out, "But you know, all the time I was sitting there, despite all those legs and bosoms and music, the only thing I could think of was the lions I had seen this afternoon in the zoo, caged and wretched."

Despite the busy schedule she also managed time for a weekend with us in the country where we introduced her to fresh clam juice, which she had never tasted and which she found delightful, and where we were able to insure her twelve hours of solid sleep, a gift she claimed to cherish equally with the pledges and donations she had received for the fund.

She had found people, deeply concerned about preserving wild life, who will contribute money if they can be persuaded that there is any stability in the native Kenyan government. Before leaving home she took the precaution of interviewing five of the country's leaders and got assurances, on paper, from Ronald Ngala, Jomo Kenyatta, Tom Mboya, Sagini, the Minister of Education, and Mr. Jamidar, the Indian Minister of Tourism, that they are prepared to act in responsible fashion in the preservation of wild animals.

Furthermore, three of the Kenya tribes have set aside land for game reserves. They are desperately in need of money but if they are successful other tribes will be encouraged to do the same. Those who might wish to contribute to the Elsa Appeal may send money to World Wildlife Fund, 709 Wire Building, Washington 5, D.C., marked for Elsa Wild Life Appeal and the money will be sent to Kenya. Contributions are tax deductible.

What had impressed her most in her television appearances was the rapidity with which the other two women who appeared with her on *To Tell the Truth,* also pretending to be Joy Adamson, had learned facts about Kenya. "They were extraordinary," she said. "In four hours they knew things it has taken one twenty-five years to learn."

Elsewhere along her line of march she had acquired the hope

that West Point was on Long Island and the unshakable conviction that the state of Connecticut adjoins Washington, D.C. We tried gently and without noticeable success to correct these geographical misconceptions.

We took her and our other guests to a friend's house for Sunday luncheon and as we stood in the front hall waiting for Norton to bring the car up we admired her coat: soft cashmere of a beautiful burgundy color. She glanced at herself in the mirror, but I felt that the zest normally inherent in the circumstances—an attractive woman complimented upon her appearance—was somehow lacking. "Yes," she said, "I suppose it's all right but when I think . . ."

"What?"

I had released the cataract. "Oh, it is too infuriating!" she cried. "I have a leopard coat, it is magnificent, it has sweep, flair, people turn around in the street, the skins are so superb."

"But where is it?" I asked.

"In the closet hanging, just hanging there. It's those World Wildlife people. They say I mustn't wear it while I'm here. It doesn't look right, a conservationist. But George and I didn't shoot the animals ourselves, we didn't even know it had been done. We never saw the carcasses, just the dressed skins when it was all over, and they were given me as a present."

It did seem a little unfair that a woman who is devoting her life to the well-being of animals should be denied a woman's pleasure when she was completely innocent of harm. I slunk sheepishly into my minks, which she eyed, I thought, a little coldly.

Joy also gave us news of the Allans' otter. They had not been able to bring themselves to part with it although they were almost separated from it involuntarily when the poor little beast was attacked by a hyena. He was rescued in time but was quite seriously mangled. George had reported the news to Joy when he got back to camp one evening after having had a drink with the Allans. "I'll go over tomorrow morning," he added, "and take some terramycin."

"Tomorrow morning!" Joy was indignant. "I'll go now, at once." She hopped into the Land Rover and drove over to the lodge. The otter was in his box in the kitchen—he was always brought in at night—but Joy cared nothing at all for the arrangement. "You can't leave him alone like that," she told the Allans. "This animal has had a terrible experience, he must have companionship, love. I'll stay here in the kitchen with him myself." The hapless Allans felt they couldn't quite accept that so they made up a cot in the living room and Joy gathered up the otter and took him to bed with her and he held on tight to her all night long with his paws and, thanks to the combination of terramycin and affection, was immensely improved by morning.

He now has a lion cub to play with but apparently that arrangement can be only temporary as, with tame animals, wild animals, and visitors, life in the game reserves gets too involved.

Our pleasant evening with the Harveys had broken up early. By nine-thirty we were on our way back to the lodge because of the ten o'clock curfew and also because we were leaving the next day and had to pack.

The rain stopped in the night and the morning broke clear and sunny. While we were loading the Land Rover, both Gordon Harvey and Jan Allan came by for a last chat and to ask us if we would take the mail. Postal service in the more distant reserves is casual so we said we would be delighted to be of service. The evening before Joy Adamson had also given us a big batch of letters. In my ears I heard the drumming hoofs of the pony express. Somehow the Boy Scout oath seemed imminent and we felt noble and dependable, promising to mail everything in Nairobi.

Gordon Harvey's morning was to be devoted to blind-sitting. He had a movie camera—Bolex 16-mm., 32 frames per second, the doctor informed me—and was going to film a new batch of secretary birdlings that had just hatched.

As soon as the roads dried out he was planning to take a posse of African rangers and go down into the Serengeti Corridor, the long narrow sleeve of the reserve into which the herds migrate and where poaching is usually heavy. The attitude of the authorities is stern although not always as firm as one might wish. The men are armed and in the Sudan, under African government, we were told poachers are shot on sight but in Kenya trial by jury pertains and there is a long legal process and sometimes culprits are imprisoned and frequently they are not.

As we were pulling away from camp a young man—another visitor—came up and asked if we minded letting him have a fifteen- or twenty-minute start ahead of us. He was in an ordinary car and with the track a morass of mud he was fearful of getting bogged down. We promised to give him a push if he got into trouble but as we never saw him again we concluded he had overcome any hazards he may have encountered.

A visit to the Serengeti Plain is a stirring experience but, since to see free animals is immediately to become concerned for their welfare, it is also disturbing. The boundaries of the National Park within which the animals may roam protected have been changed and they have been changed in ignorance. It was assumed by both the government and the trustees of the park that the animals migrated in certain directions. It has since been proven that they do not.

It was Dr. Grzimek's finding that "the largest concentration of . . . wildebeest, zebra and gazelles cross the new boundaries of the Serengeti National Park and that the whole population remains outside the park on the southern and eastern part of the central plains for several months during the rainy season. . . . Grasses which are not eaten by the large herds cover a great proportion of the area lying within the new boundaires of the Park while the grass species preferred by the animals grow for the most part outside the boundaries. The revised boundaries of the Serengeti National Park do not include the areas over which the last great herds of African plains game move during much of the course of their seasonal migrations. The migrations cannot be changed because they are closely associated with the vegetation."

It is possible, of course, that the boundaries may again be revised to advantage the animals but anybody who has ever tried to get a group of lawmakers to reverse a decision knows he is in for a long, tortuous, and discouraging tussle. In the meantime, outside the park proper, the animals are fair prey for hunters and poachers. The mistake was not made deliberately but it was made and it's a miserable business.

From the Serengeti we were retracing our steps back to Manyara via the Ngorongoro Crater. We were on the road six and a half hours and in that time passed only two cars and a gasoline truck going the other way. There were few villages and part of the time we diverted ourselves by clocking the Thommies running beside the car. They could do brief spurts at thirty-five miles an hour and quite prolonged ones at twenty-five and twenty.

Passing a little pond, we saw six hyenas and six wild dogs. One of the hyenas waded into the water and brought out what at first we took to be a stick but on closer inspection proved to be the horns and spine of a wildebeest. There was quite a tussle over this morsel and, somewhat to our surprise, the dogs won. Koske said that once, in the Nairobi National Park, he saw dogs kill an impala but that time the hyenas got it away from them.

Wild dogs have brownish-black coats, long brushlike tails, and round ears. Koske was pleased to see their fur shining and in good condition and explained that dogs and hyenas haunt water holes, not necessarily because they are thirsty, but to prey on animals who come there to drink.

When we stopped for coffee under the same lacy acacia tree where we had eaten our picnic lunch on the way to Seronera, we found our egg shells still undisturbed. We left this fragile record, feeling that since it was organic it would soon disappear, but before lunching on the edge of the Ngorongoro Crater we tidied up after litter bugs who had scattered Kodak boxes and paper.

The crater was marvelously still, cool, and sunny and we gazed for a long time at the magnificent view: the crater floor and game on one side, rolling farm and valley on the other. The fertile land in that part of Africa belongs to the Africans themselves and they cultivate with plows and tractors. Koske took a picture of Norton and me and Wamuti standing by the rim and it was dear to us but it was among those that disappeared.

Driving on after lunch, we passed a hillside blazing gold with flowers under the hot blue sky and minutes later were shrouded in chill mist and clouds.

We arrived back at Manyara in midafternoon and gloried in hot, clean water. While having tea on the terrace we noticed a personable chap peering through binoculars scanning the game below and, falling into conversation with him, discovered he was an American and something of an odd ball. He had spent many years off and on in Africa, he was a free-lance writer and sometimes acted as adviser to Americans interested in African investments. He spoke pleasantly of his wife in New York but explained that he was a passionate hunter. He had been hunting in Africa since March and was not going home till the following January. His wife must be a very understanding woman. His immediate quarry was a zebra. He had a few skins already and the perfect spot in his house for another one. There are thousands of zebra and I suppose if one is killed instantly by a shot through the heart or brain it is not a great tragedy but since they stand around like domestic horses it can scarcely be called sport. I asked him if it wasn't a little mean. "Pure murder," he answered cheerfully. He was also after hyrax, which I found shocking as they are now very rare, but he *said* that was only one kind, he was after another.

We dined together and passed the evening in argument in which I frequently found myself on one side and the men on the other, although Norton joined me in my revulsion against the custom of clitorectomy or female circumcision, a mutilation of women that is barbaric, yet several tribes practice it and Mr. Jomo Kenyatta has referred to it as a beautiful custom.

The American told us that a group of Africans had dragged a white nurse from a hospital and imposed it on her, saying, "You are always trying to make us conform to your ways, you conform to ours." She died of shock and terror and several natives were hanged.

Emerging from that wallow, we turned to discussing art and I said it seemed curious that Egypt was the only country in Africa that had had a great creative period. European and Asiatic lands had had their turn but where were the Africans? I appreciated their isolation from the rest of the world but it was odd that there should have been no flowering of indigenous talent. They had the primitive carvings, yes, but nothing of a quality to match Greece or the Orient or the Renaissance. Perhaps Africa is the land of the future.

Our companion shrugged. He felt that their way of life was perfect for Africans and he did make a point when he said they had never organized to destroy other countries as had all the nations of Europe at one time or another. They did have intracontinental squabbles but left the rest of the world alone. Whether such abstinence is attributable to lethargy, lack of opportunity and skill, or respect for their fellow man is a moot point.

According to him, the Africans' tribal life gives them great security. At thirty-five a man sits and looks upon his fields tilled by his wife and children and is content. I said he was a lazy lug but the apologist said not at all, he had to be very shrewd and adroit in council. I said I still thought the Sistine Chapel a greater accomplishment than an African's or, for that matter, anybody else's peace of mind, but both men said I was judging from my own point of view, not the Africans'. Perhaps I was but serenity can be overrated.

Our American friend had a couple of curious quirks such as toying tensely with a pencil and looking over my right shoulder all the time he was talking to me. I kept turning around, thinking he must be addressing himself to someone behind me. When I said I was going to bed my husband said he'd stay and talk a while longer and added that he was going to try to get me to think pragmatically but our companion said it was hopeless.

Despite his low opinion of me, I have to report in fairness that when he joined us at breakfast the next morning he seemed calmer and better able to focus. But he was not the only hunter we met with tensions to be worked off. There was another who stammered badly and one with a limp. There frequently seems to be something the matter with the bang-bang boys but I do not know whether it is the chicken or the egg: whether they kill because they are that way or whether they get that way because their subconscious revolts against needless slaughter.

We packed up the Land Rover after breakfast and headed for Namanga River for lunch en route to Nairobi. Our drive was enlivened by fine sights such as troops of baboons, a great herd of giraffes, and an ostrich courting. When ostriches encounter a fair maiden whom they would charm, they squat upon the ground, wings extended, balancing like seesaws. The wingspread is impressive and quite beautiful but the rather drab young female for whom the performance was offered yawned and wandered away, shaking her feathers petulantly.

We arrived back at the New Stanley about half-past five, pretty well worn by the day's journey. When we went down to dine, the grill room seemed homelike and welcoming and the food excellent.

The next morning we had our interview with Mr. Tom Mboya, Kenya's Minister of Labor. We saw him at a triumphant moment, for at 2 A.M. that morning he had successfully settled a strike among the workers on the coffee plantations and in the automobile plants.

We were driven to the Secretariat by Patricia Hoking, a chipper young lady who was Diana Howard-Williams' secretary, and shown into the anteroom of Mr. Mboya's office. His secretary, a middle-aged English spinster as correct and pleasant in her manner to her African employer as she would have been to a British M.P., made us welcome and said she hoped we would forgive a slight delay but because of the strike settlement various delegations were coming to see the Minister, and indeed, while we waited, several groups were shown in and out and sheafs of papers changed hands. Finally it was our turn to be ushered in.

Mr. Mboya's head is round and very black and he does not

often look you straight in the eye. His voice is soft and his English excellent. He learned it in his African school as a child and also of course when he was at Oxford. He was wearing a dark suit, a wrist watch with a thick gold bracelet, and a heavy ring with a symbol of Africa. His office was comfortable but small and unpretentious and on the wall behind him hung a large colored photograph of Queen Elizabeth. On his desk was a pot of African violets, single purples, the only violets we had seen in Africa. He looks and is young—at that time, thirty-one or two—and he has been a power in African politics since the age of twenty-seven. Our impression was one of coolness. I imagine it would be very difficult to rattle Mr. Mboya.

In his quiet voice he spoke bitterly of the European landowners who by disparaging the situation in Kenya are discouraging foreign capital. He made no bones about the fact that his land is entering independent status in a bankrupt condition. "They frighten away the foreign capital which we need. Investors are uneasy."

"But, Mr. Mboya," we asked, "don't they feel themselves insecure? Do the Africans want to oust the British and Europeans and take over their land and jobs or don't they?"

He moved restlessly in his chair and said, not without a certain dry humor. "The world would take a very dim view of our ousting the British. After all, many of them were born here, they feel it is their home too." And he added with force, "We understand that. Our government came into being in April. It will be stated in our constitution that anybody who was born here or who has lived here for five years may have Kenyan citizenship. We will pass this law but the average African has to be made to realize that the Englishman is not what he was ten years ago. That is not going to be easy. Many of them have bitter memories."

As far as Kenyan citizenship is concerned, many of the English are whipsawed. Emotionally they are tied to England, practically speaking they are reluctant to exchange a British passport for a Kenyan, and yet Mboya's point of view is valid. If you are born in a country and earn your living there and bring up your children there, why isn't it your country? Whether Europeans are being driven out, squeezed out, or are voluntarily withdrawing is one of the great twentieth-century arguments with semantics rampant but we are in an age of transition, classes and races at each other's throats, and transition is historically painful.

Some of the English claim that Mboya is two-faced. They argue, "You can't believe what he says."

Personally, I do not know but I should imagine that quite possibly when dealing with two races you present a different aspect to each one—or each one *sees* a different aspect even when you are showing the same face both ways.

Norton asked if any of the Africans studying abroad were interested in coming back to Kenya to carry on and build the country economically or did they only want to be politicians? We have noticed in all the countries we have visited, including the USA, that the lure of the big black Cadillac is almost irresistible. We also asked if the trade union leaders were as greedy for power as, say, our own Mr. Hoffa. Mboya shot us an amused glance from narrowed eyes. "Our trade unions are young," he said. "They must learn discipline and how to work for the common good."

We asked him his opinion of exchange students, and for the first time he sparked with genuine enthusiasm. "I am for that," he said. "I believe in it strongly. I myself am responsible for sending eight hundred students to the United States."

Knowing he had an appointment with the governor, we left shortly afterward. Our impression? Certainly he seemed all for motherhood and against the black-widow spider. Whether or not they are his true sentiments I cannot say but he did not know us from Adam, who we were, what channels of communication we might or might not command, and he received us with courtesy. If he was superficial and correct rather than confiding, who shall blame him?

As we left the secretariat, I noticed a sign in English and Swahili asking visitors please to check with the receptionist about appointments. It was the first time, outside my Swahili books, that I had seen the word *tafadhali* (please), which actually is of

Arabian origin. I asked Pat Hoking if I was right and that *was* what it meant and she said, "Yes, people say it quite a bit now. Ten years ago we never dreamed of using it." Possibly if they had . . . No! I shall not point a moral, but the temptation is strong.

The evening of the day we had seen Mr. Mboya we met for the first time a most pleasant young woman, Tatty Bell, to whom Drue Parsons in Paris had given us a letter. She is the wife of Walter Bell, an English career diplomat, and the daughter of the famous American soldier, General "Tooey" Spaatz. The Bells were stationed in Nairobi and we had asked them to dine with us. Walter was out of town but Tatty came by herself and we took her and the Howard-Williams' to Topaz, a recently established restaurant where the menu closely resembled that of the New Stanley Grill—I expect that's the food that's obtainable— but it was good if a bit on the high side. Bill Howard-Williams had remarked that he knew the headwaiter but the familiarity with which he was greeted caused him to say afterward that he had not known him *that* well.

When we learned that Tatty and her husband were going for a few days' holiday to Malindi, a popular coastal resort where Norton and I were planning to stay a day or two on our return from our next trip—Zanzibar—we arranged to converge upon it at the same time.

Our party broke up immediately after dinner as Norton and I had to be up at five-fifteen the next morning to make the plane. When I muttered about this, my husband said, "What are you beefing about? Five-fifteen is velvet. Think of those two-thirty and four o'clock jobs when we were leaving Istanbul and Djakarta." He was right. They had been awful. Five-fifteen is the *rich* people's hour but my trouble is that when I have to get up at some Godforsaken time I am awake all night wondering if the time hasn't come. Nor is this *nuit blanche* put to good use. I have read memoirs in which the authors always seem to arrive at lofty conceptions during these doldrums; they ponder on the rights of man, they turn a deathless phrase. I ponder on whether I've left out the shoes I want to wear with my gray and white striped wool seersucker that I'm traveling in or the best way to braise endive and I arise bleary-eyed and groggy. "But there was lots of time," Norton points out. "You *could* have slept." So I could, but I didn't.

I give full marks to the New Stanley however. They operate around the clock. The waiter knocked on our door with breakfast precisely on time and the food furthermore was well prepared and hot and when we went down to the lobby to pay our bill the Indian cashier was at his post, bright-eyed and receptive to our offering.

Even the travel service is the friend who never sleeps. A little apprehensive when our taxi didn't show up on the button, we telephoned them. "The man will be there in two minutes," they said. He was there in one.

Arrived at the airport, we ran into a crisis. Someone had blundered. It was June 27 and there, printed on our tickets, dark and clean, was the date June 28. Another day in Nairobi, while not our dream, could have been borne with reasonable equanimity but we boggled at the thought of unpacking and packing all over again. We appealed to the two Indians who were turning our tickets over and over and upside down and shaking their heads with "This is very bad" expressions and an air of being bowed by life's complexities. They pointed. "These are for the twenty-eighth. That is tomorrow. This is June twenty-seventh. Your tickets are for the wrong day." I curbed my instinct, which was to scream, and instead asked with what I hoped was helpless femininity whether it would not be possible to get us on *this* morning's plane, even though, as we all knew, the travel service had made a *dreadful* mistake. The Indians sighed and looked at each other and groaned and one of them went away. In a little while he returned and addressed his colleague in dialect. The colleague looked at us impassively, handed over the tickets, and said, "You can go." We went. Hurriedly. There were several extra seats, no crisis at all, and we had a good flight to the port of Mombasa, our first stop. The second was Mombo, farther inland but also farther south. Mombo is little more than a grass air strip but magnificent green and blue mountains rise around it; there is rich rolling farmland and again the sharp contrasts of Africa were brought into focus; men in long robes and round embroidered caps wandering about looking at the plane and the personnel housed in mud and thatch huts a few yards from the runway.

Since it seemed rural and remote we asked the co-pilot why we were there and he said because it was the only place in the whole region where planes could land to pick up travelers, many of whom came from great distances away and wanted to get to Dar es Salaam or the islands.

We took off for Tanga, our next stop, and I was glad that it was only cloudy rather than foggy since the route is between mountain ranges. They are not so high but their bulk is imposing and would prove, I fancy, an unyielding bosom against which to hurl oneself in flight. We could see the mountains in our vicinity, but we had missed Kilimanjaro as we flew by, for it was cloud-enshrouded. During the entire flight we discerned no animals on the plains below us and only an occasional African village. In the high plateau country the great problem, as always, is water.

Tanga is on the costal plain, flat and fertile, set amidst masses of palms. Rising from its airport, one is instantly over the Indian Ocean, and minutes later touches down in Zanzibar.

CHAPTER FIVE

Zanzibar

THERE ARE CERTAIN LANDS that have always seemed exotic and perhaps for some time to come, until brought too close by jet planes and economy round-trip fares, will continue to seem so. At least to Americans. The Mediterranean world for many, the Orient for almost everybody, the South Seas, and for some (I am among them) the island of Zanzibar. The name alone is marvelous but also it is at the requisite distance: according to the local information bureau, 9203 miles from New York. The faraway tropical island of dreams, and so it materializes. Palm trees, white sand girdled by seas of sapphire and aquamarine, and bougainvillaea, pink, crimson, lavender, and tawny rose, blazing against a turquoise sky. Some people whom we met who lived there seemed not to share our enthusiasm and I imagine it is true that one would pretty well have to make one's own life with a constant stream of books, records, and magazines coming from home and a definite job to do, but the setting itself is enchantment.

Once the world's largest slave market, populous, noisy, prosperous through its tragic commerce, Zanzibar today, and its smaller sister island Pemba about thirty miles to the north, dream and stir under the hot sunshine and the drenching tropical rains, and the population earns a livelihood as best it can through agriculture—the islands supply a large part of the world's spices—modest commerce, navigation, and tourism. The protectorate, ruled by a sultan, also includes a strip ten miles wide along the coast of Kenya and the seaport of Mombasa. The population of Zanzibar and Pemba is varied. By far the greatest number are Africans—228,000 along with 47,000 Arabs, 18,000 Indians, 5500 other non-Europeans, and 500 Europeans.

Driving around sight-seeing, we passed the sultan's palace. It was badly in need of a coat of paint but an authentic peacock lent an Arabian Nights' touch, his tail feathers a shimmering cascade of color against one of the peeling concrete pillars supporting the iron gate. The palace being built of masonry with a square tower at one end, the sultan is more grandly housed than his subjects, the majority of whom live in daub-and-wattle huts, but he is still not so grand as the inhabitants of those Spanish daydreams in Palm Beach.

Zanzibar's real architectural feature is its doors. Considered by the Arabs in the old days to be indications of wealth and position, they are magnificent, the frames and lintels richly carved in leaf and floral designs, many of them featuring the pineapple, symbol of welcome. The pineapple unexpectedly recalled Richmond, Virginia, where it adorns some of the lovely old plantation houses along the Charles River and where it has the same graceful connotation.

If, through the portals of Zanzibar and, alas, perhaps through those of Virginia too, in the days of slavery, there passed some of the most wretched of mortals, they had the chilly comfort of knowing their misery was framed in artistry.

Some of the island doors, faded to a soft driftwood gray, open into flowering courtyards, but more disclose a cramped gloomy room with children asleep on the dirt floor.

The most superb door of all, dark gleaming teakwood studded with highly polished, fluted, cone-shaped brass nails, belonged to the Hotel Zanzibar but splendor stopped at the threshold. Within, the accommodations tended to the slapdash and ramshackle but the atmosphere was informal and friendly and we were right back in the pages of Mr. Willie Maugham.

As had the plane, the hotel expected us the following day too, but they said, never mind, if we would wait a little in the lounge they could prepare a room for us. This they did, apparently kicking out an obliging young man who gallantly implied that it was no inconvenience at all, he was on his way anyhow.

While waiting, we studied the lounge with interest. The main area was the general shape and proportion of a parlor car on a much smaller scale, with alcoves and nooks opening off it, but it had rows of armchairs down either side, just like an American Pullman, except they did not swivel and were covered with faded, well-worn cretonne slips. The guests, their tea and drinks on small chunky tables, confronted each other across the aisle as they do in a train. The Pullman overlooked a narrow alley and one day, having coffee there after lunch, we heard a man singing in the house across the way, a minor melancholy chant, like the harsh flamenco songs of the Spanish gypsies that stem originally from the Arabic.

The lounge was an extension of the lobby, which contained a cramped reception desk and a small bar. A long narrow dining room gave onto a terrace, roofed but lacking screens, where tables were also set and where we ate, shooing away the flies.

Burrowing through it, we discovered the hotel to be an erratic warren of wings and ells of varying heights sprouting odd staircases, unexpected landings, and rickety balconies. Windows opened onto narrow alleys or the tiny central courtyard and while the exterior walls, thick and whitewashed, seemed built to withstand time and the elements one had a feeling that the interior partitions would yield to a sneeze. The ceilings, large squares of beaverboard, were upheld—sometimes—by lath latticing. When the lattice strips got tired they broke away and the big cardboard squares sagged and swayed precariously. One peered up into the dark, ribbed caverns above them, the attic homes of bats. The whole structure had a madly ad-lib quality that would have given the *Architectural Forum* food for thought.

Our corner room was spacious, painted a bright robin's-egg blue, boasting two large windows and an air conditioner. The air conditioner didn't seem to be working until we turned it off, when the room quickly became hot and humid. The view from the windows, mostly rusty corrugated iron roofs, was offset by the piquancy of the plumbing arrangements: open pipes in the floor running from the fixtures to a hole in the corner through which everything was sluiced. What happened to it once it vanished from our view we do not know.

We had a large tub and a shower which ran only cold water but you could have a hot bath if you worked the geyser, a small cylindrical tank in which the water was warmed by electricity. You flipped a switch and when all was ready a little bell rang like those kettles that whistle when the water boils. It had a cheerful sound and we became devoted to it.

The proprietor of this rakish establishment was a hospitable, good-humored woman, Agnes Budge, who, with the help of a pleasant elderly gentleman whose name we never got, has been running it for many years.

After luncheon, partly on our own and partly under the guidance of our driver, Ramzani, we set forth to see the sights. We quickly became aware that, as the siesta hour was strictly observed, we were a bit early. The post office and tourist information and Handicraft Showrooms would not reopen until three, but roaming the streets or popping out from their shuttered shops when they saw us go by were any number of Arabs, Africans, and Indians, accosting us and importuning us to buy. A group of five small Indian girls were playing together, giggling and reciting the Girl Scout oath in carefully enunciated English. Little Indian boys harried us like gadflys, demanding to have their pictures taken. "You take picture three little Indian boys, yes? You pay us, you take pictures, yes?"

"We take pictures, no. Now beat it, you kids, shoo." We made shooing gestures and the three picturesque tots reluctantly fell back, one of them muttering darkly, "I am very angry."

Naturally we visited the shops but it is curious—camphorwood and ivory, silver and ebony sound marvelously romantic but very few objects made from those materials seem to fit into modern Western surroundings. Out of context they become arty.

The camphorwood chests decorated in tooled brass would be

handsome in an Arab house in Marrakesh—all white cubes and arches and carved marble screens—but they are out of place in New York's east fifties. And that filigree silver jewelry—it's skillfully made, I know, but I don't want it.

When the government Handicraft Shop reopened at three, we went back there and did purchase some spicy pomander balls made from authentic Zanzibar cloves and a wooden comb with long coarse teeth. Picturesque and especially good for thick or frizzy hair, price three shillings. The next day in the bazaar we saw the same thing for fifty cents British, or seven cents as opposed to forty-two. Ah well, the thing to remember is that the Handicraft place is a kind of co-op and helps people.

The ones I most wanted to help Norton frowned on. They were the coffee vendors. They trotted through the alleys with great brass urns of hot coffee and little cups attached by chains. They rang a bell to attract your attention. I was sure the coffee was delicious but Dr. Brown looked stern and antiseptic and would have none of it.

We visited an old Arab fort made largely from blocks and stones of an ancient Portuguese church. Zanzibar's trade with India began over two thousand years ago. Arabs, chiefly from Oman on the Persian Gulf, established small colonies along the coast between the eighth and fifteenth centuries and the Portuguese took over in the sixteenth and seventeenth centuries, dominating everything in view until repulsed by the Arabs, who then recaptured the island and Mombasa.

Part of the fort is used today for the ladies' purdah club. At first the guide wasn't going to let Norton go in with me but then he thought better of it and shrugged and motioned him to come along. Norton and I felt he hadn't defiled it too much since the clubroom was quite empty.

As in the rest of East Africa, the Indians are the merchants, although there are Arabs in the stalls of the bazaars too and we saw many of them riding bicycles, their wives sitting sidesaddle on the little seat behind, swathed in long black robes, their faces either completely veiled or half hidden by a yashmak. A few women walk with their veils tossed back—they, I suppose, are the Amelia Bloomers of the community—but we never saw any of them carrying an umbrella, and when drenched by the tropical rain, their clinging garments must be clammy and uncomfortable.

One family out for a stroll consisted of an Arab in turban and white robe, his wife, a black-draped odalisque, and a small daughter in short shocking-pink organdy. Just beyond them we passed two women working at repairing the road, their babies in slings on their backs.

A public building pointed out to us by Ramzani was called the King George Club. When we expressed interest he was much amused. We had fallen for his little joke. "That is our prison," he said, waving an airy salute as we drove past.

On the waterfront, the square house where Livingstone stayed while outfitting his last expedition to the mainland in 1866 still stands and today shelters the Insect Research Section of the Department of Agriculture.

In the harbor we saw our first dhows, those sailing ships, usually single-masted with a lateen rig and yard propelled by the monsoon, that have plied the Indian Ocean between India, Arabia, and Africa since time immemorial and that are as typical of that part of the world as are the junks of China and the gondolas of Venice. Lying on the pier awaiting shipment was a long double row of elephant tusks. I was sure they had been poached but later, when we were back in Nairobi, Jack Hilton said no, careful records were kept, the authorities knew about every shipment of ivory. I think they only think they do. The human race being what it is, probably all kinds of skulduggery goes on that is hidden from the administrators.

That evening, after we had bathed and changed, we went downstairs for a drink and discovered that it is indeed a small world—teeny-weeny, you might say—for who should be sitting in the lounge waiting for the American consul to pick him up but Mr. Richard Watts. Dick Watts is a friend of long ago and many years' standing but, though we are not too distant neighbors in New York City, we had to go to Zanzibar to meet again.

We fell upon each other with glad cries, somewhat to the surprise of the doctor, who had not before clapped an eye on the distinguished drama critic of the New York *Post*, but I have known Dick since the days when he was critic of the *Herald Tribune*, before he went off to the wars. I have known him since the days of Tony's famous speakeasy, for in those more relaxed times actresses and critics did sometimes get together for a companionable drink. I believe this practice is severely frowned on at present. Mr. Taubman and Mr. Kerr, I understand, hobnob only with women lawyers or department store buyers—no *actresses*, for heaven's sake, it might influence their reviews.

I no longer remember whether Dick's and my friendship or his reviews came first but in my memory—I have not ransacked the files of the *Herald Tribune*, let us not tinker with Memory Lane—his notices were heartwarming and every time I read what he had to say about me I liked that man better.

He was on a sabbatical from the *Post*, touring Africa, and proved an entertaining and instructive companion. We had a reunion drink together and he went off to probe the night life of Zanzibar and we to partake of the hotel fare—it wasn't exactly dining—and go early to bed.

Our ambitious plans for swimming and sun bathing the next day ganged agley when it started out gray and then sprang a gentle leak which, as the morning progressed, developed into a downpour. We passed a man standing up in a little cart drawn by a bullock and holding a large banana leaf over his head by way of an umbrella. In Zanzibar, as in the Serengeti, it never rains in June but we were able to rearrange matters there too. Despite the flood, however, we persevered in our sight-seeing and at lunchtime were rewarded by a brief period of hot, welcome sunshine. The afternoon clouded over but there was no further rain.

Ramzani was equipped with a Peugeot but even though it was small we were obliged to leave it when touring the Indian bazaar; the narrow twisting alleys could not accommodate it. The bazaar enchanted me because the stalls lining the alleys are like little

stage sets, the merchandise neatly stacked or swinging on strings,
or, when it is yard goods, folded over poles or tied together in
bunches, the merchant sitting within either cross-legged or frequently at a sewing machine. One whole section of the market
was devoted to fabric, brilliantly colored cotton *khangas,* but I
did not see any pattern I liked as well as the sisal design I had
bought in Arusha.

The food stalls, as ever, were the most tempting, with tiny egg-
plants and onions and garlic, hot peppers and heaping baskets of
rice and saffron and fiery curry and delectable spices in delectable hues.

The people were as colorful as the produce. Arabs in robes
and white pajamas with the characteristic headdress, the khufiya
and okal familiar from pictures of Lawrence of Arabia or to anyone who in early youth thrilled to Rudolph Valentino in *The
Sheik.* There were delicately boned brown-skinned Indians, black
Africans, and sensuous, curiously attractive women of mixed
races. The Indian women wore saris or long, loose trousers over
which were slipped knee-length skirts.

As we left the bazaar we drove past a field crisscrossed with
clotheslines supported on poles aflutter with brilliant garments.
It was, I think, the town washing hanging out to dry.

The doctor developed the theory that it was cheap cotton stuff
and that the colors would run in the rain but it had been raining
quite hard and, as far as I could see, everything was Everfast.

One of the sights of Zanzibar is the now ruined Marahubi
Palace—it was accidentally burned down in 1889—which was
built by Sultan Seyyid Barghash for his harem around 1880. One
drives through an avenue of beautiful old trees and past grazing
cattle to get to the baths where the disrobing room and a room
with two deep tanks, one for hot, one for cold water, are still to
be seen. There are faint carvings on the high domes and walls
but the color has faded and much has been destroyed. We also
saw the baths and toilet built for a Persian princess who was the
sultan's wife but the toilet was such that, princess or no, Her
Highness had to put her feet on two stones, straddle a hole, and

squat. Our consul, Fritz Picard, told us that this is known as the Persian Version but it is more cosmopolitan than that. The system is used in present-day Japan and it was also the fashion in a Portuguese house that we visited in a modern development just outside Nairobi.

An old, ruined Portuguese fort commands a magnificent view of the Indian Ocean but it apparently could not withstand the Arab onslaught when they reconquered the island. The cruelty of the Arabs was legendary and they used it as a prison for slaves. The great iron rings to which they were shackled are still embedded in the walls. Ramzani sat down and enthusiastically thrust his arms through the rings to show us how it was done.

Although we did not get out to look because of the rain, he also pointed out the grave of a long-dead Arab sheik who was so cruel that to this day the more ignorant and superstitious Africans are leery of passing too close to it.

Driving along, we came to a plant where they were processing coconuts and got out to watch. It is a fascinating business and you begin to wonder how people who do not have coconut trees survive, for it is a plant that supplies food, shelter—the leaves are used for thatch—fuel, and money from the sale of oil and copra.

We were able to see the whole cycle of life, for the plant had a small nursery too. To start new trees, they take the coconuts, still in their big yellow-green pods, and half bury them in rows in the ground. In six months they have small trees that are transplanted to the groves. It takes eight years for a coconut to bear but once it starts there is no stopping it. It may bear for as long as sixty years and nuts can be harvested four times a year.

Men and little boys shinny up the tall slender trunks like monkeys to pick and drop the nuts, which are subsequently taken to the processing center and dumped in huge piles. They lie there drying for a few days and the outer pod is then removed by impaling the coconuts on sharp iron spikes stuck in the ground. This part is discarded temporarily but later, when still drier, is used for fuel.

From the coconut itself they extract oil, white meat, and milk. I drank a little and found it bland and quite refreshing.

The dried kernel of the coconut—and they dry hundreds at a time on top of a huge stone oven or kiln in which a hot fire is burning—becomes copra, which together with the coarse hairlike growth on the outside of the shell is used for rope, sacking, etc.

What's this about dogs? Coconuts are man's best friend.

The trees of Zanzibar are superb: flamboyants balancing their delicate freight of flame-colored blossoms, banyans, yellow flowering bamboo, enormous mangoes with their shining deep green leaves, and companion giants with dark lush foliage and pale green globes—the breadfruit. There is the kapok too. Its fiber is used to stuff mattresses and it looks not unlike the cotton blossom. A most curious and interesting growth is the low kizibani, or sensitive plant, with its long serrated leaf. Touch it ever so gently and each leaf petal closes down along the central spine and it looks very sad and as though it had pined away from lack of love and water. A little while after you have departed it perks up and is ready to start its act all over again for the next comer.

We passed through a village called Bububu, that being the sound the spring makes as it issues from the ground, and came after a time to the Agricultural Experimental Station and a lovely spot it is, even seen through mist and rain.

Pemba is apparently a more fertile island than Zanzibar and we were told that there the clove trees grow taller but the ones we saw seemed high and beautiful. It was not the season for the cloves themselves but Ramzani picked a few leaves and crushed them and the odor was authentic and delicious. So is that of the cinnamon bark. He sliced off a sliver and gave it to us. I held it with a handful of the fragrant lemon grass and a flower called ilang-ilang and grew quite drunk from the perfume. He filched a nutmeg, which one is not supposed to do, but I had never seen a fresh one. There is a great deal to be said against city living and the packaging that goes on in supermarkets. Although on a much smaller scale, the nutmeg, like the coconut, has an outer pod which before it ripens looks like a hard little yellow plum. As the pod dries, it splits and the nutmeg drops out—hatched like an egg. The same thing holds for the cocoa bean.

The Agricultural Station also grows pepper and lichee nuts and experimentation with tea plants is being carried on. The citrus fruits flourish, as do pineapple, bananas, avocados, sweet potatoes, and a small amount of rice. The produce is so luxuriant and varied, one would think the island would be rich. There is competition from Ceylon in the spice trade but it is hard to believe that with knowledgeable methods of packing and distribution the island could not become self-supporting and prosperous.

The whites claim that by temperament the Africans are lazy. They work to amass a few shillings for the very reason that their leisure is precious to them and once they have enough for a few days that's it. They wait until it's used up before going back to the job. Possibly education will make them money-mad and give them ulcers although the climate will doubtless offset any such Western hysteria. In Zanzibar, at least, the weather is hot and humid, not conducive to excessive ambition and unnecessary toil.

Besides those I have enumerated, the Africans grow another fruit which is a real little gem, the durian. When we first wandered through the bazaar I attributed the occasional rank odors that drifted under my nose to rotting garbage combined with primitive sanitary arrangements. I was wrong. It was the durian, and it is supposed to smell that way.

"But," several people assured me, "if you can get it past your nose the flavor is delicious."

"Oh, come now."

"No, it really is."

Well, I suppose even people like Winston Churchill or Bernard Baruch or Albert Schweitzer occasionally make fools of themselves. Who am I to be immune to human failing? I said I would try some.

Mrs. Budge dispatched her driver on a special mission to the bazaar to bring one back to the hotel. That should have been a clue. If they were all that delicious why wasn't the hotel abundantly stocked? The thought did flit through my mind but then I recalled the aroma. Were they kept on hand, the mass exodus of guests would have been crippling.

The driver shortly returned, bearing what looked to be a green hedgehog. "We will prepare it," said Mrs. Budge, whisking it off to the kitchen. By the time she returned, the small lobby was quite crowded. Word of the intrepid American woman had got about. As she set it down on the table before me, our hostess murmured, "I keep trying to think of ways to improve its appearance but there is not much one can do." That was two strikes against it: smell and appearance. But the taste! The thought sustained me as I looked at the revolting mess on the plate.

Once converted from the hedgehog, its appearance was still not palatable. Lying there looking up at me were two pits about the size of avocado pits, surrounded by glutinous octopus tentacles, of a strange exhausted gray. They only just didn't writhe. Gazing down at them, I thought of Romain Gary's account in his book, *Promise at Dawn*, of the time in his childhood when he ate a pair of galoshes to win the favor of a fickle siren, aged eight. Mr. Gary had survived. So, presumably, would I. Besides, I had volunteered for this, had I not? It was my own idea. What was I? Spineless? Craven? The answer was a ringing yes. But the little crowd stood spellbound. They were testing my mettle. Some wore faint sneers, others had expressions of awe—a few showed pity. I glanced around for the doctor. Upstairs, in his bag, there were, I knew, restoratives, powerful drugs, hypodermic needles. Could he bring me back from the valley? I could have done with more concern on his part but he stood on the periphery of the little throng, puffing imperturbably on his pipe.

The moment had struck! Besides, I had better do something, the smell was overpowering. Not knowing which weapon to choose for the assault, I picked up spoon and fork together and dug in. Added to its other attractions, the texture of the durian is tough. Tough and slippery. It skidded across the plate, I retrieved it by millimeters, speared it, held my breath, passed it under my nose into my mouth, and swallowed. A gasp went up from the crowd. They swayed toward me. "Well? Well? How is it?" I have heard that on the battlefields the stench of death is sickeningly sweet. So the taste of durian.

Dead, sweet, and sickening. With an unexpected aftertaste of onion.

In this world it is rare that we learn from the experiences of others but, reader, I beg of you—take this lesson to heart, engrave it on the tablets of your mind, and *never* eat a durian. I have suffered that you may not.

To recuperate from the ordeal, we decided on another drive and, although it was still raining when we came to a small pretty cove, Norton said, "Rain or not, I'm damned if I'm going to come all the way to Zanzibar and not swim in the Indian Ocean." So we did. It was wonderful too. The temperature was perfect and the water very salty and buoyant. I am not crazy about swimming in the rain but I ventured in for bragging purposes. I have now swum in five of the seven seas: the Atlantic, the Pacific, the Mediterranean, the Aegean, and the Indian.

Our drive took us through streets with names like Mkunazini, Pipalwadi, and Health Office Road. In the better residential areas there were several small new apartment houses, the windows framed in shadow boxes that taper to nothing at the bottom and apparently do an effective job of keeping out the sun, but the buildings are not attractive, which is a pity as tropical lands are the perfect setting for graceful and imaginative architecture.

Although there was a great deal of grass, the Brahmin cattle threading their way single file through the palm groves were thin and Norton said it was probably due to a lack of nitrogen in the soil; many of the trace elements have been leached out. Vitamins would help but there is no money with which to buy them.

That evening, taking the bull by the horns after a couple of drinks, we decided to be disloyal and dine with the competition, the Pigalle, which Dick Watts said was something of an improvement over the Zanzibar cuisine. True, Mrs. Budge had her difficulties: her second *mpishi*, she told us, drank like a fish. Possibly because he had to eat the food prepared by the first *mpishi*, and on the whole there wasn't much to choose between the two establishments with the exception of the Pigalle prawns, which were delicious. Also, the Pigalle had screens in the windows and they made a big difference to one's comfort.

We were puzzled by the lack of screens all over Africa, which is certainly a bonanza market for them, and at first concluded that the poverty must be appalling since screens—especially with the incomes of the white inhabitants—aren't all that expensive. Later we discovered that the English, at least, were screenless by choice. They don't think them necessary. Just as they don't think central heating necessary in England, in a climate that perennially causes chilblains and inspires thousands of them to flee their fogbound island for the tropic belts of the world. I have come to the conclusion that some discomfort is necessary to the British temperament, although I suppose if you're unaware that it *is* discomfort it isn't and there I go, judging others by myself.

The Pigalle too is run by a woman, a Frenchwoman who married an Englishman, Mr. Dyer-Melville, and who has lived in Zanzibar since 1924. When her husband died she took to hotel and restaurant management.

We had arrived a little early, around half-past seven, and discovered that life began at eight. The only people there besides ourselves were a group of Americans, not, I am afraid, our first choice as ambassadors to foreign lands, who were clustered at the bar at the far end of the room, and the proprietor who, seated alone at a small table, appeared to be slightly dazed. She disappeared for a few minutes and when she returned she was considerably spruced up in appearance and full of joie de vivre and hospitality.

She had a flair for the dramatic and told us, acting it all out with much trilling of French *r*'s, about her husband and how, after she had taken up restaurant keeping, people whom she had known for twenty years would come there to dine and barely nod to her. "Because they were English and I am in trrrrade."

It was splendid, the way she looked down her nose, impersonating the haughty English, and then the quick switch—the smile, the outstretched hand, the bonhomie of the gay and courageous Frenchwoman. We enjoyed it thoroughly and promised to telephone her son and daughter-in-law when we returned to Nairobi where they were living and give them her news.

The next morning Agnes Budge took me shopping. We called upon a Chinese merchant whose stock was not inspiring but he was a nice little chap and I didn't like to go out empty-handed so I bought an ash tray of brass and flowered green enamel. When it isn't heavy machinery—although I *realize* how *useful* that is—commerce can be fun. The trade routes of the world. I am drawn along them like a magnet. A Chinese ash tray purchased in Zanzibar, an Italian painted tray bought in Dublin, an Indian carpet picked up in Venice—they are all harmoniously cohabiting on Long Island.

In an Indian shop I was sorely tempted by a carved ivory lion but he was heavy and expensive so I resisted, settling instead for an ivory shoehorn with a carved something or other on top. I sat chatting with the shopkeeper for a few minutes until Mrs. Budge's driver, who was depositing her at the hairdresser's, returned to fetch me. The shopkeeper took an indifferent view of all the Uhuru agitation, anticipating, I imagine, little change in his own status regardless of politics. We had noticed several red roosters drawn on walls. The rooster was the Arab party symbol. The Africans had a fish; we saw no fish in Zanzibar. The Indians apparently were mugwumps: they had no beast at all.

The flag of Zanzibar, by the way, is red. A banner, square or oblong, depending perhaps on the mood of the local Betsy Ross, but a plain red field. The Birch Society would have a fit.

Later that morning Mrs. Budge drove us to her own house for coffee. Like the hotel, it had a rakish charm and was a high house with a roof terrace on which were set trays and trays of African violets, the first we had seen since the pot on Tom Mboya's desk. We were envious, for obviously her thumb was greener, pinker, purpler, and whiter than ours at home. Norton and I love and wrestle with them but we have come to the conclusion that we are not, basically, African violet people. There is a pretty technician in his office, Helen Haywood Hoolihan, and that Hooly is the queen of violet growers. She only has to look at them and they burgeon with delight. She is generous about giving us battalions of pots in full flower and we tend them exactly as she says to but they pine for their mother and we are not able to make them happy away from home. I have been asked by guess who to say that this is no longer the case. We now employ special lamps and the improvement is *noticeable*.

Mrs. Budge had some magnificent trees on her place, one as large as the mango called the rain tree. It was of the acacia family and very beautiful. She also had frangipani and allspice and great bushes with thick glossy leaves known as the croton but the most unusual was the cannon-ball, with pinky-red cup-shaped flowers growing directly out of the trunk.

As we were leaving Zanzibar that afternoon, we had already packed and when we returned to the hotel we found Dick Watts waiting for us in the lobby with an invitation from the Stuart Lillicoes—he was there with the United States Information Service—to lunch at their house. Mr. Lillicoe would come by to pick up the three of us at twelve-thirty. When it got to be almost one and he had not appeared we decided to have a drink. That, we felt, would fetch him. I have never known the technique to fail. Any time a plane is delayed in take-off, I have only to retire to the ladies' room and it is called immediately. The same thing held true with the drink. We had no sooner ordered than our host appeared, apologizing for his tardiness. He piled our luggage into his Land Rover, we would go directly from his house to the airport, and we followed in a cab. The Lillicoe house was not so large as Mrs. Budge's but it too was tall and thin as was Mrs. Lillicoe, Sr., who was visiting her son and daughter-in-law. The other luncheon guests were two young Indians, male and female, an Australian couple, and the American consul and his wife, the Fritz Picards, extremely bright and pleasant folk.

While we were having cocktails Mrs. Picard told us about a couple of small black children she had known in a school in South

Africa. They were members of the art class who had been told they could make drawings illustrating the Bible story of their choice. One small artist had selected the Good Samaritan. There, quite recognizable, was the wayfarer who had fallen among thieves—ferocious-looking they were too—and the Good Samaritan gathering him up to bear him to the inn, which was on the right of the page with a sign over the door saying: Hotel, Refreshments.

A classmate had chosen the Flight into Egypt complete with kindly old Joseph leading the donkey by the bridle, Mary on its back, the Babe in her arms, and behind her a little suitcase with the initials J.C.

We had begun getting a bit uneasy when luncheon was delayed as we had to make our plane but when it arrived it was worth the wait: an excellent curry with an infinite variety of side dishes.

Our host and the Picards drove us to the airport and although the plane was hot and humid the trip lasted fortunately less than two hours, including customs at Tanga. A sign at the Mombasa Airport made us laugh: "Passengers are reminded that immigration formalities are their own responsibility." The traveler would appear to have considerable latitude.

We were met by one William and driven to the Oceanic, which after the dégageé charm of the Namanga River and Zanzibar hotels seemed stereotyped and very Statler Hilton. Its virtues were cleanliness, modern plumbing, a balcony, and a view over the Indian Ocean.

Mombasa is an attractive town on an island connected to the mainland by a causeway. About two hundred and sixty miles south of the equator, it has two harbors and is the chief port for Kenya, northeastern Tanganyika, and inland Uganda. The spirit of modernism is beginning to pervade it but for some time after the abolition of slavery in 1887 not much went on there. The freed slaves had no intention of working, their erstwhile owners didn't know how, and the territory reverted to the bush.

With the completion of the Uganda railway in 1902 it became

again the flourishing port it had been as early as 1154 when Arabia, India, China, and Persia were the great trading powers.

Between January and April when the winds are at rest the old harbor is packed with dhows and the town must be a wonderfully picturesque Babel of tongues and nationalities. The only out about a visit at that time is that February and March are the hottest months of the year. The heaviest rainfall is in April, May, and November.

In 1498 Vasco da Gama appeared off Mombasa with four Portuguese ships but the reception he received from the Arabs was not cordial. Indeed, through the years the ensuing wrestling match was such that in 1593 the Portuguese decided to build Fort Jesus as a stronghold. They held it for another hundred years and lost out to the Arabs for the last time in a siege that endured for thirty-three months and ended when the Arabs, storming the height, dispatched the twelve remaining survivors. Today Fort Jesus is a peaceable, picturesque ruin and we wandered about taking pictures and admiring the blue-green water of the Indian Ocean and then went to the shopping center where I picked up two gaily crocheted African caps, and to the wood-carving market, which extends down the middle of a broad highway—the polished bowls and masks and little animals dappled by sunlight splashing through the thick foliage of the trees under which the vendors set out their wares. A movie house in the neighborhood must have been playing a big Indian hit, for the sidewalks for blocks around were thronged with children waiting for the Saturday morning matinee.

We also visited an Indian temple, an airy open pavilion where no men other than priests are allowed. Norton resigned himself to waiting while I crossed the courtyard and, as a sign requested, removed my shoes and mounted the two or three steps to the broad platform which was the temple floor. Godly sanctuary or no, business is still business and another sign informed the visitor that the terrazzo floor and columns costing 10,000 shillings had been supplied free by the contractor. Obviously it behooved the good Lord to remember that when toting up the score in His great black book.

A group of Indian women in saris were sitting in a circle in the center of the floor around a large flat tray of flowers, chanting and swaying. Their orisons were mechanical if graceful and did not interfere with hospitality. A couple of them brought their hands together and bowed to me in greeting and I brought my hands together and bowed back.

Beyond the circle, with her back to them, was a statue of a large cow couchant. She looked to be made of soap but was, probably, of some waxy marble. Her hindquarters, draped with pink veiling, were turned to the ladies.

A couple of pleasant young Indian schoolgirls came up to me and asked if they might show me around. When I said I would be delighted they led me to the rear of the pavilion where there was a sunken room, a kind of big oblong pit. Charming little offerings of flowers wrapped in leaves were scattered about and, sitting cross-legged on the floor, a priest in sarong and undershirt was telling his beads. A couple of flies lighted on his nose but he was so holy that he was able to ignore them. Directly in front of him a stylized cobra made of thick twisted silver wire raised its hooded head. Its mate reared in the corner. I was glad they were of wire or I should have seen little of the pavilion.

There were statues in niches on either side, one of the elephant god with a long trunk and one of a fat maiden blowing a horn. They too had the waxy look of the cow and were splashed with a good deal of red.

From the art point of view they were atrocious, yet really no worse then the vapid plaster-of-Paris figures of Christ and the Virgin that adorn many Christian churches and at least they were definite: ugly and lusty rather than bland and exsanguinated. Since the Hindus seemed greatly to revere them I thanked the young ladies with as much respect as I could muster, retrieved my shoes, and departed.

I got back in the car with Norton and we set off for Malindi. On the way we came to an inlet and while waiting for the ferry I bought a bunch of six small bananas from an entrepreneur under a thatch shelter. They cost one American cent and were delicious and so was a little heap of fresh roasted hot cashew nuts which a colleague was selling across the road.

The ferry was a flat barge that could accommodate one car and it was hauled back and forth by a gang of men pulling on a heavy iron chain stretching across the water and passed over a pulley. I was thinking the whole arrangement very Volga Boatman when William, our driver, said, "There's no charge for the crossing but the men sing and usually passengers give them a tip." Sure enough, they started up: singing, stamping, and blowing on a conch shell. It was quite a bit of bedlam, amusing and rhythmical.

I had my tape recorder on my lap and Norton, who had got out of the car, came back and said, "This is good, be sure and get it and we'll play it back for them."

"I thought of that," I said, "I *am* getting it," and I held the little microphone out the window the better to record.

"Sure you've got the button pressed down?"

"Yes, of course. Can't you see the tape turning?"

He came back a couple of times. "Don't miss it."

"I'm *not* missing it. I've got a lot, I just don't want to use up all the tape but I'll do more if you like."

I was feeling a bit testy at his lack of trust but the Africans, apparently aware that they were being recorded for posterity, sang and stamped and banged about with renewed vigor and I smiled and nodded encouragement. We were whooping it up in fine style when the barge grated on the gravel on the farther side.

The men instantly gathered around the car and peered curiously in the window at the little black box. Norton smiled benignly, a true Lord Bountiful. "*Now*," he said, "play it back." I too smiled. What pleasure we were giving these simple black folk! I pressed the key, the reel started turning, and no sound, no sound at all emerged. I stopped, I rewound, I pressed again. I bounced it up and down. Nothing. The black faces fell. I had had the Play key down but not the little red recording button. I felt so stupid and humiliated I couldn't bear to look at the bargemen as we drove off the ferry. Norton's self-control was admirable but he is a man who understands mechanical contraptions, the mind that doesn't exasperates him, and he was hard pushed. I couldn't blame him. I was deeply ashamed, especially as I'd been so cock-sure I was doing the right thing, but inept as I was, I do plead with the Webcor Manufacturers and their competition: Gentle-men, please, when you turn out next year's model, remember that some of your product will be bought by mechanical imbeciles and please, oh, please, install a little bulb that lights when the machine is recording or a bell that rings, *anything* so that dolts like me won't miss the chance of a lifetime.

Through a mist of depression I was still able to appreciate that we were passing through fertile lovely country with enormous sisal plantations stretching on either side of the road. Vipingo Estates, the sign said, and they seemed to extend most of the seventy-five miles between Mombasa and Malindi.

We spotted an African mother naked from the waist up with two small children wearing tutus just like the Gold Dust Twins of my childhood and I urged Norton to take a picture but he was a blasé connoisseur and would have none of it. "She's too flat," he said flatly and I fear she was.

We had another ferry to cross but the postman did not ring twice. This one had no picturesque crew singing the folk songs of their native land, only greasy little tugs on either side pro-pelling us forward.

Shortly before two we arrived at the Sinbad Hotel. The Sinbad Hotel is *it*. A pleasant woman greeted us and said, "Won't you drive around to the new wing?" The new wing is two stories high and our room, large and comfortable, overlooked the beach and the Indian Ocean. We had a small vestibule, a large room with a black and white checkerboard floor, a private bath, lots of closet space, cool, pretty chintz, a full-length mirror, and a bal-cony. Even the bath towels were attractive, light green, coral, pink, and blue. Rates per day: 140 shillings or $19.60 for two, meals included. Things looked pretty nice. Even nicer when the lady said, "Wouldn't you like drinks sent up?" We would indeed, a whisky and soda and a Pimm's Cup while we were getting ready for lunch.

The dining room was large and airy, opening onto a terrace and the beach, and was decorated with murals of Matthew Arnold's *The Forsaken Merman*. Little gray church, deserted children, lonely kings of the sea—very poignant. The food, while not French, was still, excepting perhaps the New Stanley Grill, the best we had had in Africa.

We had seen from the register that the Walter Bells had arrived and as we were returning to our room after a swim a note was delivered asking if we wouldn't join them in the bar a few minutes before eight for a drink.

We had tea served on our balcony and three enormous black and white crows with feet like talons appeared on the railing, demanding cake. Throughout Africa we found the animals tolerant and sociably inclined but since they did not speak English and might not be entirely aware of our winsome ways we treated them with respect, with the exception of the Treetops baboons and the Malindi crows, keeping a reasonable distance between us, and the entente was always cordiale. While drinking tea and feeding the crows we hung over the balcony, watching and gradually becoming mesmerized by the rhythm of the gardener chopping away at the grass with a *panga*, a short thick blade. In nearly two months in Africa we never saw them use either a scythe or a lawn mower. The *pangas* do the job but they take infinitely longer. On the other hand, what would the men do with the time they'd save?

It was pleasant to see the Bells again and in the bar we found an agreeable feline friend who lay on the bar proper for a while and when bored with the conversation retired to the top of the refrigerator.

We told Tatty Bell about two young African couples we had seen walking along the beach in the afternoon. They were naked from the waist up but the girls wore short full skirts, yards and yards of pleated fabric like a ballet dancer's tutu. It is originally white, eventually deepening to gray, but over it they usually drape a brilliantly colored piece of Madras, the *khanga*. This depresses it a little in front but it puffs out in back, forming an immense bustle, very steatopygic. Tatty told us that the material of the underskirt is called Merikani cloth because it is cotton, which was originally imported from the American South. When I commented on the brilliance of some of the patterns and the Africans' marvelous color sense, she said, "Yes, but that fabric is all printed in Birmingham or India." Alas, how vulnerable are one's illusions.

We dined in the Moon Garden, an outdoor terrace charmingly lighted, with a fountain and a small round marble dance floor on which one dances to the music of a gramophone. The columns are festooned with a lovely vine, white bleeding heart with red drops. We watched lightning-swift little lizards snapping up their insect dinners and had a quite good one of our own accompanied by an excellent Beaujolais '59. Walter Bell told us that French wines age two or three years in the course of their journey down the African coast through the Indian Ocean because of the heat.

When we retired to bed we were impressed by our mosquito-netting canopy—quite the most ambitious we had seen; a real little Henry V tent at the Battle of Agincourt. A bunch of plumes was all we needed. Despite its picturesqueness and efficiency, however, we still wondered why they didn't install screens.

We liked the Sinbad so much we wished we had come there directly from Zanzibar instead of spending the night at the Oceanic in Mombasa. The town was reasonably interesting but the hotel, while comfortable, was, as I have said, stereotyped. It increased expense and made for one more bout of packing and unpacking. Any time a traveler can save himself that chore without missing a vital sight or a pleasant experience, he is wise to do so.

The next morning after breakfast we drove with the Bells in their car to Casuarina Point, a lovely beach, although thick with dried seaweed, sheltered by pliant feathery pines. According to the Oxford English Dictionary, the branches of the casuarina resemble horse tails. According to Merriam-Webster, they are reminiscent of a cassowary, which is a bird. Like beauty, shape and similarity must also lie in the eye of the beholder. I could look at the casuarina the rest of my life and never think of a horse. Nor a bird, unless one were to light on it. I am like the hero of Pierre Daninos's book, *Uncertain Monsieur Blot*—an unimaginative type who could spend thirty years under an apple tree and the theory of gravity would never occur to him.

Leaving the beach, we headed for the ancient settlement of Gedi. Ahead of us on the road was a large group of Africans, members of the Giriama tribe. They had their backs to us and the brilliantly colored swaying bustle behinds of the women were an amusing sight. They were chanting and singing as they walked along and as we drew near in the car they crowded to the side of the road to let us pass and we saw that on their shoulders they carried a bed upside down, a frame on legs with a netting of rope stretched across it. On the bed lay a shrouded figure. We were in the middle of a funeral procession.

Gedi is a curious spot. The ruins rising out of the jungle growth are reminiscent of Angkor Thom in Cambodia but on a much smaller scale. It was originally an Arab city but its age is indeterminate as the only monument with a date is a tomb just outside the wall with the inscription Ah 802—in the Christian Era, A.D. 1399. Lying four miles from the sea and two from a navigable creek, the reasons for its foundation are obscure, but it may have been because there was water there although today the wells are dry. It is also thought it may have been a mineworking center and apparently the inhabitants were reasonably well off as a good deal of fine-quality Chinese and Persian ware has been unearthed from time to time, and may be seen in the Information Room at the gate.

There are ruins of an H-shaped palace, mosques, and the thirteen houses that have so far been excavated. Each house has a bath and has been named after the principal objects found in it: the house of the iron lamp, of the ivory box, etc.

Tatty and I walked along the winding jungle paths, trying not to trip over the roots of trees, and each, as we confessed to one another, keeping a sharp lookout for snakes. We didn't see so much as a worm but Tatty said that when she and Walter lived in India, whenever she took a walk she went clapping her hands and singing, hoping to shoo away any lurking serpents.

Leaving Gedi, we drove to Ocean Sports for beer, the excellent Allsops, a light lager which is delicious. Ocean Sports is a small pavilion-bar overlooking the beach, simple but done with taste. Comfortable woven rattan chairs, a few glass globes from Japanese fishing nets hanging from the rafters. We asked the Bells if the Africans themselves ever started places of the kind and they said no. Until their independence Africans had always been discouraged or forbidden outright to engage in money-making enterprises. They were not allowed to grow coffee either. Any real "money economy" was denied them, they were relegated to "subsistence economy." It will be interesting to see what they will do along these lines now that they have the opportunity.

Walter also said that there is a big influx of Japanese to East Africa. It is a solution to their population pressure, and if the Africans do not need all the land themselves, since the Japanese are not white they may not be averse to the idea.

On the other hand, there would seem little reason to suppose they won't want the land. It's what they've been fighting for for a long time and their birth rate is on the increase just like the rest of the world's.

The next morning was bright and sunny and Tatty and I drove into Malindi village for a shopping spree. I dearly love little stores that sell bright trinkets. We bought baskets and three gay *khangas*. I planned to use them as tablecloths in the country. Our purchases, though modest, were exhilarating and as I said to Tatty, "I really love spending money but men seem to hate it."

"I know," she said, "I don't know why they want to make it."

Leaving the Sinbad, I ask the nice lady owner her name. "Mumford," says she.

"Oh. Mrs. what Mumford?"

"P. My husband and I are both P."

"Yes, but . . ."

"Sinbad Hotel, Malindi, will reach us," she says briskly, and although she is an attractive woman and a pleasant proprietor I detect a slight "and none of your lip" attitude. I press no further so do not know if P. stands for Priscilla, Prendergast, Peter, Pauline, or Portland Ppfluffington Pringle pronounced Puffle. Be that as it may, I suggest making a reservation at the P. Mumfords' and visiting their delightful hostelry.

Back in Nairobi after an easy two-hour flight, we dined that night with the Howard-Williams'. Diana told us over the phone that a Mr. Donovan would fetch us in his car and drive us out to the house. He arrived in an elegant Mercedes-Benz which he drove like a crazed demon and as he careened around curves on two wheels and streamed down hills at eighty it occurred to Norton and me that we had a very good chance of never clapping eyes on our hostess. I can only say that Mr. Donovan could enter the Tokyo taxi drivers' union as president, something of an accolade since they are the most terrifying drivers on earth. Compared to them, the Italians and Portuguese, no tyros when it comes to lunacy on wheels, are as children in their kiddie cars.

We arrived at the Howard-Williams' shaking so that we could scarcely get glass to lip and were further unnerved by being introduced as Mr. and Mrs. Chase-Brown. The English love hyphenated names and pounce on any excuse to squeeze one in. We recuperated, however, under the warmth of the hospitality and the charms of a tiny Pekinese puppy. The Pekinese is one of the few breeds of dog to whom I am usually indifferent but this one quickly had the dinner party groveling under his golden paws. He was a love.

When it came time to say good night Mr. Donovan—with no noticeable regret—we had been articulate in our reactions to his driving—turned us over to another couple who had apparently been behind the wheel of a car before and who conveyed us back to the hotel in relaxed and mature fashion.

We spent a considerable portion of the next day at the offices of the air line and the United Tourist Service, for we had decided to rearrange our itinerary.

Norton had got wind of the splendor of the fishing in Lake Rudolf and was longing to go. Since, after our trip to Uganda, we would have a bit of leeway in our schedule, which called for Addis Ababa and Egypt, we decided to see if we couldn't charter a small plane, this being the only practical way of getting to the lake. The man said he would see if he could get another passenger to share the expense with us and would give us the news when we returned from Uganda.

I left Norton and went to have my hair done at a hitherto untried shop, Magda's (on the scruffy side), and when emerging was knocked down by an African on a bicycle. A bicycle may seem an innocuous vehicle but it packs an unexpected wallop. Although no bones were broken my left ankle, right knee, and left hand were badly strained and twisted. The poor young African kept murmuring, "Sorry, sorry, mem-sahib." Even in my pain that mem-sahib had a fine Kiplingesque ring but when cars began stopping and people started crowding around, darting suspicious looks at the black cyclist, I felt matters had gone far enough. I managed to get to my feet and hobble away and the young man mounted his wheel and took off like the wind—his relief at not being detained and questioned very evident.

That evening the Jack Hiltons came to dine with us. We had planned on taking them to a restaurant but because of my foot dined at the hotel instead. Jack told us of a rare case in Nairobi National Park history. A male lion attacked a female sexually, killed, and ate her. It was the first case ever recorded of lion cannibalism. They shot a hypodermic arrow into him to stun him and castrated him while he was unconscious. They were hoping for a more co-operative attitude toward the opposite sex, although if he persisted in his greedy ways they were planning to

send him to a larger reserve. I could only wonder about the fate
of the poor girls elsewhere but I suppose the wardens minded
that less so long as the shopwindow was not shamed.

After dinner we took the Hiltons upstairs to look at some of
Norton's pictures. They were enthusiastic, which I felt showed
great courtesy. Seeing wild animals must have been a real treat
for them!

Traveler's Tip No. 16. When possible have pictures developed locally. In Nairobi an Indian shop, Karmali's, does them
quickly and well. With a hand viewer you can have pleasure
looking at them and they are great whilers away of time on
airplane trips.

The next morning we visited the Coryndon Museum where we
saw the big cross-section models of elephants' heads and I learned
about the thousands of tiny air chambers which counterbalance
the great weight of the tusks. When I marveled at nature's ingenuity, the doctor said in, I thought, a rather snooty manner,
"I don't see why you're so surprised by them, humans have the
same thing."

"All those little air cells? Come off it."

"What do you think sinuses are?"

"For most people a nuisance. I'm just lucky that mine don't
bother me."

"They are air spaces, too, to balance the weight of our skulls."

He sometimes says there are gaps in my education. There are
gaps.

The museum has many displays of animals against their natural
habitats in huge shadow boxes like those in New York's Museum
of Natural History. One of my favorites was the klipspringer of
the antelope family, a beastie who walks on tiptoe, right up on
the rim of his little blunt hoofs, a ballet dancer *sur ses pointes.*
The museum also boasts a superb collection of butterflies and
moths. The owl moth is a faery creature who lives on fallen logs,
his wings of mottled white, beige, and gray rendering him very
nearly invisible. There were many stuffed little bee eaters, the
kind we had seen in the Serengeti. The cards under them said

they were the Common Bee Eater. Not to me, they're not. To me they're exquisite.

There were also copies of fascinating prehistoric rock paintings, the originals still in the caves. The skill with which the artists, dust for thousands of years, caught the movement of wild animals with whom they shared the earth has yet to be surpassed. These lovely examples of observation and fleeting kinship are the more precious because right beside them in drawings and models one sees the hideously cruel devices with which man trapped and slaughtered his lifetime companions. Spiked traps into which the animals stumbled and were impaled in agony, rocks that tilted and crushed them, rawhide strips cut from their dead predecessors that slowly strangled them—the whole obscene paraphernalia of destruction.

Fortunately, there are also examples of human ingenuity working to a better end. There are the first man-made dwellings as distinguished from caves, efforts of the Cro-Magnon Frank Lloyd Wrights. Frank Lloyd Wright as a matter of fact would have been in his element back there, he having been a great one for rock and stone and brick. I respect his talent without coveting the results since I warm to interiors featuring plaster, paper, paint, boiserie, silks, and chintzes, a little gaiety and coziness, rather than to stark red wood and native stone. I appreciate glass in moderation but let's not go mad, fellows. However, many characters are more rugged than I and Mr. Wright is their ideal and all of that kidney would have loved those houses of ten thousand years ago: they were basic stuff—what the French call *matière première*. Pits in the ground, fourteen by ten by four feet deep, covers or roofs of branches and bracken held in place by stones.

We gazed at them with more than superficial interest. Drop the bomb and we'll be right back where we started.

CHAPTER SIX

Uganda

ENTEBBE, the airport and seat of government of Uganda, lies two hours by air from Nairobi across Lake Victoria, the second largest body of fresh water in the world. The first is Lake Superior in the United States. Lake Victoria is a tricky one. Given the name, a person might well assume that Victoria Falls tumbles out of it and a person would be in grievous error. The incomparable mile-wide cascade is a thousand miles south of the lake on the upper Zambesi River and Dr. and Mrs. Brown did not see it and Dr. and Mrs. Brown are sorry.

Our Entebbe flight was pleasant, the proceedings inefficient. Instead of giving us our landing cards to fill out while we were in the air, they waited until we landed and then held us up while we did it. Also, in Africa, they always ask to see your tickets after you are down. How do they think you boarded the plane in the first place?

The system irritated Norton and me since our tickets were not a matter of a sliver of pasteboard or one small oblong piece of paper. They were like those short-snorter bills during the war. New York, Paris, Rome, Nairobi, Zanzibar, Mombasa, Nairobi, Entebbe, Nairobi, Addis Ababa, Cairo, Paris, Venice, Paris, New York. By the time all that was unfurled the entire airport was festooned, we were exhausted, and the chap who had insisted on seeing them was reeling.

Our driver in Uganda was Mohammed and our car was a

Chevrolet, another blue one. They must get a discount. The bush, basic Africa, lay behind us and we were a little sad. However, Uganda has a beauty that Kenya and Tanganyika lack, for it is a brilliant, tropical green, lush and fertile, its mountainsides clothed with hundreds of thousands of banana and coffee trees.

The Lake Victoria Hotel where we spent the night was attractive on the outside—tables on the lawn under parasols and the British clientele at tea—and inside my idea of Sing Sing. We were shown into a ground-floor room dark as the hole of Calcutta and when I yipped, the doctor, I could see, felt embarrassed. "It's only for one night," he said. "What does it matter?" But what I say is, life is short and all we are sure of is the present. If nothing can be done, bear it with equanimity, but if improvement is possible, improve.

My squawk elevated us to a pleasant room on the second floor overlooking an entrancing jacaranda tree freighted with lavender blossoms. Also the windows were screened. When we commented on this intelligent arrangement the assistant manager said, "We couldn't get on without them. Flies swarm in from the lake in clouds." The room, while better than the first one, was not exactly a prize, for there was no dressing table and the only mirror was on the inside of the closet door where there was no light.

It seems to me a woman might make a good livelihood traveling around the world demonstrating the simple routine of bathing, dressing, reading, and sleeping to hotel managers who quite possibly are Martians. Their needs obviously differ from those of the human race.

I comforted myself as best I might with hot tea on the lawn and afterward we drove through the Botanical Gardens, which are what make a trip to Entebbe worth while. Stretching along the lake shore, they are planted with superb trees from all over the world. The mimosa with their thick golden candles are among the loveliest and (I took the names off the plaques nailed to the trunks) we favored too the moraceae and microcada with their great gray roots obviously designed for children playing hide-and-seek.

Along the roads mud-and-wattle huts jostle the stucco houses built for officials, for although Kampala is the commercial center of Uganda, the seat of officialdom, the capital, is Entebbe. It's like New York City and Albany or Sacramento and San Francisco.

One immediate difference we noted between Uganda and the coastal countries was the amount of clothing worn by the women. No breasts—instead, long dresses of white and singing blue and chili red. The skirts are full and flowing with peplums dropping from the waist, under the peplum a sash, and sleeves gathered into points on the shoulders. The Ugandans seemed taller than the other Africans we had seen and the women were often statuesque, walking like queens with enormous gourds or pitchers on their heads. Their clothes have a fluid grace and their use of color is tonic, audacious.

Back at the hotel while washing up for dinner we engaged in a little ballet. Our windows, which we had opened—after all they were screened—had been closed during our absence. We reopened them. In a few minutes the room boy arrived with his Flit can, closed the windows, drew the curtains, sprayed, and departed. We opened the curtains and the windows. We proposed to fight it out on those lines if it took all summer and indeed we would have done better to stand guard than to go down to dinner. That night we struck bottom. *But.* There are ways to lick the Hotel Victoria food! You won't dine but you'll survive till morning when breakfast will be reasonably respectable. Slice everything on your plate down to the merest sliver, just enough to anchor salt and pepper. *Shower* them on. Salt and pepper quite tasty and will blot out what's underneath. Order a bottle of red wine, about three dollars, but worth it. Drink this and skip down the menu to the cheese. Cheese not supreme but at least recognizable as food. Order crackers because in Entebbe even the usually good African bread has been debauched. On way out of dining room, grab a fistful of small bananas.

On our arrival we had noticed a good many Americans at the

reception desk and Norton found out they were mostly American air force personnel. We wondered why. All kinds of things go on that Washington never tells us about.

In the dining room, heroically plowing their way through the meal, we had also seen a good many Africans. At one table was a white man, four American women, and four blacks. Norton chuckled. "I'd like to have a group of Alabamians and Mississippians here tonight," he said. "It would be a real eye opener for them."

After dinner, or rather after our interlude at table, we went into the lounge for coffee and found a conference group forming in front of a large blackboard. We asked an American lady if we might stay and she said, "You surely can."

In a few minutes an African took his place beside the board and began demonstrating an abstruse mathematical formula. We learned he was a teacher at the University of California. I was lost after the first simple digits and escaped to our room but Norton stayed for a while, assimilating knowledge, and when he got back he claimed it had been most stimulating.

The next morning in the *Argus* we read with pride and a sense of dismay, when we thought of our taxes, that the United States had given Uganda £675,000 in aid to education and that £200,000 more would be made available, chiefly for a girls' school in Toro. Maybe it was enlightened self-interest, we could only hope so, for suspicion is strong that large dollops of this delicious goo go into the pockets of the politicians, for the most part the people of the country know nothing about it, and Uncle Sam is quickly forgotten.

On the same page with the news of the school money was a story entitled "Russia Impresses" that recounted the adventures of three young trade union Ugandans who had gone to Russia and taken a four months' course in something or other that had been condensed for their benefit from the normal ten months' period. They said they had been greatly impressed by the absence of poverty, friendliness of the people, and complete equality.

We fled the Hotel Victoria with first light. Even the beds were awful, the springs screeching so loudly with every movement that one was awakened a dozen times during the night. It only occurred to us when we were under way that we should have taken the mattresses off the bedsteads and slept on them on the floor.

Kabale, our destination, was seventy-five miles to the west and while a picturesque spot we were vague as to why we had been booked there. There was no natural feature of spectacular beauty and no animals but later we decided the tourist bureau probably had not had *only* the welfare of the hotel at heart—they do tend to spread the largesse whenever possible but the distance from Entebbe to Katwe, our goal, is great. Driving it in a day, while perhaps possible, would be exhausting. Also, we had the treat of crossing the equator for the fourth time (the third was in the plane flying from Nairobi to Entebbe) and found it extremely cold, colder than it had been when we went to the Mount Kenya Club.

Unpacking my bag that night, I had a poignant moment. The Bells had told us we would find Uganda *much* warmer than Kenya. I had brought a fan. Eying it and fingering the heavy blankets on our beds, Norton gave a hollow laugh.

Almost all the country we passed through was a banana-growing district and women went by carrying enormous loads of green bananas on their heads. There were also occasional groves of tall, slender blue gum trees as well as coffee trees starred with white blossoms. In Kenya they already bore red berries.

There was a good deal of rain and heavy mist but the Africans did not seem to mind it. Sometimes they would shelter under banana leaves but for the most part they strode along impervious. Umbrellas are apparently unknown or are regarded as effete.

As in Kenya and Tanganyika, the women carried loads on their heads, but we saw fewer bundles of wood such as the coastal women had borne on their backs in slings, a strap across their foreheads. Occasionally boys might try the balancing act but they were not so skillful as the females, they had to steady their bur-

June, the landing crew and assistants

The Waldorf—main lodge
at Lake Rudolf

Bar at the lodge

Ilka wrestling with
sixty-eight-pound Nile perch

Vanquished adversary,
the Nile perch

Father John Ridyard

The lion of Judah—Addis Ababa

Addis Ababa market place

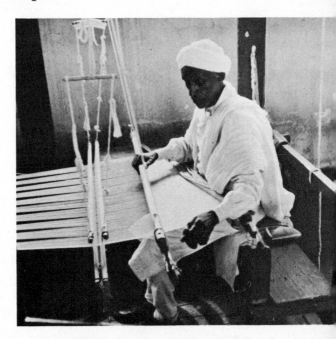

Worker in the Handicraft School,
sponsored by the Empress, weaving the
gauzy fabric for the shamas

Ethiopian women in native dress, the shama

Ethiopian farm

Cairo street scene

Galabias and striped pajamas for street wear—Cairo

Suleiman in the mosque courtyard

The Nile, a dhow, the fretwork tower seen from
our balcony at the hotel

Little boats on the Nile—in foreground bridge where the
trucks and tanks waited their turn the day of the parade

Nasser passing in his car—chaps hanging overboard in following cars
are police ready to jump off and attack any would-be troublemaker

2

den with one hand. The girls were always, "Look, Ma, no hands."

Bicycles were plentiful and there were even a few cars driven by Africans. The whole atmosphere of Uganda is more prosperous than that of the coastal countries but also more Westernized; to our way of thinking, unfortunate.

Any land should have the good Western things, obviously. Prosperity, education, sanitation, all the rest of it, but when the equivalent of rock and roll invades every area, obliterating local color and tradition, whether in architecture or dress, food or manners, it seems a pity. It dissipates the strength of a people without giving them anything very satisfactory in return.

Some of the men wore the picturesque and comfortable *kanzo* but many of them, even far out in the country, might have been walking the streets of a European capital. Now and again, though, came a moment of piquant contrast. We saw a young man striding along the dirt road wearing shoes, trousers, a shirt and tie, and with a book in his hand. A mile farther on we passed one clad in a goatskin carrying a spear.

Uganda has her rondavels too, many of them whitewashed, but there are a greater number of square mud huts as well. Occasionally we passed a rondavel made of tin. Mohammed said they were shelters for road gangs; I should think they would be blistering hot in summer and cold and bleak in the rainy season but Norton thought they were made of metal to prevent pilfering of tools.

In all our long day's drive we saw only one billboard to mar the beauty of the countryside. It was a Coca-Cola sign. Shame on Coca-Cola.

We were sighting the Ankole Hotel at Mbarara for luncheon and on the way were surprised by the herds of longhorn cattle grazing by the roadside. We wondered if they might be descended from the Texas longhorns or vice versa but when we suggested this to the proprietress of the White Horse Inn at Kabale she said coldly, "I shouldn't think they came from the States. If they are imported *at all*, it is from North Africa." We found this rather surprising, always thinking of that part of the world as desert. We had got accustomed to the Africans asking for money when we wanted to photograph them but Dr. Brown's patience wore a little thin when he started to photograph the steers and their owner came running, indignantly demanding *pesa*.

In the bar of the Ankole Hotel we met a stocky, florid man who, from his speech, we took to be either Australian or Cockney, deciding on the former when it developed he was the district education officer. African districts correspond to our counties. He had been in those parts for eight years and told us he had twenty-eight thousand children in primary schools when he should have eighty-five thousand. They had a few truant officers but the distances were so great that rounding up the children was an impossible task.

When asked how he felt about African young compared to those in the rest of the world, he said, "They stack up just the same. Very bright, normally bright, slow, and stupid."

He had also been the education officer in Alexandria during the war and had personally marked and graded the papers of fifty thousand British soldiers. This seemed a formidable achievement and we drank a toast to his patience and ability.

Nearing Kabale, the road lay through rolling country, every hill terraced to the very top with beans, bananas, and millet. The farms were all African-owned and looked prosperous and well tended. Unlike Kenya and Tanganyika, in Uganda, at least since the protectorate treaty with the British signed in 1890, the whites have never been allowed to own property but only to lease it.

We arrived at our destination, the White Horse Inn, at about a quarter to five. Half the way had been tarmac, the rest dirt, and despite the unusually heavy rains the red dust lay thick as ever on the leaves of the trees and bushes bordering the road. We had a small cottage with private bath and the water, while brown, was hot and plentiful.

Traveler's Tip No. 17. Carry a transistor radio with you. There will be areas where you'll be able to pick up an occasional broadcast which can be enjoyable while bathing and changing in the evening.

Traveler's Tip No. 18. If you are game people a couple of packs of cards and traveling chess and checkers sets may be welcome in the evenings, especially when the lights are inadequate for reading.

At dinner that night we met a very nice American girl named Ann Sullivan. She had been traveling around Africa for five months quite alone, and was planning on another three before returning home. She went everywhere by bus, was usually the only white person and always the only white woman aboard, and she said that never once had she been molested or annoyed in any way. "The only time I feel at all nervous or lonely," she said, "is when we arrive someplace at night and I don't know my way around or quite where I'm going to be staying."

Remembering the bloodthirsty column by Mr. Robert Ruark that we had read on the plane the night we took off for Paris, we found her account of her adventures interesting.

We were sorry to say good-by to her the next morning but our ways separated and as she was heading toward a city she took along our postcards and letters, promising to mail them.

African mornings are lyrical. Leaving Kabale, we drove along a ridge, the valley to our right filled with shadows, the dark wet trees, the smoke rising from the morning fires, and the African silhouettes looming out of the mist, creating an atmosphere that was a pure Japanese or Chinese print—Asia and Africa artfully allied.

As the sun rose higher and the mist cleared, we saw the carcass of a small animal, a goat or calf, hanging from a tree, a fire in its belly, a direct, common-sense way of drying and smoking it.

There were charming little vignettes along the road: four or five whitewashed rondavels with thatched roofs in a grove of banana trees; women in dresses of blinding pink or orange, the colors we use on phosphorescent billboards—if ever they were lost at sea they'd be instantly discernible. Groups of school children waving as they passed, their flower-colored uniforms, pink and green, blue and lilac, far gayer than the dreary blue serge skirts and middy blouses of the European schoolgirls.

As we were passing a bus, the driver leaned out and waved to Mohammed, who waved back. The bus slowed, stopped, and so did we and both drivers jumped out, greeting each other with joyous shouts and hearty handshakes. A couple of other chums sprang up from the roadside like Cadmus' dragon's teeth, only they locked in friendly embrace, and the people in the bus leaned out, laughing and chattering and cheering them on. It was a far cry from Fifth Avenue. Norton and I could imagine the attitude of the passengers were the bus conductor and, say, a taxi driver pal to indulge in a comradely get-together. After a fairly prolonged exchange of pleasantries the old friends bade each other farewell, the bus driver called out good-by to us, and we shouted back, *"Waheri"*—he might be practicing English but we were determinedly practicing Swahili, and we continued on our ways.

Encouraged by such good will, even the sun came out in splendor and we rolled along, lolling out the windows and enjoying ourselves immensely.

Crossing a great plain, in the very middle of nowhere, we saw a sign in French, *"Tenez la Gauche."* Whence came this intrepid son of Gaul and whither had he gone? We found no further trace.

Farther on we passed a range of bare undulating hills, the few trees they nurtured seeming to spring from their flanks at right angles. Uganda was beginning to seem more and more like Wonderland and we shortly became convinced we had arrived there. We passed a long migration of people all streaming in one direction, many with heavy loads on their heads. When we asked Mohammed what was going on, he said, "Market day." He spoke truly. A rise of ground, a bend in the road brought us to an explosion of colors and life and sound, for spread along a hillside was a great outdoor market. There must have been a thousand to fifteen hundred people milling about, buying and selling wares ranging from bananas to teakettles. There were combs and soap and hardware and a man selling big hunks of salt. It came in rock formation from a nearby lake and when he had a customer he pounded it into granules.

There were babies galore in slings on their mothers' backs or lying naked on a bit of cloth spread on the ground. The most colorful merchants were the vendors of material. They had bolts of every shade and pattern and at intervals on the slope, where a flat place had been trodden out, were men with sewing machines. It's a fine system. You buy the fabric of your choice, take it to the sewing machine man, who quickly stitches it up, and there you are: instant clothes! They do it differently in Africa: the men sew the clothes, the women sow the fields.

We wandered about buying bananas and a few trinkets and people looked at us with brief curiosity and went on about their business. Throughout all our travels in Africa we were greeted with either indifference or friendliness, never with animosity. Driving indeed was a delight, for wherever we passed the people along the road waved us a greeting and we waved back, jouncing as we waved; although there are more paved roads in Uganda than in Tanganyika, mostly they are dirt and we could hear and feel the stones banging and clattering against the undercarriage. "Glad we don't own this," observed the doctor. "It's taking one hell of a beating."

We passed three leper camps in the course of our journey but they were off the road, we did not see any of the sorry inmates, and Norton says that a cure is now possible.

The Ugandans have a curious system for keeping you in the path of righteousness. They plant a row of rough posts down the middle of the road on the turns; serviceable enough in the daytime but a real hazard in the black night when there are not even those metal buttons to reflect the headlights.

About two in the afternoon we arrived at Queen Elizabeth National Park, I regret to report in foul moods induced by hunger. We could happily have spitted, broiled, and eaten Mohammed, we were so mad at him. Ann Sullivan had told us that the distance from Kabale to Mweya Lodge was about sixty-five miles.

Mohammed said, no, it was ninety-five. A longish morning's drive in that country but still possible. It turned out to be one hundred and fifty. What made us mad was that, had we only known, we could perfectly well have arranged a picnic lunch instead of listening to our stomachs grumbling and growling.

Our bad mood lifted, however, when, driving through the gates, we saw a large yellow sign: "You are entering Queen Elizabeth National Park. Elephants Have the Right of Way." Who would dispute them? Almost immediately we saw two of them having it, a mother and child under a tree on our left. We began to see other game too, our first Uganda kob, a charming creature whom we did not stop to photograph owing to hunger pangs, and we still had several miles to cover.

By the time we arrived at the lodge luncheon was over and the kitchen locked up but the manager and his wife very decently managed to get us some cold meat. The staff, despite that traditional and, we discovered, now largely fictional mem-sahib and bwana business, behaved just as they do any place else when they consider they are being worked overtime: banged the plates down on the table in front of us, expressing their displeasure with black looks and insolence.

The bar was closed and while the food lockers might be violated there was no question of opening that until six o'clock.

Traveler's Tip No. 19. Never be without a little portable sustenance. In our cottage we sneaked a couple of pink gins and carried to the dining room two cans of warm beer to cheer the cold, begrudged meat.

The Mweya Lodge, with a terrace, dining room and bar, cottages and bunkhouses nearby, is magnificently located on a bluff overlooking Lake Edward and Lake George, connected by the Kazinga Channel, the abodes of our first water animals. The next day we would take a launch trip to see hippos and crocodiles but that afternoon we settled for unpacking, driving about, and watching a fearsome battle between two small local beasts, the gray lodge cat and a lizard. The lizard, while not minute, was not very big either and he was full of pluck. The cat kept dabbing at him with his paw and the lizard roared silent defiance, his little red mouth wide open, his little front paws jabbing the air. When the cat's attention was diverted for an instant he slipped away like mercury. He was doughty but drab of color whereas one of his cousins, whom we later encountered on a whitewashed wall, glittered like a rajah's treasure. His head was turquoise, his tail, at the tip, sapphire and, where it joined his body, gold. The body itself was emerald green. A Cartier lizard if I ever saw one.

Mweya Lodge offers a great deal in the way of location but the people who built it and those who run it haven't thought things through. If we had been roughing it under canvas we would have expected and accepted primitive conditions. But if you're going to go to the trouble of building bunkhouses, what is so difficult about making closets two inches wider so that hangers may hang straight, at right angles to the wall, instead of at a slant because of congested space? Cross ventilation had not been considered either and the electric light was inadequate and distant from points of usage. Our beds, as at the Victoria in Entebbe, were lumpy and full of backchat. The quality I most admire in a bed is taciturnity. All I ask of a bed, besides comfort, is that it keep its lip buttoned.

They did have running water for the tubs. Behind each cottage was a brick and plaster kiln in the top of which was inserted an old Mobil oil can filled with water. A fire laid underneath warmed it very satisfactorily.

Our room boy, Joseph, was a darling: old, gnarled, snaggle-toothed, endowed with charm as a flower with fragrance. The tape recorder entranced him. We showed him how it worked and had him speak into it and then played his own voice back to him—this time I pushed down the button. His wrinkled pixy face lighted in amusement and he laughed like a child but a child with a sense of the ridiculous.

Mweya has other attractions too, including proximity to wild animals. One day we watched two cyclists approaching the lodge and at a place where the road rose and dipped over a hill an elephant stood. He stood there for quite some time, languidly browsing the overhanging branches of a tree, and the two young Africans balanced on their bikes, one foot on the ground, eying him with a wary and respectful glance. When he was good and ready he moved away and the cyclists peddled the last hundred yards to the lodge with the devil at their tails although the elephant utterly ignored them.

Queen Elizabeth National Park grows a cactus called euphorbia or candelabra tree. They do somewhat resemble candelabra when young but the older trees are like gigantic round tight bouquets. They are characteristic of many parts of Africa but do not have the grace of the thorn trees.

We felt very proud when we learned to distinguish the Uganda kob from the female waterbuck. Just to show I can do it—and I hope I'm right—the kob's neck is longer and her ears, though rounded at the top like the waterbucks', are set on her head so as to form a V. The top of a lady waterbuck's head is flat, the place between her ears is square. They are both dear girls.

One of the delights of travel is the bars, not only for the refreshment obtained but for the company as well. Travelers pick each other up without introduction and the encounters are frequently rewarding.

Our first night at Mweya we met a very interesting Belgian, a Mr. Van der Plass, whom we asked to join us at dinner. He was a magistrate in Ruanda-Urundi on a brief holiday and had seen his family off for Belgium the previous week.

Although Belgium has given up Ruanda-Urundi, she still contributes $10,000,000 a year to the country but at least another four or five are needed. Here, of course, is where the small emerging countries play power politics, often shrewdly blackmailing both Russia and the United States. "All right for you! If you won't give us the money we know who will."

In Ruanda-Urundi apparently the Russians stir up trouble by going, for example, to the bar boys and saying, "You should revolt. You see how poor you are now? That's because the head barman and the hotel owners are keeping all the money." The sad truth is there's no money to keep, the country is bankrupt. Industry is virtually nil although they do have natural gas but no oil and there are few visitors.

In a country of several million there are four doctors and nineteen law-enforcement officers and, according to Mr. Van der Plass, none of the officials has gone beyond high school. Whether they were not permitted to or weren't bright enough to or whether there were no higher schools I do not know.

Even in our brief and superficial meetings with those who had spent years in Africa, Norton and I became convinced of one thing which American liberals are reluctant to believe and that is that many Europeans do genuinely wish Africans well. They are not fools so whether it be with open arms or deep regret they accept changes in a world in which many of them have passed a lifetime. But they do think the Africans have a longer way to go than the do-gooder white outsiders or the Africans themselves are willing to believe. And indeed one has only to be there a few days to realize that Western schoolteachers are vitally necessary until the African nations are able to educate at least one generation of the native population.

European teachers are willing to come but they obviously must be paid. Before Uhuru their own countries footed the bills. Now the Africans must do so or, if they are lucky enough to have the withdrawing Europeans willing to pay the lions' share, even after their departure, they themselves must contribute something and they are finding, just as all young people do when first living independent of the parental roof, that the bills come as quite a jolt.

Norton, trying to think how countries like Liechtenstein and Luxembourg managed financially—although Luxembourg of course has coal—suggested a broadcasting station, a sort of Radio Africa. Mr. Van der Plass seemed to think the idea had merit because the country is high and centrally located. On the other hand, there is the problem of language, and at the present time the people are touchy and superstitious. An American company paid five thousand dollars for permission to take films in the

Albert Game Park which they proposed to show on television as propaganda for Ruanda-Urundi and to stimulate tourists to go there but the inhabitants were so capricious and created so many difficulties that the Americans finally said, "The hell with it. Give us back our money and we'll get out."

Van der Plass himself loves the country and hoped very much to be able to continue his life there. Also, having been there for nearly eight years, if he could hold his job a few months longer he would be entitled to eight months' vacation with full pay. We wished him well.

Another encounter was more touching: a Scotch-Irish woman, a Catholic in, I should say, her middle thirties. She had two children aged about ten and eight and a nine-month-old baby. She was charming with them and obviously loved them dearly but when her husband went off for a bit we fell to talking and she said, "Oh, I do hope so much we won't have any more children. We shouldn't have had this last baby and now I'm worried to death for fear I'm pregnant and I don't know what we'll do if we have another one, how we'll ever manage. We're just barely scraping by as it is. We've saved and saved for this holiday. . . . I don't know how we'll get by, I just don't know." Her hands twisted in her lap and her eyes filled with tears. Sometimes to non-Catholics it seems odd that the dogma of intensive breeding advocated by the Roman Catholic Church should be propounded by celibates and by celibates who, as individuals, do not have to make good economically in a competitive world.

A Norwegian-American was staying at the lodge too. He came from Coeur d'Alene in Idaho. We had never heard of it but he was living proof that it exists. He was a cultural economist for the United States Government and had just come from Madagascar. His job is to survey land, study the agricultural situation, and assess the ability of the populace to be self-sustaining. After his brief holiday he was returning to Washington to hand in his report and did not know where he might be sent next.

Norton and I are lifelong Americans but we always seem to have to travel several thousand miles to find out what our government is up to. Mr. Reicard impressed us as an able chap and we were glad he was on our team. He had lost his right arm in the First World War and ordered only soup and fish at dinner. I asked if he wouldn't like some meat, I would have been glad to cut it for him, but he said no. Perhaps he was shy about his disability or perhaps he just didn't want any. It wasn't very good.

At eight-thirty the next morning we started off for our day's game drive through the park. In Queen Elizabeth Park the stars are elephants, waterbuck, and water buffalo. They claim there are lions but we saw none and there are no zebras, giraffes, or wildebeests.

Elephants are leisurely lumbering creatures but with an objective in mind they move and it is uncanny the speed with which anything that size can melt from view.

When it became obvious that a group of them were going to cross the road in front of us to go down to the river, I asked Norton to take some pictures but he wasn't in the mood. He said, "Not now. We'll see others just as good and I'll get them then." Well, we didn't. I learned that if ever there was a place where "a bird in the hand is worth two in the bush" holds good it's in Africa. Literally. A bird, or an elephant, in the lens is worth a baker's dozen in the bush where they swiftly disappear.

Another time my spouse was more alert. We came upon two elephants who, even to the unpracticed eye, were obviously in amorous mood. "Oh, look," I said, "they're courting, they're in love." Norton swung his camera into position. "I certainly hope they're going to copulate," he said. He's a doctor, they talk that way. You just have to get used to it. I got a real shock the first time when I heard him, speaking to someone on the telephone, ask, "Where's the body now?" Or he'll say something like, "I have a double nylon zipper on my blood cuff." That's the thing they wrap tight around your arm when they take your blood pressure. Doctors have different possessions and a more basic approach to life and death than non-pros.

For our Uganda trip we were not in a Land Rover and, although our Chevrolet did not do too badly, it was not fundamentally—pardon, General Motors—the car for the job.

A Land Rover had been suggested, indeed pitched at us the night before in the bar, by the manager of the lodge but we felt that two shillings fifty the mile was high when we were already paying for a car. Also, Queen Elizabeth National Park is better landscaped for a conventional automobile than are the Ngorongoro Crater or Serengeti, but even at that I'm not sure we didn't make a mistake. With that sliding roof, the Land Rover is infinitely better for picture taking and in it one can get very near the game.

We had asked for a ranger to accompany us because we felt he would be better equipped than our driver, Mohammed, to find game. As it developed he wasn't necessary but he and Mohammed, like Koske and Wamuti, made a happy little team and since we never did get his name we called him Lone. In a way he justified himself. He guided us to a large pool filled, so we thought, with tiny islands but the islands shuddered and heaved and lo! Hippopotami. Hundreds of them. Huge comical creatures who exist almost totally submerged, only their rounded backs, shrewd little eyes, and mouse's ears showing above water. They elevate, yawn, and submerge again. If ever there was a community free from ulcers it is that of the hippo. In the midst of tension or a subway rush I now think of them and relax, adding, I am sure, several minutes to my life.

Lone heaved a stick or two and they reluctantly roused themselves, moved a few feet away, and sank back into the calm water, their great forms settling like bulging parachutes.

Flamingos lived in the pond too and beige ducks with handsome orange and black tail feathers. Pure white tickbirds used the hippos' backs as restful perches.

Near the pool on a hillside were about ten elephants. We felt a renewed sense of wonder in looking at them as a family of three wandered away from the herd. One was a new baby—two and a half weeks old, the ranger said. As they got our scent the mother reached out her trunk and with a tender, gentle gesture herded the baby beneath her. The big bull closed in and the baby walked snugly protected under its mother's belly, its father close beside it.

Later we saw hippopotami in the bush a mile or two from the pond, for they are herbivorous and wander far afield to eat. Mud wallows are popular with both them and the water buffalo and we would see them lumbering up from a bath plastered with mud, blissfully happy. One hippo, rolling about playful as a kitten, so startled a water buffalo that he stared, gave a snort, and departed at a gallop.

A fascinating aspect of Queen Elizabeth Park and the adjacent country, the area known as Katwe-Kikorongo, is its geological youth, the gigantic earth movements and eruptions which resulted in its present form having taken place in the past million years. This may not seem like yesterday until one realizes that the Alps are between twenty and thirty million years old and that the mountains of Scotland and Scandinavia were hurled from the depths of earth and ocean five hundred million years ago. Compared to them, the great Ruwenzori range is positively skittish. Professor L. C. Beadle, in his introduction to a booklet on the Uganda National Park, says, "The remarkable fact that this huge mountain mass springs almost directly from the plain and has no real foothills, is evidence of its youth and of its origin by some kind of upthrust."

Nor was the Ruwenzori the only result of the vast convulsion. There is a section of the park that is pitted with craters, some shallow depressions fifty to a hundred feet deep, others five hundred feet deep and many miles in circumference. Occasionally they form concentric circles overlapping each other. Some of the slopes are densely forested and the crater floors flat, grass-covered, and dotted with trees. Sometimes they drop away into a still deeper crater, the deepest always heavily wooded. One drives along a high winding ridge road peering awe-struck into the immense holes and marveling at the titanic rumblings and regurgitations that must have gone on as the volcanoes erupted and gas and steam roared their way upward through the earth's crust. There are a couple of crater lakes we wanted to see but they smelled so strongly of sulphur that the road leading to them was temporarily closed.

Today the area is marvelously quiet. We shut off the motor and listened to the faint murmuring sounds of nature and watched the tall grasses, as high as the car, moving in breeze-woven patterns against the sky.

In the course of the morning we also visited a small round pavilion on a hillside dedicated to Queen Elizabeth and the Duke of Edinburgh when they visited the park in 1954.

Much of the country traversed was remarkably beautiful but the burnt earth we had already seen so many times never ceased to distress me. Africans apparently are terribly obstinate about fertilizer even when it's available. According to Pieter Lessing, a journalist who has lived most of his life on the continent and has written a book called *The African Kaleidoscope*, as soon as the African gets Uhuru he refuses to use fertilizer because the English have told him to do so. Each to his own revenge, I suppose, but talk about cutting off your nose to spite your face!

Our launch trip through the Kazinga Channel came after luncheon but there was a bad moment when we thought we might not make it. This was because the floating islands of weeds, sticks, and matted grasses sometimes drift against the launches and their weight is such that departure from the dock is impossible. Happily that turned out not to be the case and after negotiating a short palm-log pier, the logs rolling under our feet, about ten of us set out in a weather-beaten launch strongly resembling an espresso machine.

The crew of two native boys pushed off into the channel and we passed through thick stands of papyrus with their long pliant stems and heads like feathery green chrysanthemums.

Our first subjects for photography were a marabou stork and an elephant accompanied by his faithful pages, the white tickbirds. A little farther along, grazing on the banks, was another enormous elephant and one of the children on board, a little girl named Lorraine, called out, "Jambo, Jumbo," and everybody laughed and shouted, "Jambo, Jumbo," too. *Jambo* is Swahili for "Hello" or "How are you," or "Hi, there," usually accompanied by a delighted grin, since meetings in Africa seem almost always pleasurable.

The channel was thick with hippos, their round ears and round eyes pushing up through the lily pads. Considering that they are monumentally unlike a horse, it is extraordinary, when they are entirely submerged with the exception of the upper half of their heads, how like a horse's that half head is. Hippos are the aquatic comedians of the animal world as wart hogs are the land-bound ones.

Thousands of birds live along the channel and we saw flashing kingfishers and saddle-billed storks, black cormorants with white throats and gleaming black bodies, clean-looking and noble in sharp contrast to the unclean, mean-looking vultures.

We felt certain that hippos were rolling underneath us and that we were being propelled by twin hippo power which, while not without risk, seemed more reliable than the gurgling, coughing, sputtering coffee maker that was our gasoline-driven engine.

Norton was using his big telescopic lens to get the animals on shore and everybody was admiring it and he said modestly, "Yes, it is quite nice. With it I can see what the animals are thinking." Three water buffalo standing on shore only a few yards from the launch gave him a dirty look.

The next morning, leaving Queen Elizabeth Park on our way to Fort Portal, we drove over the wide plain, passing candelabra trees and occasional grazing animals shrouded in mist like a landscape in a dream.

The Ruwenzori range, the Mountains of the Moon, lay ahead and theoretically we should have been seeing them but it was the same old story of fog and clouds enveloping the heights. Some people do see the top of Kilimanjaro, we ourselves saw Mount Kenya, but nobody ever sees Mount Stanley. I don't know how they can be sure it's there.

The long road from Katwe to Fort Portal is hard-surfaced and an hour out of Mweya we were back in thorn-tree and banana land. At Fort Portal we turn off the main road, heading into the mountains and Bundibugyo, home of the Pygmies. Dr. Brown is not happy about this, saying he knows what Pygmies look like and how they smell and why are we wasting our time? I hadn't actually planned it but somehow they seemed to be on our itinerary and as the country itself was so beautiful why not have a look?

The Ruwenzori Mountains are spectacular and the road we were traveling, the Barunga Pass at 4000 feet, although only dirt is still a feast of engineering. How the tiny rondavel settlements, perhaps four or five houses clinging to the mountain flanks at a dizzying angle, overlooking the vast plain far below, were ever anchored to their precarious perches is a mystery.

The plain is partially carpeted with banana plantations and dark trees. The Semliki River winds through it and in the distance stretches the endless green savanna with occasional columns of smoke rising into the still air. I assumed the tribesmen were at it again, burning the grass, but Mohammed said no, the smoke was from sulphur springs.

He was quite knowledgeable but he wore glasses and had a prissy mustache and an abrupt disapproving manner and I did not like him. Norton was much more tolerant, adopting a noble "There's so much good in the worst of us and so much bad in the best of us" attitude that I found hard to bear. I had to admit he made sense, however, when he said Mohammed's trouble was probably that his English was limited. That's why he seemed abrupt. God knows, if I had had to speak Swahili it would have been basic, lacking in refinements and grace notes.

The mountainsides were completely covered with trees, the boughs balancing in horizontal layers over the ravines, the light dropping through the higher branches splashing lovely patterns on those below.

After a long gradual descent we reached level ground and drove over narrow but surprisingly good roads through a thick jungle. We were in a district called Bamba and most of the men we passed carried spears but they were not so long and businesslike as those of the Masai. A little while later we began meeting Pygmies who ran beside the car, arms outstretched, yelling, "*Pesa, pesa.*" Both sexes wore only brief sarongs and had shaven heads so the only way one could tell the women was by their long pendulous breasts, which flapped as they ran.

There was one normal-sized African girl wearing a blue cotton dress and a charming smile and balancing on her head a minuscule pot of what looked to be green vaseline. African and Asian women have it all over their Western sisters when it comes to carrying babies and possessions. The babies are in slings on their backs, the possessions on their heads, and their hands are free.

We finally came to a halt, stopped by a large group of Pygmies gathering in the middle of the road. I looked at my dear one, who was obviously on his way to the guillotine. True, the atmosphere was getting a little aromatic, if not as much as I had anticipated, but they were ugly little creatures and madly voracious. One whom we had met earlier and who had directed us along the road had an intelligent face and soft blue eyes with long lashes but his relations were a rugged breed. The head man, who was stone blind, was voluble in speech and demanded forty shillings if we were to photograph the group. His sense of values appeared inflated.

While Norton and Mohammed were bargaining I got out of the car and gave a few cents to a mother and her baby and to a tiny wrinkled old crone who were willing to pose. All the Pygmy women crowded around me, pointing at and touching the strands of pearls I was wearing, indicating they would like to have them. I indicated that I would too and we seemed to have struck a snag in the negotiations when Mohammed said we had better give them something or they would make trouble. Considering the size of them and the size of us and that we had a car, Norton and I were vague as to what trouble they could make but, mindful of Gulliver, we said all right, we would give them three shillings if three people would pose. They wanted five and the whole group would pose. Take the picture first and bargain later, Mohammed suggested.

By this time Dr. Brown's patience, which had been thin at the start, was beginning to shred. "No," he said, "I will do as I say, I will give three shillings for three people and the chief or anyone else can pick them out." This caused such an uproar—everyone wanted to be chosen—that, uttering a short, potent oath, the doctor herded Mohammed and me back into the car, slammed the doors, and drove off. I myself would have been willing to haggle a little longer since they are strange and unusual folk but after a good many years of marriage I know when we are at the boiling point and it seemed wiser to desist.

Traveler's Tip No. 20. Especially good for Africa but applicable in other lands too when the birds are wary. A Polaroid camera plus whatever others you use is a good idea. If one of you diverts the quarry with pictures instantly developed which you give them, the chances are they will be enchanted, ignore money, and your accomplice will be able to get a permanent record.

As a matter of fact I had a qualm about the unpleasant little chief. They had all been as short on appeal as they were in stature but would he perhaps lose face with the tribe because he had not got any money? I worried but I need hardly add that we did not go back to see how things were working out.

We had to get out of Pygmy land by the same way we had come in and on the return journey passed a broken-down Dodge pickup truck. We stopped and a group of young men asked if we had a pump they could borrow for their tires. They were funny and gay, one getting down on his knees in the road, pretending to utter ardent prayers for help. We were able to lend a hand and, looking around a minute or two later, saw that, in true African fashion, quite a group had congregated. We had been eating a picnic lunch in the car so I gave cookies to the children. "You know," I said to Norton later, "those cookies were good. Perhaps I am creating the African palate of the future. Someday one of those little boys may say, 'Long ago a white lady and gentleman drove by the jungle hut where I lived as a child and the lady gave me the most delicious food I had ever eaten and I then and there determined to become a famous chef so that I too could make marvelous things to eat and here I am today, the owner of the Pyramide, the greatest restaurant in France.' Do you think that might happen?"

"I doubt it," said the doctor. I shed a bitter tear.

During weekdays there are hours when the traffic on the winding mountain road is all one way as it was in the Ngorongoro Crater but not on Sunday, which was our day. Rounding a sharp curve at a good clip, Mohammed missed by a hair an enormous truck rounding from the other way also at a good clip. Norton and I gulped. Had we gone hurtling down the mountain together the result would not have been savory. Throughout much of Africa they use a special kind of dirt for surfacing the roads called murram. It packs hard and is very practical.

We arrived at our night's lodging, the Ruwenzori Hotel, at about half-past three. It was a big conventional hotel rather than a lodge, and reasonably attractive with broad verandas and well-kept lawns. After reconnoitering a bit I decided to work on my diary and try to nap. Later Norton came back from the bar to report that I would hate it. "It was jammed with young men slapping each other on the back and shouting," he said. "They must have just won a cricket match."

Once refreshed by hot baths—clear clean water this time—we decided that boisterous youth might not be so bad and perhaps we should join the gaiety. On the way down we saw dozens of cars parked in the driveway and anticipated a cheerful bedlam. It was therefore quite a shock to push open the bar door and enter the tomb. Not a sound, not a human being. I said to Norton, "You must be dotty. This is like that famous story about the American girl and her mother in Paris years ago. The girl leaves their room for a while and when she returns her mother has vanished, the furniture has been changed, the very paper on the walls is different, and the management claims they never heard of two American women. Ma had the plague or something and they had to erase the evidence."

Norton himself looked discomfited. "I swear there was a gang in here. All those cars . . . where are the people they belong to?"

The barman who came in just then restored our tottering reason. "This is Sunday night, sir. The hotel shows movies every Saturday and Sunday, that's where they've all gone."

I too would have liked to go, a British comedy was playing, and from the dining room we could hear occasional bursts of laughter. However, by this time they were better than halfway through and we were hungry but the dining room lacked sparkle, the only guests beside ourselves being two middle-aged Englishwomen who, it developed, were also en route to Paraa Lodge and Murchison Falls National Park.

We departed next morning in a great hugger-mugger over luggage and effects. I had lost my dark glasses and was in a state of shock. I had another pair but they were my special pets. Through them I had gazed upon the Bosporus and the Aegean Sea. They had filtered the glittering gold of the temples of Bangkok and dimmed the blazing sun along the causeway leading to Angkor Wat. As with well-seasoned omelet pans or salad bowls, what passed through them was enriched by what had gone before.

Without them I was deprived, bereft. Later I found them in another suitcase. Norton's "Thank God!" was heartfelt.

All that morning he was thoughtful about the wealth of Africa. The terrain inspired him—sedimentary deposits and such. He thought there might be oil under the plains, water tables below the mountains, "but," he added, "I cannot doubt that the idea has occurred to geologists long since." Perhaps it has and I find it a depressing one. With water one might still be able to exert some control; with oil the game would be abolished overnight, wealth greater than any viscous fluid destroyed forever.

That particular drive was quite rich in natural lore. Having few bulldozers, none in the part of the country we were in, the Africans have an ingenious trick for breaking up big rocks and boulders. They drill many small holes into which they insert sticks. When it rains, or they wet the sticks enough, they swell and after a while the rock breaks into fragments, easy to move.

Norton said that when he first bought his place in Connecticut, years ago, he'd put a kerosene torch against a rock for several hours, then pour cold water over it. A great cloud of steam would rise and the mighty boulder split into pieces. I think it a brilliant idea but he says *everybody* knows about it. I didn't and I mention it in case anyone is thinking of going back to the grass roots. It's a handy nugget of knowledge in a New England pasture for instance.

The road to Hoima runs between steep grassy banks, the grass well trimmed by the trusty *penga* and assisted by many goats, who fancy it for grazing as the new young shoots are tender. Hoima itself is a pretty town and the center of Bunyoro, one of the three kingdoms of Uganda. The public buildings are attractive, set among lawns, green playing fields, and superb acacia trees alight with golden candelabra. In the little shops men were busy at the sewing machines and there was a stimulating air of prosperity and activity. Passing through the town, we came to Monkeyville. The trees on either side of the road were alive with Colobus monkeys, handsome citizens with long silky black and white fur. The word *kolobus* in Greek means maimed or mutilated and the monkeys are so named because, unlike all other breeds, they lack thumbs. Their babies are entrancing and I immediately added them to my imaginary zoo.

We lunched at Masindi at the East African Railroad Hotel. It was clean and nondescript in appearance and the food was the best we had in Africa: excellent steak and kidney pie freshly made and piping hot. There was even the wherewithal for a salad. We complimented the manager and his wife and learned with regret that they would soon be leaving as the hotel was to be run by Africans. Farewell, I am afraid, to the outstanding cuisine.

We had passed the two English ladies from Fort Portal on our way to Masindi and just as we were leaving they arrived and asked us if we would tell the Paraa Lodge people at Murchison Falls that they would not be getting there that night. They had run their car off the road into a ditch and while it was somewhat accordion-pleated in the front they fortunately were unhurt.

Traveler's Tip No. 21. We did not realize it until we were in the middle of the trip but with a little enterprise tourists can manage without a chauffeur. Not quite so easily in Kenya and Tanganyika, perhaps, but in Uganda the roads are good and well marked. One has to have a ranger or a guide in the reserves but they are always available. For the most part Africans speak enough English to give directions and our own experience was that the Natives are Friendly. In Tanganyika and Kenya you have to know how to drive a Land Rover, in itself no trivial accomplishment, but in Uganda almost everyone travels in regular cars.

Murchison Falls National Park encompasses an area of about a thousand square miles. A colony called Fajao, more or less its nucleus, was established at the foot of the falls in 1896 and was visited by Winston Churchill in 1907 but he found it almost extinct as a result of sleeping sickness. Before World War I the few stragglers who remained were removed, a sleeping sickness area was proclaimed, and the bush closed over such traces of civilization as had been established.

That particular malady turned out to be a Godsend, for it preserved the wilderness and the animals to this day. Now there is no epidemic and there is wild life in abundance.

It is partly due to this happy state, however, that one's first impression of Murchison Falls is slightly sinister. There are thousands of red ant hills and there are the ground bill birds: black, evil-looking creatures, one of whom must have been the inspiration for John Collier's eerie story, "Bird of Prey," in *Fancies and Goodnights*. There are more and larger elephants in Murchison than we saw elsewhere but there are also thousands of dead trees—their tortured black limbs jutting into the sky. This is partially the result of the fertilizing fires but partially also it must be attributed to the elephants, who rip off and eat the bark. The young English warden whom we later met told us they were going to have to shoot some of them to reduce their numbers so they would not entirely destroy their own habitat and starve as a result.

We had laughed at the Mweya Lodge in Queen Elizabeth Park when we saw the boys on bicycles held up by an elephant but we ourselves were in the same spot at Murchison. Two or three very large Republicans were swinging their trunks, flapping their ears, and having a happy graze by the side of the road and we waited courteously until they were ready to leave. When they turned, Mohammed would try inching forward but the instant they heard the motor they would swing toward us again, eying us suspiciously while their ears flapped forward and their trunks rose to the ready. Never dispute an elephant whose trunk is raised in anger. We learned later that it is not so much the trunk one must be wary of as the tusks. When they are up, look out but to a novice a raised trunk has an aggressive air and it was not until they had finished that particular course and moved on that we did too.

The road followed a rise of land, dipped, and we were on the shores of the Nile. While we waited for the ferry that was chugging toward us, Norton watched its mechanism with interest. It was not as picturesque as the ferry of my shame, no Volga boatmen or iron chains. This one was propelled by an ancient greasy tug nudging it from one side.

Like Mweya, Paraa Lodge is also situated on a bluff, overlooking the Nile instead of a lake. The cottages, although very simple, are a little grander than those at Katwe and we were told ours was the one in which the Queen Mother had stayed when she visited Uganda. It was situated about four hundred yards down the road from the main house and they said they would send a car for us at dinnertime. We explained we were stalwart types who didn't mind footing it a few yards but they explained we weren't stalwart enough to ward off wandering hippos and elephants. Many of them are of friendly persuasion and enjoy an evening stroll through the camp. Nobody minds much and they told us not to be alarmed by an clattering sounds we might hear. It would just be elephants at the garbage cans. There was only one they ever got mad at and that was because he was careless. He had learned to open any outside water taps he came across, which wouldn't have been too bad if he would have taken a drink and closed them again but he left them running and water is a luxury that *nobody* can be allowed to waste. "If we've told that elephant once we've told him a hundred times . . ."

We stepped from our cottage onto a narrow terrace and then the ground fell away to the water. About halfway down the slope was a big tree and in the early evenings two elephants used to come and stand under it only a few yards away from us. The pool at the bottom was inhabited by hippos and a little low mud island was the home of a crocodile. He lay all day without stirring, his mouth wide open. When we came in one evening Norton took his binoculars and peered down at him. "Any change?" I asked.

"Yes," he said, "big activity. He's closed his mouth."

The lodge was run by a couple named Thurgood. He was a good many years younger than she and an extremely handsome man. She had had three daughters by a previous husband and they seemed a curiously matched pair. I felt a story coming on.

We discovered that there are fishing launches available on the river but one must bring one's own tackle. The catch is Nile perch and the record at that time was 160 pounds, a single fish taken in 1961. There is smaller fauna too, of course. At tea we met a charming lizard with an orange head and body and tail of deep brilliant navy blue. He was an agama in dress uniform, his breeding colors, and Roger Weater, the young English park ranger, told us that the reason he did the push-ups that so amused us, raising his body up on his front paws and looking curiously about him, was to attract insects. Fascinated by his acrobatic skill, they would draw near, his long thin tongue would shoot out, and that was the end of them. He had catholic taste, that lizard, and appreciated cake and crumbs too.

There were several Indians staying at Paraa, the women draped in their saris. They are picturesque but somewhere along the way that design got garbled. The tight-fitting embroidered

bodices are attractive and the skirts are all right and the drapery
or sari itself can be lovely but what about that expanse of person
through the midriff? Usually there is too much of it and it bulges
and no provision has been made to accommodate or shelter it.

That night at dinner we had a small domestic contretemps,
my dear one claiming that it would embarrass him to go to the
dining room bearing half a bottle of red wine left from our dinner the night before. I maintained that it was good, expensive,
and why waste it?

"I wouldn't dream of doing it at the Century Club," he de-
clared grandly.

"I should hope not," I said, "but we're not *at* the Century
Club." We took it, they had some, but I am a strong believer in
waste not, want not.

Men's attitudes in these matters, I have found, differ strongly
from women's. I remember my first husband never could adjust
to my asking for oil and vinegar, salt and pepper in a restaurant
so that I might make plain salad dressing instead of eating that
nauseating orange gook from a bottle they serve under the guise
of French dressing, and I once had a beau who broke off our
romance when, on leaving a hotel in Beverly Hills, I said I would
like to stop by a friend's house on the way to the airport to leave
four or five unopened quart bottles of soda I had bought and
paid for but had not used.

A charming exception in these matters is my friend Richard
Lewine. I once left Mr. Lewine a half bottle of scotch when he
and I were both staying at the Beverly Hills Hotel and I was
going back to New York. Mr. Lewine *appreciated* it and I appreciate him.

My first night's slumber at Paraa Lodge was sporadic, owing
to the hippos. They are herbivorous in theory, which doesn't
mean they won't open that vast maw and swallow you if annoyed, and they strolled up the hillside from the Nile in search
of delicacies. Honking under our low windows, they sounded
exactly like porkers and despite their reputation as vegetarians
I drew the covers over my head, hoping to stifle any human

scent. The lodge people *claimed* that they never tried to make their way inside but as we were to learn later they have very affectionate natures and are not averse to a bit of cuddling.

Chai arrived at seven—we had neglected to hang out the Do Not Disturb sign—but we didn't mind too much as we were anxious to get under way for our falls viewing.

At breakfast a lean, rickety native warrior appeared outside the dining-room windows wearing moth-eaten ostrich plumes in his hair and a cloak of leopard skin. He feinted, pretending to hurl his spear through the window, but he was not very convincing and Norton took his picture out of pity—he seemed so anxious to get a little attention. We thought him the local lunatic but learned he was paid to go through this little act, the management hoping wistfully that the tourists might get a thrill.

The distance from the lodge to Murchison Falls is about twenty-one miles and the going is rough. Everybody does it in ordinary cars rather than Land Rovers but I would advise this only if the car is rented. Had ours been our own we would not have dreamed of subjecting it to the rigors of the route. As it was, we bumped without qualm. Who shows to another's property the solicitude he displays toward his own? I can't think how they manage in Soviet Russia where nobody owns anything. The place must be a shambles.

After an hour or more of swaying and jouncing through the bush we reached the top of the falls. The rapids, churning and foaming between narrow banks, rush onward to the drop and hurtle downward through a twenty-foot cleft in the rocks in a roaring, boiling cascade, striking the bottom with such force that a trillion snow crystals are flung upward, glittering through the smoke and spray, a shimmering rainbow arching over them.

It is a fabulous sight and its spectacular quality was enhanced for us by the unusually heavy rainfall in the days preceding our visit. We walked along the rocky face of the slope through tall grass and stood at the very edge staring down into the erupting depths until we turned giddy.

A young German couple whom we had noticed the night before at the lodge were sitting on a bench looking at the falls too and after a while the bride got up and wandered off into the high grass. Mohammed started to follow her, saying to Norton, "Sometimes hippo come up from the water to graze, someone should be with her."

"If I were you," said Norton, "I would leave her alone. She is pregnant and I imagine she wants to go to the toilet."

Mohammed looked absolutely astonished. A peculiarity of white women perhaps?

We returned to the lodge at lunchtime to find twenty-five Americans, mostly women, who had come in that morning by plane. They had been driven through the park to see game, were about to have a hurried luncheon, and would then be taken down to the Nile and shoved aboard launches for a couple hours of river game viewing, after which they would pile back into the plane and take off again.

I would rather see the marvels of Africa that way than not at all but there is no question that if one is relaxed and has more time the pleasure increases proportionately.

In the party was a homey little body from Idaho. In the lounge after luncheon I poured her a cup of coffee and she peered into a pitcher. "I wonder if that's real fresh cream?"

"I doubt it," I said. "I imagine it's out of a can."

She looked dismayed. "Mercy!" she cried. "Canned cream. I wouldn't dream of it."

Quite possibly she lives in the downtown shopping center of Boise but in my imagination I placed her on rolling farmland amid fat herds and huge crops of the potatoes her state is famous for. A farm where they gathered fresh eggs in a basket and churned their own butter and skimmed real cream from the top of real milk and the milk came out of cows and the eggs out of chickens and cardboard containers were unheard of. I hope someplace in the world such a farm still exists because today it is doubly precious, not only to its owners but as a symbol for the disenfranchised who walk on concrete instead of earth and who dream of a place where they know how to prime a pump and where, if you mention a backlog, they do not stare at you with uncomprehending eyes.

Hoping to plant figurative seeds that might someday be translated into the real thing, we asked the Thurgoods if it wouldn't be possible to grow fresh vegetables for the table. "The soil looks so fertile," we said hopefully. "Of course we can be wrong, possibly it isn't?"

"Oh, but it is," Mr. Thurgood said. "Things would grow beautifully. Our difficulty is the elephants. They pull everything up." Well, there you are, Japanese beetles in the roses, rabbits at the lettuce, birds in the corn, elephants amid the peas and beans. We were learning gradually that sophisticated visitors don't necessarily always know more than the benighted folk who live in a place.

At two o'clock, about half an hour after the flying Americans had departed, we boarded a launch with an English couple from southern Rhodesia, the Newberrys. The launch was smelly and oily but effectively manipulated by two native boys.

We liked the Newberrys at once. They were pleasant and intelligent and seemed very companionable despite the fact that she was obviously several years older than he. Her first husband had been killed in the war when her daughter was a baby of eighteen months. The girl was now twenty and they were hoping she would come to live with them when they got themselves re-established. They had met in Khartoum and had been living for several years in Salisbury. "Life used to be very pleasant," Mr. Newberry said, "but conditions are changing. We feel we should get out now while I'm still young enough to put down roots elsewhere."

They had found they would be able to draw £1500 a year of their own money although there was no guaranty from the government that the arrangement would last forever. They were going to sell their house as the chances were they could keep what they got, or a good part of it, and with this stake they were thinking of settling in São Paulo in Brazil. Mr. Newberry was an economist and in a vigorous growing community thought he would have a good chance to establish himself.

It can't have been easy to leave a home where they had been happy but they were practical and courageous and felt they were making the right move.

Their plan, or rather *his* plan, was to drive through the Sudan but Mrs. Newberry knew the long, tedious, bakingly hot trip and was hoping to persuade her husband to put the car on a boat and sail down the Nile instead.

The Nile is confusing. Since the delta lies more than four thousand miles from the source to the south one would think that going north would be going up the Nile, but the Upper Nile and the Upper Kingdom of Egypt are south and the Lowers are north.

Despite the fact that their lives were being entirely discombobulated, the Newberrys held no ill will against the Africans. "They'll want the whites back in twenty years or so," they said. "But first they've got to push everybody out and have a whack at it themselves."

I suppose no one can judge the timetable. I would think they would be more likely to want the whites back in five or ten years but by the time twenty years have passed the Africans may have become reasonably expert in a good many fields themselves. Who is to say?

The launch trip was a feast of thrills. Oribi and bushbuck watched us from the shore and all around the launch the hippos milled. There was one born ham who raised himself up on a sand bar, stood broadside to the camera for a few minutes, turned, gave us the full impact of his entrancing front view and, after a gracious bow to his subjects, submerged.

Passing close by a fish eagle with his sleek white head and black shoulders, we saw that his underbody was brown and near him fluttered hundreds of little birds with orange beaks, white breasts, and brown wings. There was a lovely water bird who appeared to be wearing a blue toupee edged with black stripes. His head and throat were white, his plumage reddish brown.

We watched a baboon on the bank with her baby and moments later had our first close-up of a crocodile, a huge, yellowish-gray fellow lying on a mud and reed island. There were countless numbers of them—both islands and crocs—and the boys nudged the launch right up against them. We could literally reach out and touch a thousand dollars' worth of shoes and handbags but did not. Seen close to, the jaws of the crocodile are scalloped where the fangs of the upper jaw close over the lower. Studying them carefully, we could discern no tear. They are terribly lazy, these great reptiles, and completely unafraid. What would they fear? Who could get past those jaws? Mrs. Newberry and I lacked something of crocodilian equanimity when the launch was smack up against an island so that there was no slit between us and them through which they could slither should they decide to move. Eventually, they almost always did if the boys shouted enough or threw sticks. They would open a mean little eye and with a movement like quickly flowing oil pour themselves off the island under the launch.

While still some way from the falls we began picking up spume and more hippos. In one pool we counted sixty, seventy, seventy-three . . . we lost count. The falls thundering into the river are impressive but from above one can get closer and the view is more spectacular.

On our return journey we spotted two giraffes among the trees on the riverbank. They were graceful and darker in color than those of the Serengeti.

At dinner that evening we noticed the young German couple saying grace. They did not speak throughout the meal, after dinner in the lounge each picked up a book and read, and in about an hour, without a word, they rose and withdrew to their cottage. We hoped that when the baby came it would give them a topic of conversation.

The next day was sunny and lovely and we set out in a Land Rover for a game drive along the Albert Nile. The launch trip had been on the Victoria Nile, the one at Katwe on Lakes Edward and George. One cannot but feel that the British explorers overdid the royal family or that, though filled with courage, they lacked imagination. After all, the natives must have had names of their own for their rivers and lakes; what was the matter with using these?

There was an agreeable elderly Welsh gentleman, a Mr. Browne, with us in the Land Rover and a pretty English girl named Miss Collins.

Our first animal was an oribi, shy swift little antelope, a grayer sort of Thommy. Miss Collins said Thommies are good eating. Gossiping about the curiously mated managerial pair at the lodge, we quoted Benjamin Franklin's remark, "In the dark all cats are gray."

"That may be," said pretty Miss Collins a bit acidly. "Some of our directors seem to think so but they certainly smell different." We had learned that she was secretary to an executive on her holiday and her reaction was so sharp that Norton and I concluded she was in love with her boss and perhaps had a dusky rival for his affections. We were convinced of it when she told us that she and a friend, another girl, were sitting in a café one time and two Africans sent drinks over to them. The girls were furious and Miss Collins said to us, "If I owned land, rather than see them get it I'd burn it."

It must have been hard for her, living in a country where she hated the native population so bitterly.

There were lovely birds along the drive, Nubian bustards, gray with black dots, and a brilliant flashing scarlet bird with black wings, a chap doubly holy, a cardinal-bishop.

We turned off the track with the ranger to find the carcass of an elephant dead about a month. There was nothing left of him but a big piece of hide and a few bones. Vultures and hyenas had done for the rest. I wanted Norton to take a picture but he said the subject was not pictorial. It would have been a record, though, and an interesting conversation piece when we showed pictures.

In a way, the drive was maddening because we were driving through country teeming with game but could see only a little because of the extraordinarily high grass resulting from the heavy rains. We did come at last to a big pond that looked almost like land because of the density of the water lilies. Happy hippos wallowed about and nearby stood an elephant with four tick-birds perched on his head.

Marjorie Kinnan Rawlings in her book *Cross Creek* speaks of the irreducible minimum she requires in life in order to be happy and says that she can do without a great deal but that she must have a tree against the sky. I have always agreed with that but after seeing Africa I would add, with an elephant standing beneath it. The elephant is the inevitable word, he is the final flick of the artist's brush that completes the picture.

I would also hope never to be so poor that I could not afford a saucer under my cup. A saucerless cup lowers my morale.

When we reached the banks of the Albert Nile the grass became much shorter and the view of the game greatly improved. We came around a bend to find a large water buffalo barring the way but he took off before we could get a picture. It was too bad to miss him because he was very near. However, there were oribi and wart hogs, waterbuck, and the smaller, redder, and charmingly graceful Uganda kob and at one moment a group of frantic guinea fowl.

Nearing camp, we came upon a ginger-colored patas mother monkey and her baby crossing the road. The mother was already across and the baby was by himself but when she heard the car she dashed back, snatched him up under her belly, and leapt away. Roger Weater told us the patas spend more time on the ground than any other monkey.

On our return to our cottage we discover that a handsome blond American boy has moved into the room next to us. He comes out on the terrace to view the crocodiles and hippos and we fall into conversation. He tells Norton he thinks he will charter a Cessna and fly himself to the Serengeti. We learn later it is unlikely he will be allowed to do so as even local pilots have difficulty pinpointing the Serengeti airstrip. It also develops our young man is booked for a month's safari with Ker and Downey.

We decide he sounds rich. Looking in the register, we discover that his is a well-known American name. He is rich. Also very nice and keen on Africa and Egypt. I am aware that Egypt is in Africa but somehow, when safari-minded, the continent below the Sahara seems an entirely different world.

Roger had invited us to tea but as Mohammed was nowhere to be found we had to walk about a mile to his house along a hot dusty road. However, we had only ourselves to negotiate. After seeing several African women with heavy loads of wood on their heads I decided my troubles were skimpy.

The warden's house was small with a fine view and assorted pets. Three baby crocodiles, a puff adder—in a glass box, I am happy to say—a parrot, a baby white rhino. The baby crocs reminded me of my childhood. I once had a little alligator as a pet at the same time we had a cat. Coming into the sitting room one morning, we discovered half an alligator. The front half. It could not have been a pleasant demise.

Roger kept the rhino in a big pen and he proved to be a most affectionate companion, but in a way affection presented as much of a problem as animosity would have. When Roger scratched his chest he would lean upon him full of love. When we saw him he weighed a mere six or seven hundred pounds. As he grew older we felt his master would have to major in calisthenics if he were to hold his own. White rhinos are not white, more of a dusty brownish gray, but they have a square lip and are rare.

On our morning game drive we had seen a water buffalo who had broken his leg some time previously and although he had enough to eat he was in great pain. Roger observed that he was going to shoot him one of these days.

"Why not today?" we asked.

"Oh," he said, "I'm not going all the way over there just for that. I'll do it when I have to be in the neighborhood anyway."

My liking for the young man chilled. Perhaps he was afraid, which would certainly have been natural as wounded buffalo are notoriously vicious, but he had wanted the job of game warden, was trained for it, and knew what it involved. Letting an animal in his care continue to suffer seemed to me a bad business.

In the early evening before dinner we sat on our terrace with two elephants shuffling and swinging their trunks very near the cottage and a hippo grazing just below us on a small semicircular patch of grass. It seemed the most normal domestic scene in the world. The next morning, waiting for Mohammed to bring the car, we were again on our terrace. It was a peaceful gray-blue day but there were no elephants in sight nor any hippos either. The stillness was broken only by a little bird with a plaintive cry. Car-pay-thi-a, Car-pay-thi-a, the accent on the thi. He sounded as though he were calling for his lost love.

We left the lodge about ten, heading for Kampala, but were held up at the ferry by a group of Indians, gay in native costume. The ferry had to get them across the Nile and then come back for us. About a quarter of a mile on the other side two boys on bicycles and ourselves were stopped by a herd of elephants shuttling back and forth across the road. We waited our chance and when there was a gap we forged ahead in the car, acting as interference for the cyclists, who followed hard on our wheels.

Once out of Murchison Falls Park the countryside, while green with many trees, became fairly monotonous but we passed waves of the rising tide of Africa's future: frequent groups of school children with their books although Norton was amused by a sign proudly proclaiming Senior Elementary School.

In general, illiteracy is high but fortunately some five hundred British and American teachers have applied for the Teachers for Africa scheme. Some had already arrived when we were there and others were on the way. Their salaries are paid by the three East African countries implemented by the Agency for Internal Development.

Arrived in Kampala, we went to the Imperial Hotel, spacious, old-fashioned, rambling, and comfortable. In the restaurant there were two or three tables with white girls and colored men dining together.

At Masindi on our return trip, when we again stopped there

for luncheon and it was again delicious, we met an American,
Bob Axelby, a professor of English at Beirut University, who rec-
ommended the Top Life night club as the Kampala hot spot. The
night before when he had been there it had been very gay, a
big gathering of local officials preparing for Uhuru, which was to
come on October 9. We decided to pay a visit. We took a taxi
as it is about two miles out of town and when we went in a
fellow sitting at a table asked if we were members. When we said
we had not the pleasure he announced we could join for twenty
bob. We said that seemed a bit high for only one night. Couldn't
we become non-resident rather than proprietary members? He
replied with some disgust that we could. Six bob.

We went downstairs to the club proper, which appeared to be a
long corridor. The bar ran along one side and on the other were
several doors opening into rooms marked private. However, as
windows as well as doors gave into the hall all of which stood
open, Private seemed a courtesy title. At the far end the hall
widened into a small square dance floor. The six-piece combo
—guitar, bass fiddle, saxophone, drums, maracas, and trumpet—
was good. The trumpet player also had a piece of bamboo
wrapped with wire on which he strummed. Sounded fine. We
learned later that the musicians were from the Congo. Since there
wasn't a score in sight, when there was a pause in the dancing
I went up to a member of the band and asked if the music was
written down at all. The saxophonist answered politely that it
was not. They rehearsed a bit during the day and played at
night. Back in my chair, I glanced over at them. He had evidently
translated my question into Swahili as the rest of them were looking at me, slapping their thighs, and chuckling with glee. Written
down? *Music* written down? I was as riotous a comedienne to
them as I had been to the girls in Manyara when I wore my
Masai necklaces.

We apparently made a conquest because two or three times
a plump young African woman came swaying over to us. "What
is your name?" she asked in a soft sibilant voice.

"Our name is Brown."

"I am Bernadette. What is your name?"

"Brown. We are from New York."

"My name is Bernadette." Along in there we began to suspect that Bernadette was blotto. She was convivial, though, and eyed my modest pearls with the same avidity shown by the Pygmies. As she was reaching out her hands to touch them a friend came along and propelled her away.

The night before may have been official but when we were at the club the clientele lacked distinction. It was what a liberal friend of mine would refer to as a different socio-economic group. He would be accurate, I expect, but I find modern jargon difficult to master. It's like dialectic materialism and dichotomy. What kind of English is that? In more idiomatic if possibly class-conscious terms, I should say the people were of the working class: household servants, petty clerks, and mechanics. They danced a very respectable twist and mostly drank beer. The doctor kept muttering that we didn't go to places like this in New York and why were we here and couldn't we leave and I have to admit the atmosphere was not very festive but we were the only white people there and they treated us with courtesy. I thought of what would be likely to happen were the situation reversed and two colored people had come into an all-white night club in New York.

Back at the hotel, when we mentioned to the Indian desk clerk that the Top Life had seemed rather quiet he said that things usually picked up after midnight but to see it at its best we should go on Saturday. Saturday night at the club—the same the world over.

The next day we tried to reach a Mr. Ntiro to whom we had a letter of introduction but to our regret he had left Makerere University for a visit to England.

Failing to establish intellectual contacts, we drove about seeing the city. Kampala is built on hills with spendid views at every turn. The House of Parliament and Post Office, which serve Bunyoro, Toro, and Buganda, the three kingdoms of Uganda, are as fine as those of any architecturally conscious Western city and they have a new modern hospital of which they are rightly proud, for it is a handsome building. It was due to open in October, on Independence Day, but we couldn't help wondering about the staff. Where would they come from? Would the doctors and nurses be well trained?

We had been told that the place to visit was the Kasubi, the burial place of the *basekabaka* or kings of Uganda. Set within a compound, the tomb is an enormous rondavel made of reeds and elephant grass, the conical roof coming all the way down to the ground.

It had been sprinkling during the morning and as we crossed the compound the sprinkle increased to a downpour. We knew we must take off our shoes, which we did, as we reached the door of the tomb but when we tried to place them a little way under the great thatched roof so they would not get full of water we were sharply reprimanded by a gnome dressed literally in rags. He was the guardian of the dead and slept on two or three goatskins on the floor of the anteroom. Why three kings should have such a destitute creature as their guardian was mysterious.

We enter the tomb proper, a spacious round chamber, its vaulted reed roof upheld by many pillars wrapped with strips of red cloth. "Sit down," says the gnome peremptorily. We sit on mats on the ground. The torrential rain is drumming a deafening tattoo on the roof but it does not blot out the keening of three or four women seated near us in the gloom whom we take to be professional mourners.

The three tombs, covered with carpets, are set behind a fence of spears of varying lengths which the kings carried in life and upon which hang their shields. In front of each coffin is a photograph of the incumbent and to the right is a curtained alcove which we rightly guess is to be the burying place of the present *kabaka*.

We waited there longer than our interest endured, hoping the rain would cease, and when it began to slacken, just a little, we decided to make a run for it. The tourist bureau had instructed us that under no condition were we to tip the guardian, that was the order of the *kabaka*, so we did not do so but as we hurried across the drenched compound we felt his resentment piercing our backs like one of his masters' spears. I think both the *kabaka* and ourselves were wrong. Why shouldn't he have had something? His lot was wretched enough, God knows.

Another visit was to the Uganda museum where they have interesting archaeological tidbits, including beads and cowrie shells which were once used as money. That we knew about; we did not know that wild banana seeds had also served the same purpose.

There were drawings there too as there had been in the Coryndon Museum, showing the hideous brutality of the traps used to snare animals. They had mostly been used in ancient times but today's poachers, if they cannot afford or obtain guns and are not apprehended by the authorities, use methods equally horrifying.

No century and no nationality has a corner on cruelty although I think we may assume that in the assessment of history our own time will rank high.

A less shattering exhibit is the divining pots used by the Madi and Lugbara tribes in judging the guilt of a man accused of a crime. Small pots were heated to a high temperature and medicated water was poured into them. If the water boiled over the man was innocent, if it stayed in the pot he was a dastard. The method at least had the virtue of being easily accessible to bribery. You got to the fellow with the fire and arranged a deal on the temperature.

Later in the day we drove back to Entebbe to take the plane, passing under the partially completed triumphal archways already being erected for Independence Day. Landing in Nairobi for the fifth time, we felt we knew the airport pretty well. And there was more to come!

The next day we joined a large buffet luncheon party at Muthaiga given by the Jack Hiltons and afterward went to the races. The course is very pretty, especially the paddock, which is filled with trees and ringed by flowers.

Another guest at luncheon was Lady Delamere. Hers is a large name in the history and politics of Kenya, for it was with the advent in 1898 of Hugh Cholmondeley, third Baron Delamere, that the white settlement of the country really began. Her ladyship being quite grand in a meticulously tailored suit, hat, and pearls, I assumed the races would be the local Ascot but there was, on the contrary, a charmingly informal quality about them, with children galore and many dogs (on leashes) racing around the paddock and across the grass to stand cheering at the rail. The turf track is a big one and, the day being chill and cloudy, I bet on a horse named Mink. We were both left out in the cold.

It may seem a curious thing to say of a grown man but Norton had never seen a horse race. When he was telling this to the Hiltons I said, "Why, darling, you're crazy. Don't you remember that time, shortly after we were married, when we went to Santa Anita with Millie Raines?"

"I remember it perfectly," he said. "What you don't remember is that as the first race was called a man in the stands a few seats away from us had a heart attack and I spent the rest of the afternoon in the clubhouse looking after him."

He was quite right. The Kenya races were his initiation. Just to whet his appetite, he won a small amount on the first one and lost consistently thereafter.

The afternoon was pleasant but greater excitement came the next morning when we took off in our chartered plane at seven-fifteen for Lake Rudolf. The travel man had been as good as his word and sharing the flight with us was a gentleman named Sinclair, Scottish born but African bred for most of his life. Our plane was a four-passenger Piper Comanche, our pilot a young woman named June Wright, quiet, slim, excellent at her job. We learned, although not from her, that she had been awarded the King George medal of courage as in the turbulent days she had flown countless people out of the Congo, more than once risking her life to do so.

We flew just under two hours during the early part of the trip completely befogged. When the clouds broke we saw we were over densely wooded, mountainous country with Mount Kenya off to our right. Gradually the landscape changed, becoming tawny and cloud-shadowed. We flew over a crater lake and a dry river bed. Mr. Sinclair laughed. "It's like most African rivers. You fall in, get up, and dust yourself off."

Now we were over the northern provinces, a wild and desolate landscape of dark escarpments and arid plains, the country of Elsa, the lioness, near Isiolo.

Mr. Sinclair told us that in the early days people were only allowed to travel through that part of Kenya in convoy. Not because of the hostility of any natives they might encounter but because, if their car broke down and they were alone, they were doomed. They could not possibly hope to walk the terrain on foot in the frightful heat and aridity and once their supplies gave out they would die of thirst and hunger.

Today a single car may go in but not a single person and there must be ample water, fuel, and extra tires. At certain check points travelers are requested to notify the authorities of their arrival by radiotelephone. If they are not heard from within an allotted time a search party goes after them.

That is the curious thing about Africa. It is an enormous country, yet everyone knows where you are or where you jolly well ought to be at a given hour. Any travel project is your neighbor's business and it is comforting and reassuring.

Flying always northward, the earth's surface began to assume more and more the contours of a relief map until we spotted Lake Rudolf. We flew over its irregular, deeply indented black volcanic shores and picked up the landing strip we were aiming for, a ribbon of black sand that had been cleared of the short yellow grass that is the province's sparse vegetation.

June set us down neatly and we taxied along to park beside another small plane and to greet the landing crew, which consisted of two young gentlemen aged about six and ten. With the exception of a topknot on their small shaven heads and a tasteful string of red beads around their necks, they were naked as the day they were born and intensely black. Not coal black—coal has a sheen—but wool black, dense and without highlights. Although charmed by them, we were dubious of their ability to secure the plane but June seemed insouciant and in a few minutes four or five young adults came along who were obviously able to cope.

We also met a short, bowlegged little chap in blue trunks named Guy. He spoke idiomatic English with a heavy French patois accent and came from the Seychelles Islands off the east coast of Africa. He was the camp manager. We piled into a Land Rover for the short run up a hill to the main lodge, a long shed with a high pitched roof of palm thatch upheld by posts set into the concrete flooring. Stretched along the posts, a four-foot sheet of papyrus matting acts as a wall. It isn't much of a wall but in that intensely dry hot climate it is perfectly adequate, serving as a background for chairs and shelves and allowing the maximum circulation of air. There is a well-stocked bar ornamented with fishing nets and glass floats and behind the bar the dining table. Electric lights are attached to the posts and the current is strong enough to power a freezer and refrigerator. Tables, books, and ancient magazines give the place a homely air and we liked it at once.

Our room was another palm shack about fifty yards from the main house with a gable over the entrance but no door. It too had cement flooring and the tentative wall arrangement. Big nails for clothes were driven into the stout center pole that upheld the roof but we mostly flung our things over the top of the papyrus matting. There was a rude washstand with running water and I cherished our small splotched mirror. Mosquito-netting canopies covered our cots and at night we tucked ourselves in with care. We knew there were small snakes about and hoped the netting would act as effectively as a snake baffle as it did for lions. Incidentally, Mr. Sinclair subscribed to that theory too. "You people probably think us barmy," he said, "but many's the night I've slept in the bush with lions about and been safe as a church under my netting."

Mr. Sinclair's right arm was off below the elbow but we never did find out how it had happened.

Another little thatched shack housed a shower (it was a big tin can with holes in it), and a chemical toilet or long drop, as Guy called it, was reached by threading one's way through a labyrinth of papyrus matting. A crude wooden arrow painted red and nailed to a post was supposed to be raised when this sanctuary was occupied and one lowered it on departing. Small lizards and a hoptoad sometimes came to visit.

After depositing our scanty luggage in our room we returned to the main house for breakfast, an excellent one of pineapple juice, tea, coffee, bacon and eggs, and delicious wild honey.

To our intense disgruntlement Guy proclaimed it too windy for fishing so we unpacked and lolled about, chatting, reading the old magazines, and playing with Moth Ball, the camp dog, a vague member of the bazenji family. In Swahili *zenji* means mongrel and *ba* is son of. Two cats, a Siamese and a smoke-gray wraith, completed the family. They had names but Guy smiled when he said so and Sinclair observed that they were doubtless not for feminine ears. Lake Rudolf, of course, is a lonely place; who knows what may go on?

In one of the magazines, a year-old copy of *Wild Life*, there was an account by Betty Roberts of how, during a period of bad drought, she and her family kept alive a small herd of hippos by feeding them hay and lucerne. The Robertses became devoted to their ungainly pets, who were affectionate, not at all stupid, and cozy as domestic pigs.

After some months of happy communal life Mr. and Mrs. Roberts were obliged to leave their farm overnight to place their children in school. They returned to find that in that one night poachers had killed their big bull and a cow. They hadn't taken away the carcasses to eat, they'd simply killed them and left them there. When such senseless slaughter is involved, Jehovah's point of view about an eye for an eye, a tooth for a tooth, seems sound philosophy.

Our disappointment over not being able to fish was relieved, to a considerable extent, by our meeting with a Catholic priest of the Maryknoll order named John Ridyard. When June introduced him as Father Ridyard I thought I couldn't have heard correctly. He was a youngish man, tall and heavily built, dressed in khaki trousers and a short-sleeved khaki shirt. We learned later that he used to weigh 300 pounds and had slimmed down by an encouraging 110. Possibly his non-priestly bearing—non-priestly at least as far as non-Catholics were concerned—stemmed from the fact that before he took orders he was a fighting pilot in the Pacific in World War II. He was good-looking when we saw him and in a photograph of himself taken some years before, when he was in uniform and had not yet attained corpulence, he was quite breath-takingly beautiful. I cannot think what American womanhood was doing, letting him vow celibacy, allowing such magnificent material to lie fallow. Piety is all very well but celibacy is a great waste of noble gifts; God's gifts at that. Father Ridyard's parents were dead and his family consisted of some sisters "whose husbands," he said with a chuckle, "don't want me around." As it would be impossible not to like him personally, their feelings must have been a matter of principle.

In his extreme youth my own father joined the merchant marine for a few years and, although the most easygoing of men for the rest of his life he would glower whenever he was obliged to ride a public conveyance with a man of the cloth. Denomination didn't matter—it was the clergy he mistrusted. "Damn sky pilots—they're bad luck." He would mutter and grumble and nothing could shake his conviction that with a cleric aboard doom impended.

In any event, Daddy to the contrary, Father Ridyard, or Father John as we soon came to call him, was an asset to our party. Warm, outgoing, earthy, and intelligent, he proved a delightful companion. He had been at his post, a parish south of Tanganyika, for six years and was now on a six months' sabbatical, although part of that time had to be spent in propagandizing for the order. He too had come to Lake Rudolf for a bit of fishing and relaxation—he had flown himself in in a small chartered plane, the one we had parked next to on the landing strip, and was going on to the States. It was our good fortune, a month or

two later, to have him as a weekend guest at our house in the
country.

After a revivifying beer we sat down to an excellent luncheon.
Norton and I glanced at each other and our spirits rose. The
food, especially the fish, delicately flavored, perfectly cooked, was
top-notch. Later it developed that meals were top-notch two
thirds of the time: breakfast and luncheon. By dinner the staff
had shot its bolt. Meals, however, were but an interlude in the
serious business of fishing, and happily after lunch Guy announced that the wind had died enough to make it possible for
us to set forth.

Eight of us piled into the jeep: Father John, Sinclair, June,
Guy, Norton, I, and two African boys. It took us about three quarters of an hour of jolting to reach the lake. I had taken a vow
that in describing the landscape I would not use the word "lunar." I broke the vow. Pitted in texture, gray, tan, black in color,
a bleak, barren, desolate prospect—it's lunar.

A small village, fifteen to twenty low mud rondavels, is strung
out along the lake shore, sheltering, according to Sinclair's com-
putation—a man, two wives, three or four children per hut—about
a hundred people, give or take a few. The tribe has cattle (not
many) and, like the Masai, live mostly by drinking their blood
and milk, a diet they occasionally supplement with fish, herbs,
and insects.

Few can read or write but they are adroit at arithmetic, especially when dealing in units of five, because of five fingers to
a hand. When bartering for cattle or wives or whatever may be
in question, one man will hold out a fist and another will put
down a stone. When they have a pile of five stones they start
over again until the requisite number of piles is arrived at.

Sinclair told us that even with the most elementary of educa-
tions native tribesmen are sometimes brilliant in examinations as
they have an uncanny ability mentally to photograph a printed
page but, having learned a lesson visually rather than rationally,
they tend to forget very quickly. A good many of them can be
persuaded to take a three-year course at a university—they con-

sider four too long, a point of view concurred in, as I seem to
recall, by Dr. James Conant—yet they easily become bored, and
reasonably well-educated Africans may drift back to the bush
without regret. This is discouraging to Western idealists and adds
fuel to the endless arguments for and against missionary work,
proselytizing, and poking one's nose into other people's business
but, the white man being what he is, the African has small hope
of being left in peace.

Arrived at the lake shore, we clambered out of the jeep and,
in twos and threes, into the dinghy that took us out to the fishing boat. Her name was the *Lady of the Lake* and her history
was unlikely. She belonged to the May Company, the string of
American dry-goods stores, and had been used by an archaeological expedition which the company had financed. For obscure
reasons, or perhaps lack of forethought, like the man who con-
structs a boat in his cellar and finds, on completion, that she is
too large to get out the door, the *Lady* had been built far inland
and had had to be transported, morsel by morsel, to the shores of
Lake Rudolf. Nobody seemed to know anything more than that
about her and it was rather as though she had materialized out
of a bottle but, being so handily there, she got a great deal of
use.

Once aboard it took us about three quarters of an hour to arrive at South Island, the fishing grounds. With few exceptions
the inhabitants are Nile perch and Nile perch are *large*. I, who
have done very little fishing in my life, caught a 68-pounder.
It was a real tussle and I was proud. My sense of guilt in destroying wild life was assuaged by the knowledge that perch are delicious eating and not game fish caught merely for the thrill of
battle and who, once dead, are stuffed to form dubious decora-
tion for the self-conscious "dens" of suburbanites.

I hooked another one too; he was even bigger, Guy said, nearly
a hundred pounds, but he was the one who got away. I hauled
him right up to the boat but one of the African boys made a gaffe
with the gaff and at the same moment the fish swallowed the

first cluster of hooks, snapped the lure, and in a powerful lunge broke free.

Truth to tell, once assured that he had not escaped owing to a foolish error on my part, I was glad he had won and only hoped the poor creature would be able to vomit up those dreadful hooks that must have been caught in his throat or stomach. What had he ever done to me that I should come 6600 miles to destroy him? Also, I find that while there are some things I can enjoy for prolonged periods—reading, writing, sight-seeing, looking at pictures, or witnessing a theatrical performance—in sports or games, whether watching or participating, my attention span is limited. That is one reason, aside from a total lack of talent, why I would never make a good card player. When you're losing you're not supposed to quit, when you're winning you're not supposed to quit. When can you quit? Apparently it has not occurred to those who formed these conventions that boredom can set in, sometimes quite early.

In any event, having won my spurs in the fishing contest, I could relax and watch the others. Mr. Sinclair was fascinating. Bending his amputated right arm at a sharp angle, he held the rod in the crook of his elbow and expertly manipulated his reel with his left hand. He caught a 95-pound perch. Norton got three but they were not so large. One of the African boys speared two much smaller fish, tilapias I believe they are called, which we were told are also fine eating. Father John brought in a couple and when we got back to camp and weighed the catch we found we had altogether 272 pounds. This was respectable but nowhere near any record. Sometimes the take is as much as a thousand or fourteen hundred pounds.

Cruising along South Island, it was interesting to see that despite the seemingly total lack of vegetation there was life on shore: crocodiles, several mountain goats—how they got there was mysterious—and Egyptian geese.

Heading back to camp, we ran afoul of a major blow; waves increasing in height and violence, wind racing across the water at knots galore per minute. We were drenched and the good doctor became irritable. It was, he said, totally unnecessary to go crashing through the swell as we were doing but Guy was at the helm, driving full steam ahead into the teeth of the blooming gale. Remembering the sea chanteys my father used to sing me to sleep with when I was very small, I felt that the name of our boat should be changed to the *Walloping Window Blind,* whose "man at the wheel was taught to feel contempt for the strongest blow-ow-ow."

We finally reached harbor without capsizing and a company of little naked black kids waded into the water to beach the dinghy as we came ashore. We left them some fish and drove back to camp.

It was now dark but June and I were longing for a dip so we hopped into the small swimming pool shaped like a fat comma. The water was so hot—literally much hotter than a tub—that we couldn't take it for long, yet curiously enough, despite the heat, it was refreshing. Once out, the air seemed cold in contrast. Later, over drinks in the bar, I remarked that the power of the desert sun was extraordinary. "I never dreamed it could get water that hot."

"Yes, it is very hot," Guy agreed, adding with a twinkle, "Also, of course, the pool is fed by hot springs. The water runs underground through lava beds and gushes into the pool in that little waterfall. It is constantly fresh and changing." Travel is indeed instructive.

In the course of the evening someone observed that everyone arrives in Africa full of zeal. "The first year the African can do no wrong. The second year he can do no right. The third year you don't give a damn what he does." And also, "The longer you spend here, the more you see and hear, the more confusing it gets."

We went to bed early but our cots were uncomfortable and all night long the wind blew relentlessly, whistling through the thatch and rattling the dry palm fronds till we thought the trees would be uprooted.

Unfortunately it did not die with the morning and Guy said

the lake was so rough there could be no question of taking the boat out. We wandered about disconsolately, our only diversion the departure of Father John. He was taking most of the fish back to Nairobi to be frozen and sold. That is a very pleasant arrangement at the camp. If you are agreeable to the idea they will sell the fish you have caught and the number of shillings it brings in the market is deducted from your bill. For those who might be interested in a trip to Lake Rudolf, doing it as we did cost $178. That included two thirds of the cost of the plane—Mr. Sinclair paid one third—the use of the boat, and a day and a half in camp.

We all went down to the landing strip to watch Father John take off. He sped down the runway, rose, circled above us, tilting his wings in farewell, and as the speck that was his plane disappeared in the distance we wandered back up the hill to the Land Rover. We were going to drive to the lake and try casting for tiger fish but when we got there the wind was so strong that we had no luck. I sat in the car waiting for the men, and five Africans of the village came and sat down on the ground beside me, their togacloaks around them. After a time they got into conversation with the camp boys which became more animated the longer it lasted until finally they were laughing and chattering and hugely enjoying themselves. They must cherish company, for theirs is a wild, meager, lonely life, one that might be thought desperately boring but they are accustomed to it.

Before too long Norton and Sinclair gave up on the casting and we returned to camp. While waiting for luncheon there was an unexpected spurt of activity via the radiotelephone; much cranking of the little handle—Guy animated and loquacious. On bad days of wind or storm you sometimes get skip areas so that while a person who is listening in may hear both parties to a conversation the people having the conversation cannot hear each other. It is then up to the eavesdropper, and highly welcome he is, to relay the gist of the message. On our day the matter was a shipment of cattle, the health of animals, and the new district commissioner who was moving into his quarters for the first time inquiring, on behalf of his wife, about the furniture and linen in the house. It was vital and basic and, to me, interesting.

We ate some of our own perch for luncheon and shortly before it was time to leave the wind died. Naturally, the fishing would have been perfect but by then it was too late. The afternoon became very hot and still and June said we would take off at four when it would be cooler and there would be less turbulence over the desert.

Our little naked landing crew waved good-by and we headed into a clear blue sky. All went well for a while and June deliberately lost altitude so we could better see the countryside which—once we were out of the desert area—rolled green and lush beneath us.

Over Nyeri we peered down, looking for Father John's plane, as he had told us that he'd go there in case the weather closed in as had been predicted. June circled the field in vain, we couldn't see a trace of him or his plane. "He'll have gone on to Nanyuki," Sinclair said comfortably. "There are a couple of butchers there who have deep freezers where he can store the fish." Again we found that in enormous Africa everybody knows where everybody is. As matters turned out we didn't, but it wasn't until Father Ridyard visited us in New York that we learned our error. When we told him we had looked for him at Nyeri he said, "Oh, I was there all the time. When I didn't like the looks of the weather I came down, just as I said I would. I'd put the plane in the hangar, that's all. That's why you didn't see it." A logical procedure that had not occurred to us.

We saw several rondavel villages from about a thousand feet and while we were studying them the trouble began. The few dark scattered clouds surrounding us began merging and thickening until finally we were completely closed in. June kept climbing and talking constantly to the ground over the radio. Even in so small a plane we could not hear her but we could hear the man on the ground and one thing he said in his chatty well-bred English voice brought me no comfort at all. "You are now at a dangerous altitude," he said. Norton was being helpful too. "That means other planes are lost up here in the clouds at this same level. He wants us to know that so we won't collide."

"Thank you, dear," I said. June continued climbing. Once we broke through the overcast into the bright sunshine I felt better even though I suspected the fuel must be running low. I learned later I was wrong, there was plenty of fuel, but how do I know how hungry a plane gets?

A bit later we could hear the ground in communication with another plane, this one lost in the overcast. "Tell the bloke to look out the window and report what it's like up there." Bloke reports, "Looks pretty sticky all over."

I noticed that Mr. Sinclair and Dr. Brown, both of whom have piloted planes themselves and who had been most expansive in the early stages of our flight, grew quieter and quieter and began looking at steady June as though she were a combination of the Virgin Mary and Charles Lindbergh. My own apprehension being at the brim, I sought surcease in an old Agatha Christie I had brought along, *The ABC Murders.* I was fighting fire with fire. We descended again into the murk and were enveloped in a thick impenetrable gray blanket. Radar has us, radar hasn't us, we are on the beam!

June, banking, timing her downward spirals, eyes glued to her wrist watch, is making a perfect instrument approach to the field. "She's great," murmurs Norton. As though I didn't know! Oh, please God, if we get down I'll give her something lovely, a handsome alligator bag, a big bottle of perfume! At that instant we break through the overcast. Fear? Panic? What nonsense! There is a 1500-foot ceiling, room to burn. We ease down onto the tarmac and roll to a trim halt. What I give June is my warmest thanks.

I must have looked a little shaken, for she said with a smile, "Were you nervous? I *am* sorry but there was really nothing to fear, you know. We were quite all right the whole time."

I had heard of her heroism, I had firsthand knowledge of her skill, but was she really experienced?

"Have you been flying long?" I asked weakly.

"Twelve years," she said. I shut up.

The truly African part of our African holiday was drawing to a close and we spent the next morning packing our safari gear and souvenirs, things we were sending home. Taking our biggest suitcase and a carton to the freight department of East African Airlines, we got a bitter blow. What had cost us $83 to ship over was going to cost $138 to get home and it was only four pounds heavier. These are the vicissitudes of travel and one is stuck with them. Right in the USA I have sometimes had to pay excess charges flying one way and nothing the other, the weight of my luggage being precisely the same both times. It depends on the caprice of the individual behind the counter. Unaccompanied freight, of course, is something else again.

Later in the day Tatty Bell came by the hotel to drive me out to see Baroness Karen Blixen's old house, the one she wrote about as Isak Dinesen in *Out of Africa*. It is quite Danish in feeling with tiles and gables and a clock on the front. Unfortunately, at that time, I had not read *Out of Africa* but I did so after we got home and it is a beautiful and poignant book written by a woman whose love of Africa and devotion to the native Africans who lived on her farm sings from every page.

And that they loved her one cannot doubt when reading one of the most moving passages in letters which her unlettered cook, Kamante, has written by an untutored scribe and sends to her when she has left her farm and returned to Europe. "I was not forget you Memsahib. Honoured Memsahib. Now all your servants they never glad because you was from the country. If we was bird we fly and see you. . . . Write and tell us if you turn. We think you turn. Because why? We think that you shall never forget us. Because why? We think that you remembered still all our face and our mother names."

It seems that shortly after her marriage the baroness was brought out to Africa by her Danish-English husband who planted his bride and departed on safari for a year at a time, returning home only to order new shirts in Nairobi. I believe she was able to console herself—one sincerely hopes so—for she must have been an enchanting woman and obviously she was popular and her great talent much appreciated, for today everything around there including roads and a golf club is called Karen.

The house is set in a charming garden and adjoins many acres of woodland where water buffalo roam. It is wonderful to be able to live in full country only twenty minutes from a big city but I do not doubt that within the next five years these delightful conditions will have disappeared. Indeed, since the days when Karen Blixen lived there urbanization has greatly impinged on the land. When bad times came to the farm the baroness, heartbroken, was obliged to sell. We were told it was still owned by the daughter of the people who bought it, but when we saw it, it was rented to a woman who, while amiable about showing us around, struck me as being somewhat sparsely furnished in the upper story. She was English with a high shrill voice and went into paroxysms of laughter as she told us that her children loved America and wasn't it *too* hilarious! As Americans, Tatty and I were able to control our mirth.

In the late afternoon Norton and I went off for a farewell visit to the Nairobi National Park and enjoyed a bonanza of fifteen lions. There was a group of five surrounded by twelve cars to which they paid absolutely no attention. Two of them were males with magnificent manes; one of them got up, wandered over to a female, nuzzled her gently for a minute or two, and then returned to flop down again with a contented yawn on his bed of long grass. Farther on we came to another group, three this time, who had the same playful, affectionate attitude toward one another, and across a gorge—we needed glasses to see them—we spotted a pride of seven. That last day was one of our best, producing ostrich, impala, hartebeest, wildebeest, Thommies and Grant's gazelles. Driving out the park gates, we saw a particularly savage specimen, a mother cat with a dead rat in her mouth trotting home to her kittens.

Leaving the New Stanley the next morning caused us a real pang and aroused in us the staunch determination to return. We had been comfortable there and from its doors we had emerged to adventure. While perhaps not a luxury hotel, the essentials are in good supply. Beds comfortable, water hot and abundant, service efficient—they could speed up the telephone a little and no harm done—and the food in the grill good.

Traveler's Tip No. 22. Put a card or a piece of paper with your name and the address of your next stop inside your suitcase on top of your clothes. That way, if the tags or labels on the outside become detached, your chances of eventually getting your luggage are still good.

To reach the Nairobi airport one must pass the game park and across the road, standing solitary against the sky, we saw our last giraffe. We felt sentimental about him and hoped he would quickly get back into the reserve before harm befell him.

CHAPTER SEVEN

Ethiopia

THE FLIGHT to Addis Ababa, or New Flower in Amharic, the native tongue, was pleasant. The Ethiopian airline is a subsidiary of TWA and the plane was comfortable, the luncheon hot and good.

Starved for newsprint, Norton and I fell upon a five-day-old copy of the Paris *Herald Tribune,* little suspecting that a few months later we would have to brace ourselves for a total blackout of news when nine New York papers would be suspended by a strike. We also devoured a *New Yorker* in which I first read an excerpt from Rachel Carson's remarkable book, published later that season, *Silent Spring.* Being, as we were, particularly sensitive to animals at that time, it was painful to read her account of the vast numbers of American birds being destroyed by the indiscriminate spraying of pesticides over the face of the country.

Driving into town from the airport, we received an impression, later implemented by further exploration, that what the Ethiopians have on their hilly terrain is the blueprint for a city rather than an actual city. To the impressionable tourist eye it is a conglomeration of nothing much. Two or three impressive modern buildings and in front of the opera house one dramatic and quite beautiful piece of sculpture, the lion of Judah, which was done by a French artist in 1955. He is splendid. One paw rests on a stone, his tail curves downward, a crown adorns his head, and he wears his magnificent stylized mane with pride. The opera house shows movies more than operas. Two or three fine broad paved boulevards are bordered either by empty real estate or by clots of miserable huddled shacks with rusty tin roofs. Outside the center of town there is no paving and, as we were there in the rainy season, when doing any sight-seeing we walked ankle-deep in mud.

We had been told that the Hotel Ghion was the place to stay and we found it comfortable and the personnel willing. "What room shall I give you?" the clerk inquired pleasantly when we arrived and asked for our reservations.

"Well," we said, "we really don't know. Which one would you suggest?"

He guided us to a quite attractive suite in a little bungalow but because of the rain we thought accommodations in the main building would be more prudent and ended up in considerable splendor, being installed in the apartment occupied by Haile Selassie when he had stayed there in the past.

The sitting room was semicircular in shape with six enormous windows shaded by venetian blinds, a wood-burning fireplace innocent of wood, and walls painted a rich throbbing orchid. Adorning them were pictures of Austrian Alpine villages inhabited by buxom maidens in dirndls.

The bedroom was equally imposing with a big old-fashioned double bed of carved wood and two enormous wardrobes. The Ghion had its shortcomings but it is the only hotel I have ever been in in my life where there were enough clothes hangers—masses of them, far more than we needed, and proper ones too, well shaped and of wood, not loathsome twisted wires. The bathroom was early De Mille: black tiles and turquoise fixtures. The functioning of the plumbing was sketchy but we felt imperial nevertheless and considered we were getting a good deal for our sixteen dollars a day, meals included. They were American dollars. The Ethiopians also have dollars. Value, forty American cents.

As we were registering, a letter was handed to us from Mrs. Tolson, the wife of an American general stationed at Addis. It was a cordial and charming letter but threw us into something of a state as it became evident that inadvertently we had badly garbled the plans of several people.

We had been due in Addis on the fourteenth of July but because of our unexpected side trip to Lake Rudolf our arrival had been delayed by two days. The Ethiopian Airlines office in Nairobi had promised to notify the hotel, which, since Addis is a small community where everybody's business is known, would have aided matters considerably, but had neglected to do so.

Mrs. Tolson had invited us to a dinner party the night of our supposed arrival and the American ambassador, Mr. Arthur Richards, had arranged an audience for us with His Imperial Majesty Haile Selassie I, Emperor of Ethiopia, King of Kings, Elect of God, and Conquering Lion of Judah. We profoundly regretted missing such an occasion as it would have been a memorable experience but now, unfortunately, it was too late. His Imperial Majesty, trailing his titles like a comet's tail, had left town the day before.

We phoned Mrs. Tolson immediately but got no answer. When we told this to Hapte Selassie Tafessa of the Ethiopian Tourist Bureau, who had met us at the plane and with whom we should have conferred in the first place, he said at once that Mrs. Tolson was now in Nairobi.

We then called her husband, the general, at the American Embassy and had the good fortune to speak not only to him but to His Excellency, who invited us to dinner that evening—a farewell party for the retiring British ambassador. It was black tie but Norton would have to go in his neat blue suit, that being all he had.

Our social life arranged for, we went on a tour of the city guided by a flip young man from the tourist bureau to whom we did not warm. He had, he said, gone to school in New York and worked at the Hotel Taft. As a bellhop, would be my guess.

Addis Ababa is a lofty city lying at an altitude of 8200 feet and sprawling over fragrant eucalyptus-covered hills. Considering that more than 450,000 people live there, the condition of the streets is puzzling but is perhaps to be ascribed to intense poverty as well as to the fact that before the arrival of the airplane, because of the mountain ranges that ring the country, Abyssinia was stringently isolated. Ideas, raw materials, and products penetrated slowly.

With the exception of the Italian occupation (1936–41), the land has never been invaded, although now and again an intrepid explorer such as James Bruce ventured into the country where, as Alan Moorehead says in quoting his diary in *The Blue Nile,* in the year 1771 he witnessed men and women in drunken rout slashing steaks from the flanks of living animals whose legs were tightly bound so they could not escape but were mutilated, screaming in agony, as the feast progressed.

Today Ethiopian cattle are respected as a source of wealth and are being developed as a future export "crop" to supplement the coffee which has, so far, been the country's export mainstay.

Of the public buildings Africa Hall, headquarters of the United Nations Economic Commission for Africa, is the most imposing although the Addis Ababians are very proud of the palace, the official residence of the emperor. It is an enormous biscuit-colored building, one façade boasting twenty-three large windows. It used to be the official guest house but Haile Selassie gave his original palace to the university on his twenty-fifth anniversary as sovereign and now lives there. It can scarcely be considered a comedown.

The emperor owns a zoo and I was pleased to see that his two lions are not caged but move around quite freely on a rocky platform jutting from a hillside. They have dens into which they can retire and are separated from sight-seers by a moat and railing. For captives, they are well off but their lot is poignant compared to their relations roaming the bush in Kenya and Tanganyika.

Besides his lions His Imperial Majesty is also a cheetah man. He owns two who wear collars and leashes and whom one may pet. They play, like kittens, with a wooden croquet ball. The zoo also contains monkeys, antelope, and two small gray kangaroos.

They are smaller than any other kangaroos I have ever seen, possibly a dwarf variety.

In the palace grounds a Japanese garden was in the making with an arching bridge over a small pool where three white swans and one black floated serenely above their reflections. There was a charming one-room Japanese house that smelled of clean tatami and the Japanese architect, who was there supervising this unexpected little vignette of a foreign land, told us the mats had just been laid. Our smart-alecky guide, looking at a tiny carved chest, asked if it held a transistor radio, winking and guffawing at his own witticism lest it should escape us. The architect said soberly that it did not. Neither he nor we were amused. From Japan we went with a company of colored schoolteachers from the States to visit the tomb of the Emperor Menelik II. Menelik I was the son of Solomon and the Queen of Sheba, so that the line may be said to be even older than the Grimaldi of Monaco, whose family supposedly extends back a thousand years.

Menelik II's tomb is in a vault beneath the church which he shares with an empress or two and the eldest daughter of Haile Selassie. The atmosphere is cozy.

The Ethiopians are Christians, having adopted the Coptic branch of the faith when it was introduced into the country in the fourth century A.D., and we went to visit one of their round churches built in a series of circles, the innermost one of which houses the ark. It had a reed roof reminiscent of the tomb of the *kabakas* in Kampala, was of recent construction, and not particularly interesting.

After a visit to the art school where there were one or two eye-catching posters with flat stylized human figures we returned to the hotel for tea. The tea itself was excellent and I imagine that the little cakes, when they had been freshly baked, a month or so previously, must have been very good.

Around seven Mr. and Mrs. Paul Barringer picked us up in a car to drive us to the embassy for dinner. If I understood his job correctly he was a kind of aboveboard, recognized, and, I should imagine, popular superspy for the American government. He checks up on our embassies abroad, appraises the kind of job being done, and reports to Washington. He was leaving Addis on Friday. Everybody was leaving on Friday, including the British ambassador in whose honor the dinner was being given.

The American Embassy and assorted outbuildings are set in a seventeen-acre compound which used to be the home of the dowager empress and which was given to the United States by Haile Selassie after World War II.

The residency is attractive and our absent hostess, Mrs. Richards, obviously a woman of taste, the parts we saw—the drawing room, dining room, and a bedroom to which the ladies retired after dinner—were charmingly furnished. The bright fire crackling in the hearth and the promptly served cocktails were welcome on a cold rainy night.

We had come a little early as Mrs. Barringer, in the absence of Mrs. Richards, was serving as hostess. In about ten minutes the other guests began arriving, a pleasant mélange of Ethiopians, Egyptians, Indians, British, and Americans, twenty in all.

We dined at one long table and with the arrival of the dessert and champagne His Excellency the American ambassador rose and proposed a toast to His Excellency the British ambassador, saying how deeply he would be missed. I imagine he was missed and that he was enchanted to be leaving his post at Addis. In all likelihood the city has charms not apparent in a forty-eight-hour visit but, having got ourselves into the place, the doctor and I devoted a good deal of time and effort to getting out of it as speedily as possible.

We were struck, however, by the number of Americans we saw in the streets and in the hotel dining room. We have various missions there and are, I suppose, trying to help the country to develop along our lines rather than along those of you know who. We didn't spend enough time there to find out *why* we are so eager to win its allegiance but possibly we are adhering to the principle of any port in a storm. As far as I know there is no oil; maybe uranium or something in the mountains but, despite increasing air travel, air bases, because of the mountains, are limited, although Addis and Asmara will eventually be able to accommodate jets. Of course there is that stretch of coast along the Red Sea and maybe we have an eye to the defense of the Suez Canal.

I should have liked to have an opportunity to talk at greater length with some of the dinner guests, several of whom were obviously interesting, but the sexes separated for coffee and liqueurs and the party broke up minutes after we reassembled. I expect the British had to pack.

The next morning we went to visit the Jubilee Palace, the one given by Haile Selassie to the university. It is vast, uninteresting, and official. Inside, an enormous throneroom brings to mind large convention halls of large hotels in the American Middle West. Upstairs several rooms cover the same area.

One piquant feature of the building is a narrow staircase of twenty-four steps winding upward around a flagpole in the front courtyard. They wind up and stop in mid-air and on the top step is a small bronze lion couchant. Norton and I concluded that when he addresses his people the lion is booted off and the emperor stands on the little platform.

The palace architecture alone would suffice to inspire any resident to give it away but the emperor had a reason more cogent than mere lack of homeyness. There was that revolution against the throne in 1960, during his absence from town, when eighteen of his ministers were killed in the building and his wife and eldest son were upstairs. Afterward he had a disinclination to live there. Despite an occasional upheaval, however, His Imperial Majesty is very much the country's boss and has been since he became regent in 1916. Anyone old enough will remember the slim, straight dignified little figure protesting the invasion of his territory by the Italians before the League of Nations in 1936. He made a deep impression on world opinion and maybe his rule has been what Ethiopia needed but he is an emperor and the ways of democracy are not his ways, which is by no means the same thing as saying that he is not bright. In his seventies, he is extraordinarily alert and shrewd. He just doesn't seem to have done much for his country.

Near the palace a big circular cage full of lions is considered one of the city's outstanding sights. A tiny pen nearby into which ten or twelve lions were so tightly jammed that they could not all put their feet on the ground but had to stand on each other, milling about in intense discomfort and misery, made me physically ill.

The city has, of course, its less repulsive aspects and one of them is the native dress, the *shama*. The women wear swinging skirts of gauzy white bordered with a bright band of color and little round turbans or caps of brilliant malines (cerise is popular) over which is draped a veiling of the same gauzy fabric. Swaying down the street or trotting past in the low horse-drawn two-wheeled vehicles which we call sulkies but they call gerries, they are a pretty sight.

The open-air market covers many acres with hundreds of stalls and shacks, the alleys between them stone-studded mud wallows. The vociferous and constant haggling is intensified by the braying of donkeys and the rapacious barterers are sneered at by the supercilious camels, their feet squelching into the mud as they go stepping by, their high humps laden with their masters' wares.

I had a small triumphant haggle of my own although I achieved victory by the coward's method rather than the attack direct. Most of the merchandise is not very tempting but the classic canvas scrolls on which is retailed the story of King Solomon and the Queen of Sheba are primitive and amusing and travelers to Ethiopia usually want to take one home. When I asked the price the man in the stall said sixteen dollars Ethiopian. That would have been $6.40 American. On hearing this I gave a derisive "Ha!" and started away.

"Fifteen dollars, fifteen dollars," he called after me.

Seeing that my ruse had worked, I stopped, appeared to consider, and then, with a "No, no" started off again.

"Thirteen dollars, thirteen dollars," he shouted. "See beautiful pictures. Queen of Sheba, Ethiopia land of Queen of Sheba and picture of king."

I was beginning to feel my oats. "I pay no more for king than commoner," I said. "Six dollars."

The merchant writhed with indecision. "Twelve dollars," he said but I was grand.

"Eight," I countered, starting away again.

"No! Wait, lady, wait. Ten."

"Done," I cried. "Ten." I might, I suppose, have got it for less, but I was giddy with pride. It was virtually the only time in my life I had ever haggled, I had been successful, and I would be a magnanimous victor, not demanding the last drop of blood, the last smidgen of flesh. I would treat the Ethiopians better than they treated animals. I paid with a flourish and the scroll now hangs in the library bathroom in our apartment.

It consists of four rows of pictures, eleven to a row, telling the tale of the visit of Queen Makeda to the great King Solomon.

Solomon, it seems, was much upset when he discovered his people were worshiping a big fat serpent as a god. He went into conference with his ministers and the result was that they fed the serpent a poisoned goat. In the pictures the goat is pretty fat too, and stiff-legged to boot, as though he had caught wind of what was afoot and was resisting to the inevitable end. Anyway, after the serpent had swallowed the poor beast he instantly curled up and died, thus convincing the people that he was not a god after all.

Well, news of this tour de force reached Queen Makeda in her southern kingdom, of which Aksum, in northeastern Ethiopia, was the principal city, and she set forth to meet the man of wisdom. According to the tenth chapter of I Kings, she did it in style, too, for "she came to Jerusalem with a very great train, with camels that bare spices, and very much gold, and precious stones."

She was beautiful and seductive and Solomon, having eyes in his head, fell in love with her but she was virtuous and said, "No." Personally, in view of what happened later, I think she was playing hard to get. The rebuff miffed Solomon but he made the best of it, saying merely, "Very well, so be it. But if you take anything in my palace, any tiny thing at *all* which I do not offer to you, I shall bend you to my will."

Since, in return for the goodies she had brought him, he in true kingly fashion was plying her with every gift and luxury, she pooh-poohed the idea merrily enough. She already had the sun, moon, and stars and the little red wagon. What could she possibly want?

Aha! Canny old Solomon knew. That night he served a great banquet of highly spiced and extremely salty foods, all the while offering Makeda everything with his own hands.

He then retired with one of her serving maids to whom he had taken a fancy. It was Makeda's turn to be miffed. Still, having denied him, she couldn't very well make a fuss if a servant eagerly grasped what she had turned down. The first half of the night Solomon spent with the maid but he was obviously something of an acrobat and there is a piquant picture of him peering through the curtains, keeping an eye on the queen to see what she is up to.

What she was up to was petty larceny, or so Solomon construed it. Unable to resist the thirst induced by the spicy, salty dinner, Makeda was surreptitiously reaching for a goblet of water. As she brought it to her lips Solomon pounced. "Aha! You are taking something from me that I did not offer you! *This* time you shall not escape your fate."

Well, under those circumstances what is a girl to do? My guess is that, thinking about all the fun the serving maid was having, she had a change of heart, kept a sharp eye on those curtains, and when she saw them billow ever so gently she reached for the goblet *hoping* to be caught in the act.

Be that as it may, the second half of the night belonged to Makeda. Shortly afterward she and her train returned home and nine months later, to the day, the queen and the maid gave birth to sons. In the picture they look like two heavily bandaged thumbs but that is because of the swaddling clothes. There was no rivalry between the mothers, the boys were brought up together, although, to be sure, Makeda did appoint her son King Menelik I during her lifetime. She was a lot more generous than Queen Victoria. Menelik was the first flower of the Solomonic line and grandfather several hundred times removed of Emperor Haile Selassie.

I felt this was quite a lot for four American dollars and that I had made a good buy.

From the market we went to the handicraft school sponsored by the empress. The school consists of rows of sheds where goldsmiths work and where men as well as women loom carpets, some of them very handsome, and weave the white gauze for the native dresses. In the school shop we bought a gay little basket and two flat thin silver forks for fishing out olives and onions.

Colonel Crosson of the American Embassy had kindly arranged to have a car put at our disposal and in the afternoon, driven by an embassy aide, we ventured a little farther afield. The aide, an Ethiopian, seemed a bit taciturn—conceivably he had had plans more engaging than chauffeuring two strange Americans around his country's capital—but he was nicely dressed and very good-looking in an aquiline fashion.

Since Colonel Crosson had felt we should see the sharp variety of the countryside adjacent to Addis we headed for Modjo in the arid belt, first passing through green and fertile fields just outside the city. Ethiopia is a large country, the size of France and Germany together, and parts of it are of spectacular beauty but only nine per cent is arable and only about thirty per cent is fit for grazing. In the limited portion we saw the poverty was appalling. Most of the houses were rondavels or mud huts with corrugated iron roofs. People in dirty ragged clothing sat about in the mud, seemingly devoid of any drive or ambition, the result, possibly, of malnutrition. The country is being modernized and the government seems at last, with foreign aid, to be making a heroic effort toward education but I believe I am correct in saying it is not yet compulsory. People find the tuition costly and many families are apathetic about sending their children to school in any case. They want them in the fields and looking after livestock, so illiteracy is still shockingly high; according to one Ethiopian with whom we talked, over ninety per cent.

The animals are pitiably thin, sheep, cattle, and goats along the roadside trying to find provender in areas already grazed over. Since we did see many haystacks, however, we assumed the farmers were doing what they could.

We returned from Modjo, where there was little to see, the way we had gone, passed through the city, and started the ascent of Mount Entotto. The mountainside is covered with hundreds of thousands of eucalyptus trees which, economically speaking, are to the Ethiopians what the coconut palms are to the inhabitants of Zanzibar.

The framework of their houses is made from peeled saplings plastered over with grass and mud and we saw men carrying enormous bales of dried leaves which we assumed were for thatch but our embassy aide said no, they were used as fuel for baking bread since they burned hot and quickly.

From the top of Mount Entotto one has a beautiful view of Addis Ababa which, although lying on hills itself, is set in a vast bowl surrounded by mountains. Norton got out of the car to take pictures and a group of men and women strolled by, staring at us curiously. When they saw and heard me at work on the tape recorder their eyes popped out of their heads. I was lucky not to be grabbed and burned as a witch. At best they must have thought me close kin to a fruitcake.

Rolling down the opposite side of the mountain, we entered a broad fertile valley where the grazing was excellent and where the cattle looked content. We drove for several miles but in all that sweeping expanse there were few houses, only now and then a tiny community within brush or thorn enclosures, and it was hard to tell the rondavels from the round hayricks. Everyone seemed friendly, however, laughing and waving hospitably as we drove by.

When it began to get dark we turned back to town, passing

streams of people walking home from work. The few hovels that showed one dim electric light bulb hanging from the ceiling were shops: shoe stores and butcher shops. In the butcher shops the carcasses hung from hooks and there was no refrigeration. The system made me a dash apprehensive and indeed at dinner Norton having, imprudently I thought, ordered pork, got a bite halfway to his mouth and sent it back.

The evening passed in a state of depression. The rain poured in solid sheets and apparently we had not endeared ourselves to any of the people met at the embassy the night before to the extent of their inviting us over for a drink. We were lonely and blue. We had been trying hard to move up the time of our departure but after our forlorn evening we were still scheduled for another two days in Addis and there seemed scant hope of hurrying the mills of the gods.

We understood that Debra Zeit, where there is a lovely lake, and—if one wants to go farther afield—the ancient cities of Gondar and Aksum, with its mysterious inexplicable obelisks, are interesting places to visit but we were in one of those moods that sometimes assail the traveler; we wanted out.

Early the next morning we phoned our life line at Ethiopian Airlines but he was dubious in the extreme. The plane was filled with a tourist party and in a group like that nobody ever canceled out, unless of course he was ill. We thought wistfully of plague. My sigh traveling along the telephone wire must have touched a responsive cord, for presently the man said, "There's one slight glimmer of hope. Yesterday's plane overflew Asmara owing to weather and there's just a chance it may be going back today. If it does I think we can manage something."

"You'll let us know?"

"The instant I know."

"Let's start packing," said Norton. "Serendipity and all that, the prepared mind."

He was right. We had barely opened our suitcases when the phone rang. The plane *was* going and there *were* places and we were confirmed! Our spirits soared.

We rushed downstairs, breakfasted, rushed up again, finished packing, and were paying our bill at the desk when the car arrived. Toting up the charges, Norton gave a slight start.

"Good Lord," he said.

"What's the matter?"

"That telegram we sent to the Nile Hilton in Cairo saying we'd be there ahead of time . . . know what it cost? Ten dollars."

"A telegram saying 'Arriving tonight'—that's impossible."

The clerk at the desk chimed in, "Please, sir, I explain. Here are telegrams quite expensive but then also was the taxi."

"What taxi?"

"The taxi taken by the boy from the hotel to the telegraph office to send message and return."

They do it differently in Ethiopia. With a good deal of vehement muttering the doctor paid and we departed for the airport.

The airport was chaos. The tour that our man had spoken of was American and it was booked to the limit. What appeared to be five hundred people were struggling to get their luggage assembled and their passports stamped, and to board the plane. As they were taking off before we were, we stood on the side lines observing our fellow citizens far from their native habitat. What struck us forceably was the almost universal wearing of glasses. Surely American eyesight can't be that bad! Yet, excepting the Japanese, I do not think there is a nation on earth so dedicated to spectacles as we are. We, so prideful of our hygiene and vitamin civilization. Our faith in American ophthalmology was shaken but I still hold firm to American dentistry. There *no one* can beat us.

In that same *Un Certain Monsieur Blot,* which I have quoted before and which I had been reading on our African tour, Pierre Daninos suggests that the English should police the world, the Russians take charge of space travel, the French man the kitchens, and the Americans direct public services. To all this I would agree, only adding, and I hope not from a sense of false pride, that the USA might also monitor the planet's dentistry, cigarettes, and musical comedies.

Our compatriots' tour once off the ground, it was our turn to board and, as has happened before on our travels, the moment we leave a place the rain ceases and the sun appears in hot and brilliant beauty.

Although Asmara lies above or north of Addis Ababa, our flight was, so to speak, downhill, since Addis is at 8200 feet while the altitude of Asmara is 7600. The few villages we saw lying in the folds of the hills we were aware of chiefly because of their glittering tin roofs, as unsightly and out of place against the green and brown earth as beer cans in the woods. When we came down at Asmara we found the air to be dry and pleasant and the atmosphere seemed lively, the all-pervasive apathy of the southern city had disappeared. After a brief stopover we took off for Cairo.

For a few minutes the flight was pleasant. In my lexicon a pleasant flight is one on which nothing at all is happening. You stay up here, you forge ahead, and everything is smooth as silk. That's what I like. Unfortunately, this nirvana lasted only minutes. The border between Ethiopia and Eritrea is a bleak and formidable mountain range. We passed over great heights, between great heights, and along deep ravines. The mountain flanks glimmered gray and brown and dark mustard through shredded clouds of inky black. As the plane banked and bounced and missed the peaks by seeming inches I was aware of the savage beauty of the scene and I was also terrified. I reached out and took the doctor's hand. "Calm down," he said. "Two hours ago you couldn't wait to get on this plane." That I considered a non sequitur. Two hours ago in Addis Ababa, between showers, it had been hot and sunny. Now we were storm-tossed over a sullen and inhospitable mountain range. I had a *right* to change my mind but Norton thought me fickle and was pleased, I know, to sense, a little later, a recrudescence of affection, a condition induced by the fact that, once clear of the mountains, the elements relaxed. We flew over a slice of the Sudan and at Luxor crossed the Nile. Looking out the window, we could see how literally true it is that the Nile is the life of Egypt. The green belt on either side stops abruptly where the water no longer permeates the soil.

CHAPTER EIGHT

Egypt

ABOUT EIGHT O'CLOCK we arrived in Cairo. The drive from the airport to the center of the city is quite long but even in the darkness we liked it. The air was balmy and delicious and with the lights and the crowds in the streets the place had a truly cosmopolitan air. Suddenly we were glad to be back in the sophisticated world.

The gladness petered out when we reached the Nile Hilton. It is enormous, vulgar, brash, and noisy and you'll travel a long way before finding worse service or a more slatternly or insolent staff. The bellboy who carried our bags to our room was in need of a shave and stood fingering his crotch as he talked to us. Elevator and room service are slow and in the dining room Norton waited fifty minutes for a chef's salad.

On the plus side, one can say that the hairdressing establishment is large and efficient. There are many operators, it stays open until 8 P.M., and a shampoo, rinse, set, and manicure cost five dollars. The rooms are comfortable with pleasant balconies overlooking the river. Cairo is a big city, about 4,600,000 inhabitants, and at night the lighting is lovely. Golden spears thrust deep into the Nile and on the shore directly across the river from us an airy fretwork tower pierced the sky, its lights shimmering in the water. It has only recently been built and we were told that from it one has a beautiful view of the city. Since we saw a good many handsome views we did not test it, settling instead for the pyramids of Giza seen from our balcony.

The next morning we went to the American Express Company to work out our schedule and then to the museum. I have been to a good many of the world's treasure houses and they are magnificent, yet on seeing Cairo's one's first impression is that the others may as well shut up shop. The Cairo Museum is unique.

Against our will we had acquired a guide at the door. He irritated us but as he *had* to know more about the exhibits and where they were than we did we reluctantly accepted his services for "One American box, that all it cost you." We were vague as to what the box might be but, eager to get inside, we thought we'd take a chance and when it came time to pay him all was made clear. A box was a buck and there were to be two of them, one for each of us. Muttering, "That's not what you said," Norton thrust two dollars into his hand and a few piasters extra to get rid of him. Egyptian money is pounds and piasters. The Egyptian pound is worth about $2.87 and there are thirty-four piasters to the dollar. These amounts are subject to a fluctuating exchange.

Our guide led us first to one of the more sensational if not the most beautiful exhibits: the mummies. Some of them still have hair on their heads—not a thatch, a few sparse wisps, but after three thousand years . . . One is a woman who died in childbirth—a caesarean section—and the baby's tiny body wrapped in linen lies at its mother's feet. When preparing the dead for mummification the Egyptians would fill the belly with pebbles after removing the viscera, and the throat and skull were filled with precious stones, which is why the faces are sometimes broken and torn. The grave robbers defiled them to get the jewels.

One touch that we found beguiling was the eyes painted on the mummy cases. This was so that the dead might look out at their visiting friends and relatives.

It is somewhat tricky trying to keep track of Egyptian dynasties, since they married not only their brothers and sisters but their fathers and mothers as well. To the Egyptians, Oedipus, carrying on like that merely because he had had sexual relations with his mother, would have been incomprehensible. Doesn't everybody? Furthermore they don't appear to have been any crazier than lots of people who wouldn't be found dead marrying a first cousin. And whatever their morals or power plays, there is no gainsaying the fact that they were a beautiful race, slender linear creatures living their lives in profile, only the eye gazing full front unabashed, in friezes of incomparable beauty, moving with measured tread down the hurrying years of history.

There was only one disappointment in the Cairo Museum and that was caused by my own ignorance. I couldn't wait to see the head of Nefretiti, who was so perfectly named, for her name means "the beautiful woman has come," but the lady, we were informed, lives in Berlin. Nefretiti married Akhnaten, who was probably her brother. For eleven years they lived in Akhetaten, a city her husband built south of Thebes, where they took great interest in the tombs their nobles were constructing and where they walked through the sun-flooded streets and gardens in naked beauty. The king wasn't as beautiful as the queen, for he had a paunch which is shown in the sculptures and paintings of the time. They loved beauty, pleasure, and good food and if they had no warlike inclinations they had others equally strenuous, for Akhnaten married one of his and Nefretiti's daughters while Nefretiti still lived and she bore her father a daughter.

Nefretiti was also the mother of Tutankhamen and when her husband, from whom she was understandably estranged, died she married her son to his father's widow, who was also his sister and his father's daughter. Is that clear?

Tutankhamen ascended the Egyptian throne at the age of nine and died at eighteen. The most celebrated treasures of the Cairo Museum are the objects found in his tomb when it was opened by Howard Carter in 1922. The tomb itself, which we saw later at Luxor, is very small and it seems almost incredible that such a constricted area could have contained such a number and variety of objects, large ones too, including three golden coffins —enormous chests really—one inside the other like Chinese boxes with the mummy cases inside the innermost box of all. There

Large economy-size Russian rocket

Gold statues of Tutankhamen in a case in the Cairo Museum

The Sphinx at Giza

Norton, Ilka, camel

Tomb at Sakkara

Tomb of Mera

Nile at Luxor

Camel at Luxor

Temple of Queen Hatshepsut

A tomb painting

Figure at the temple of
Medinet Habu, Luxor

Temple of Karnak

Temple of Karnak with Colossi

Courtyard, Medinet Habu

Temple of Karnak

Luxor—women in black
not wishing to be
photographed

Crescent at Alexandria
the day of the parade

were three beds, a chariot, chairs, and countless small objects, including an entrancing alabaster barge; jewels and gloves and sandals, even mechanical toys and a golden mask that covered the king's head; as well as any number of statues of him in all sizes, including a very large one that stood at the entrance of the sepulchre; himself guarding himself. It has an Irish lilt, I know, but that can't be helped. Everything was jammed in helter-skelter and may well have served the young monarch on his journey to the next world but the first stages would surely have had to be devoted to getting them sorted out in order that they might function. These objects are of fabulous beauty, gold, ivory, and semiprecious stones, organized and united in matchless harmony.

The museum also has a series of ostraca—fragments of pottery or stone—dating from the sixth century B.C., engaging beyond belief. They are enchantingly colored paintings, mostly of animals: a monkey eating, a lion biting off the head of a bound prisoner—Norton and I thought of the hapless camper in the Serengeti—a hyena and a crocodile disputing a fish and, among others, one I especially fancied, a cat on his hind legs, a little stick in his hand, driving a flock of geese.

These things are gay and witty and adorable but I think one must admit that, gazing upon the gigantic sculptured sarcophagi, standing speechless before the pyramids, one is infiltrated by the trickling suspicion that the Egyptians were megalomaniacs or, in today's psychiatric jargon, sufferers from awesome inferiority complexes. Who needs that much security? That much of a build-up? Echo answers, "No one." Yet the world owes the pharaohs an incalculable debt. Art needs a peg, a focal point. In Christian countries primitive, medieval, and Renaissance art revolved around a very simple idea: a mother and a baby or a man on a cross. In Egypt, despite lip service paid to the gods, it revolved around oneself if one were grand enough and rich enough, and there is small point in arguing monotheism versus pantheism when both are such rich sources of artistic achievement.

Some of the most endearing exhibits eschew the gods entirely to center on the daily life of long-ago Egypt. One morning we went to the museum at eight-thirty when we thought the light would be right for pictures. The authorities are civilized in this respect and, unlike many museums, that of Cairo welcomes cameras. Norton was especially anxious to photograph a company of archers and one of infantrymen. Little figures, about ten inches high, they march four abreast in glass cases and used to be entombed with their owners.

The ancient Egyptian army had an idea that today's military might imitate. Each soldier's shield was painted with a different pattern so that each man might recognize his own equipment. I think today's warriors are very smart to pick their personal possessions or weapons from vast piles, every unit of which is exactly the same color, size, and shape.

There is also in the museum an enchanting model of a landowner reviewing his cattle, who pass before him in parade while he sits on his veranda, attended by slaves and scribes writing down the numbers of his four-footed wealth. Besides beasts he owned a tree-planted pleasure garden and a swimming pool which doubtless rang with the laughter of children and neighbors through the long hot days.

The museum, by the way, is open only in the mornings. There is no air conditioning, the better to preserve treasures which endure largely because of the climate, and the building becomes too hot in the afternoon to make visiting practical but the Egyptian early mornings are magical. Waking once at six o'clock, I stepped out onto our balcony. Dawn crept slowly up the sky and four dhows glided imperceptibly over the glasslike surface of the Nile. The men working them wore turbans and the long robes, the galabias of old. The masts of the dhows are now hinged and they are lowered to pass under the bridges and then slowly raised. The sails may drag in the water but in that air they dry quickly. With the exception of the hinges and of course the change along the riverbanks, everything is as it has been for nearly five thousand years. The pyramids and the dhows, the robes of the men and the eternal Nile.

After luncheon on our first day we went with our dragoman for a drive around Cairo. His name was Suleiman. He was an aged party with a limp acquired in World War I and he was quite a bore. On the other hand, like our guide at the museum, he knew things that we did not.

On our way to one of the many mosques we passed the palace of ex-King Farouk; covers twenty acres, has five hundred rooms. "A copy of Buckingham Palace," Suleiman assures us. We are able to assure him it is not.

Our first mosque, built in 1356, is one of the twelve largest in the world and a cannon ball shot off by Napoleon's army when he was in Egypt in 1798 is still embedded in the wall. One may also view a great Koran written on goatskin with the black ink shot out by squid mixed with gold. Don't raise your eyebrows, that's what Suleiman said, and although we did not warm to him he imparted another bit of information that quite shattered our sang-froid. When the mosque was completed the sultan invited the architects and chief builders to a great banquet where he served them doped coffee and had an arm cut off each one so they could never work for the competition.

Our second mosque was a replica of St. Sophia begun in 1824, but we had seen the original in Istanbul, which was built, virtually as it stands today, by the Emperor Justinian in 532. This made us feel superior, although the interior of Cairo's St. Sophia is beautiful: marvelously spacious, no columns supporting the great dome, and glowing crimson carpets covering the floor. Three thousand crystal lamps hang from gigantic iron hoops and when Suleiman switched on the lights the result was faery.

Despite the spectacular effect we were sad in a way that the twinkling wicks of old had been abolished in favor of electricity, but then that is so of many aspects of Islam. Today the muezzins no longer call the faithful to prayer from high on the minarets. One still hears their voices five times a day but they do not mount the spiral staircases. They record in an office on the ground floor and mechanical amplification sends their voices floating over the city. I expect the muezzins, at any rate, prefer it that way.

Having appreciated the sweeping view from the terrace, encompassing the entire city and the distant pyramids of Giza, we took off from the mosque for the market in the oldest part of town. The narrow alleys are of dirt and cobblestones and with the exception of the spice quarter we did not find it particularly tempting but the spices were fun. Every kind of grain and exotic produce of the Orient and a man with a big stone mortar and pestle pounding peppercorns to powder. What with the pepper and the drifting dust of grain, Norton and I were sneezing our heads off. This was unfortunate since it gave our dragoman an excuse to lead us to a perfume shop.

Traveler's Tip No. 23. When shopping around Cairo, stick to the open markets. Once indoors, you're trapped; bound, gagged, and laid on the altar.

Our shop was tiny and the atmosphere suffocating, doors and windows closed, and the owner exuding oily charm and cheap scent. Suleiman said something about our traveling with the American Express Company and that as we were friends of the management everyone had been instructed to take *especially* good care of us. This sent the shopkeeper into transports. But of course! He had the highest esteem for *all* the members of the American Express, a *superb* company. His daily prayer was that these splendid men would never leave Cairo and what kind of perfume did we prefer? A floral scent or perhaps something a little more exotic? The exotic accompanied by much hand washing and a truly frightening leer. What in God's name did he have in mind?

He was, we said, more than kind but really we didn't want anything. We were terribly sorry but Suleiman must have misunderstood and as we were traveling by air and our bags were already filled to bursting even a single bottle was impossible. That one he had heard before. His pudgy hands against our chests, he tenderly but with iron determination pushed us into chairs. I could see Norton's fist clench and for a moment I feared a swift one to the button.

Only once in my life have I ever been fought for by a man and my husband was the one. We were dining in a neighborhood bistro in New York and a drunk passing our table made some remark to me which, while alcoholic, was not unflattering. My love, however, took exception to it. He followed my admirer out to the street, returning moments later rubbing his knuckles and looking smug.

"Wh-where is he?" I asked. "Wh-what did you do?"

"He's in the gutter," said Norton. "He's fine. Don't you worry about a thing."

Once in a lifetime at home might have been all right, but Cairo! Nasser! Help! Fortunately Dr. Brown restrained himself, if only just.

"Let us forget about the perfume," said our jailer-host. "What will you take to drink? Coffee? Lemonade?" Norton, looking as though he were being offered hemlock, shook his head but I weakened. Besides, that cloying atmosphere made me thirsty.

"A lemonade," I said, "would be very pleasant."

The depository of all the perfumes of Arabia pushed a button and when a boy appeared at the street door he was dispatched for the refreshment. A rather thick wait ensued, during which the virtues of the American Express personnel were again extolled and points of sight-seeing interest discussed. All the while little phials of perfume were conjured from cases, drawers, under the counter . . . we would not have been surprised had the merchant whipped one from behind our ears. There must have been easily several dozen on display when the boy returned with the lemonade. It was sickeningly sweet but it *was* cold so I was able to manage a few swallows.

While thus occupied our host took one of my hands in his and started smearing it with the glass stoppers from the bottles. My palm, the back of my hand, my arm, a little extra flourish for the drop that went into the crook of my elbow.

"You understand you need only a trifle, madame. It is the

essence, the pure essence. Buyers come from France for these essences, they take them back to France, to Grasse itself, to make their perfumes." For all I knew there may have been some truth in that. Certainly the fragrances were so strong that more than a drop would prove overpowering.

In the end, of course, the proprietor won. I succumbed, saying I would take one phial of lotus and one of sandalwood. "And you will have great *bottles* of perfume," he assured me, "once you understand the formula and how to dilute it." An ounce and a half, he had said earlier, would cost us one hundred piasters and if I would buy one he would give me one. I didn't want the bonus but $2.87 was no great sum. If we could get away with only that we were lucky. What is annoying about the Cairo merchants and guides is that, while the amount involved may be small, when you come to pay it is never what they said it would be. As Norton drew out the money our man explained that it was a pound and a half for one ounce, in other words $4.31 American, and in the course of the transaction the promised other ounce somehow disappeared.

Norton had given in to the museum guide but this time he stood his ground. "No," he said coldly. "You said one hundred piasters or one Egyptian pound and here it is."

Our man looked tense for a moment, then he shrugged and burst into good-natured laughter. One can but try. Another moment and I would have been glad to double the price, triple it! Any ransom to get out of that odious little sweat box.

Perfume, I know, is supposed to act as an aphrodisiac but for a couple of days Dr. Brown seemed to have no trouble restraining his ardor as, no matter how frequently I showered, the cheap penetrating scent still clung to me. Indeed the following day I went to the hairdresser in the hotel. I got back to find our room empty but minutes later Norton arrived.

"You just got here, didn't you?" he said.

"Yes, how did you know?"

"I came up in the same elevator."

Another shop Suleiman guided us to was fascinating but we

were able to resist its lures. Actually it was a workroom where they made inlaid furniture, boxes, and trays. The job requires great patience and skill as each piece of mother-of-pearl must be set by hand, using the tiniest and most delicate of tools. A writing desk, the proprietor told us, had taken over a year to complete.

It is unfortunate that that much effort cannot be co-ordinated with modern taste but excepting, perhaps, the French and German bourgeoisie I cannot think mother-of-pearl inlay finds many takers.

Since we found the Nile Hilton unsympathetic, returning one day from sight-seeing, we decided to have tea at the new Shepheard's. The old Shepheard's used to be one of the most famous hotels in the Near East but it was destroyed in 1952 during Egypt's Emergency-Trouble period when the Egyptians were ousting foreigners as well as Farouk and just as Nasser came to power. The hotel that has been erected in its stead is a barracks of a place and, at least on the day we were there, not overpopulated. It is next door to the Semiramis where an acquaintance of ours stayed and where, he said, he had a superb room and bath at very moderate rates. Like the Hilton, both the other hotels also overlook the Nile.

A well-beaten tourist track leads to Memphis and we drove there one morning, following a canal much of the way. In that hot dry climate where inevitably they are powdered with dust, most of the women wear black robes and draperies. It is an ancient tradition but an impractical one. Also black is hot and while the predictions of our friends—that we would die of heat in Egypt in July—were not fulfilled, it is indisputable that white or pastel shades are cooler.

Camels, donkeys, sheep, goats, and water buffalo wandered along the canal or stood in the shade of the trees but the poor creatures were terribly thin, foraging for themselves in the sparse vegetation of the roadside. It did not look to me as though the Egyptians grew any fodder for their animals at all and I was in a perpetual state of misery.

Once the capital of the kingdom, Memphis today is a small

straggling community sunk in desuetude. When we got out of the car to look at a sphinx (not *the* Sphinx) filthy little children crowded around us nattering for money. When they realized they weren't making much headway they grabbed hold of a small puppy and set him on the low branch of a tree where he was stranded and where he whimpered pitiably. I started to the rescue but Suleiman stopped me. "They do that to attract attention, so people will notice them." I noticed them with stern looks and admonitory words until they put the puppy back on the ground.

A building near the sphinx houses a colossus, that of Ramses II, mighty in the XIXth Dynasty, ruling from 1292 to 1225 B.C. Ramses was unearthed in 1856 and was a sturdy type, weighing in at 280 tons. Time was when the gigantic figure stood upright but today he lies supine, his carved eyes staring up through the roof of his mausoleum into the blue vault of the Egyptian sky.

From Ramses we went to Sakkara, walking over some reasonably burning sands to view the Step Pyramid which, as its name implies, is a series of giant steps in pyramid shape and the ancestor of all the others, and to get to the enchanting tomb of Mera, who was once a famed prime minister. His tomb has many chambers and is decorated with delicate bas-relief carvings on which faint traces of color still linger. There is a delightful frieze of animals—birds, leopards, and bulls, plus crocodiles and hippos engaged in swallowing each other.

Mera's wife had her own suite of chambers and there is a charming relief of them playing chess together. The tombs of the kings depicted life after death but the nobles were content to record their daily doings and the pictures are gay and sometimes strangely touching.

In every tomb we visited our guide would dwell at length on how the rogues broke in and desecrated these homes of the dead. "And who are the rogues? The antique dealers!" He was forever asking himself questions and answering them in the same breath. We gathered that by rogues he meant robbers but it was near enough and he was not the first man to excoriate antique dealers.

In 1600 B.C. the Egyptians were worshiping bulls, and near

Sakkara is an underground tunnel 1200 feet long with great crypts dug even deeper which were the bulls' graves. A few feeble electric lights seemed to intensify the gloom and after we had walked a few minutes peering into yawning gulfs on either side of us we felt we had had enough. Apparently the bulls were allowed to live for twenty-five years. If at the end of that time they did not die natural deaths they were drowned in the Nile and after a brief period, to allow their spirits to escape, they were interred in their communal grave.

Having spent the morning with the dead, we repaired to Mena House for luncheon. This is a funny old-fashioned hotel built, I should say, in the eighties at the foot of the pyramids of Giza. There we found a cold beer, called Stella, very mild, awful food, and life aplenty. The place was crowded with tourists. I do not know if many of them stay overnight but the hotel does a roaring trade at lunchtime and here one discerns the fine hand of the Egyptian Tourist Bureau. We discovered later that one may easily see what we had seen that morning, visit the pyramids, and be photographed in front of the Sphinx in three or four hours, returning to Cairo for a decent luncheon. I am a passionate sight-seer but it is tiring work and I am not for wasting time that might be spent resting or eating good food.

The tourists, mostly college students, looked weary, poor children, and lolled about with their shoes off or sat with suitcases on their knees, writing postcards home.

After luncheon we concentrated on the pyramids, particularly the Great Pyramid built by Cheops, but not to the extent of entering them. It can be done by slithering along the cramped passageways on back or stomach but it didn't seem worth the effort.

One gazes, stunned, at the pyramids, trying to comprehend the Jovian labor involved in building them and the psychology that desired them.

According to Suleiman whom, although Egyptian, we did not feel to be a sound Egyptologist, the pyramids were constructed entirely by slave labor and the authorities' treatment of the thousands of human beings involved was so heinous that once a man started on the job he could expect a life span of about three months.

I do not doubt that cruelty and coercion existed but the architects and artists could scarcely have been slaves and a theory that holds that the great mass of Egyptians worked on the pyramids during the annual three months' flooding period of the Nile, when they could not be working in the fields, would seem to make more sense. Also, since the Egyptians were strong believers in life after death, it was to the people's advantage to have their kings well housed so they might continue to watch over them once they had passed to the spirit world.

Regardless of how they did it, the results are awe-inspiring. Throughout the five-hundred-year period from 3000 B.C. to 2500 B.C. the Egyptian technological progress was unique. To quote Leonard Cottrell: "At the beginning of this period neither the Egyptians nor any other peoples on earth could build in stone. At the end of it the Egyptians had erected the Great Pyramid, composed of nearly two and a half million blocks of stone, each weighing about two and a half tons, cut and laid to an accuracy of a fraction of a degree, oriented with such precision that compass errors could be checked against it. For 4500 years it was the highest building on earth."

And, mark you, "It was built in about twenty years, with no mechanical appliances apart from the lever, the roller and the inclined plane. No cranes, no pulley blocks, not even the simplest machinery. At this period they did not even possess the wheel."

Another group apart from the architects and artists who couldn't have been slaves were the mathematicians!

The Sphinx is not far from the Great Pyramid but nearer that of Khafre, and at close quarters what one sees best is the underside of her chin. She was sculptured from a mass of natural rock and, powdery gold against the blazing blue of the Egyptian sky, she is a gigantic and matchless figure.

As it was early afternoon and frightfully hot we stepped between her paws to get into the shade and went from there into the inner chamber, a temple carved out of rose granite and alabaster.

It is commonly believed that a cannon ball fired by Napoleon's troops broke off her nose but a respected authority on Egypt and the Nile, Alan Moorehead, claims that that is not so; the lady had been desecrated long before the arrival of Mr. Bonaparte.

According to a guide we had in Alexandria, most of the Sphinxes' noses were mutilated by Saladin, the Moslem conqueror from Mesopotamia who later tangled with Richard the Lion-Hearted in the Crusades and who went to Egypt in 1164.

His reason for vandalism, according to the guide, was that he chose to regard a sphinx as a sort of god, which in a way it sort of was, but to a Moslem, God (Allah) is a spirit not to be given representational form, either human or animal. Finding a god who was both a woman *and* an animal made him very cross. On the other hand, since he seems to have been a man of culture and a patron of the arts, such an act of desecration scarcely jibes. I think we must leave it to scholars or slow time to make the decision.

To be honest, the magic of ancient Egypt is dissipated to some extent by the throngs of tourists who, I suppose, are ubiquitous regardless of season, although possibly less so in winter when fewer people travel.

A large group of Americans mounted on camels were having their pictures taken in front of the Sphinx and one woman kept yelling at the photographer, "Not glossies, we don't want glossies, we want them dull."

"All right, no shine," agrees the Egyptian.

"That's the ticket," the woman shouts down from her camel, "now you're getting it."

It ill becomes me to make fun of her, however, for I too had my picture taken atop a camel, Dr. Brown on foot.

We went back to the Hilton for drinks and sandwiches by way of dinner and then returned to the desert for a performance of Sound and Light. We had excellent seats on the roof terrace of a café-resthouse directly across from the monuments. Viewing the pyramids and the Sphinx at a little distance and in perspective was deeply affecting. How many thousand times has she seen the sun rise? How many thousands of times have the stars wheeled across the heavens before her unflinching gaze? The lights dimmed and flooded and if the taped voice of the British announcer, swept away by the grandeur of it all, was a bit mellifluous he nevertheless raised goose pimples when he said, "Caesar saw it and Antony and Cleopatra. Here Alexander stood and here the armies of Napoleon clashed in battle." Actually they clashed eight or nine miles away but a little poetic license is permissible. The presentation lasted about fifty minutes and despite the fact that I nodded once or twice—all that heat and fresh air and sightseeing—I enjoyed it thoroughly.

July 23 was a brilliant morning, sunny, cool, and delightful, and the Egyptians and the Browns were happy. The former particularly since it was their Independence Day and preparations for the parade had been going on for a week.

We watched the final *i*'s being dotted and *t*'s crossed as we sat at breakfast on our balcony.

The reviewing stand was just below us and in front of it the drive bordering the Nile was empty but a bridge to our left crossing the river was packed solid with trucks and troops ready to fall into line when their turn came. People were massed in the streets and the hotel balconies were crowded with spectators.

A contingent in khaki dress uniforms stood across the street from us for three and a half hours, much of that time at attention. Poor devils, my heart went out to them. The early morning was cool but as the sun rose higher so did the temperature, although in that dry climate the discomfort is modified. The band also was opposite us and as the time drew nearer for Nasser to appear the police force, glistening and immaculate, sprang up like a file of white exclamation points, faces to the crowd, alert for would-be assassins.

At last we saw a cavalcade of cars coming toward us from the right, moving between the packed crowds at a snail's pace. A wave of shouting and cheering rose, gathered volume and, as the cars passed in front of the hotel, broke over us with a crash.

Nasser was standing up bareheaded in the front car, a black Cadillac convertible with scarlet upholstery. It looked very sleek and grand and we were proud of Detroit but in view of the rock-bottom poverty of so many of his countrymen we felt that it would have been more becoming and indeed more dignified had the head of state been riding in a Ford or Volkswagen.

As the cars rolled slowly up the river side of the road, looped around the island, and passed by us again on the way to the reviewing stand President Nasser waved at us and we waved at President Nasser. He waved at several thousand others too but even if one does not always approve of his actions it would seem churlish not to greet him on a big anniversary—his tenth.

As he and the other dignitaries took their places our personal little army across the street, which we had been watching with sympathetic interest, sprang to attention, the band played, and the cannons boomed out a salute. I suppose there were twenty-one, I didn't count, but the needle on the tape recorder leapt like a seismograph in an earthquake.

An American television man mounted on the island was raking the scene with his camera, and from high platforms built beside the road especially for the occasion other cameramen were recording the event for world consumption.

When the noise subsided Nasser came to the microphone to speak. He went on for some time and the occasional cheers and applause were moderate. He was nothing like that case history Castro but as time ticked by I couldn't help thinking of Mr. Lincoln. The Gettysburg Address took a minute and a half and I doubt if what those other gentlemen have said in several million words will survive the test of time as well.

After a final burst of applause the parade proper began with a mounted band rolling by at a brisk clip on red and green motorcycles. They were followed by white horses, followed by brown, ridden by men carrying fluttering red and green banners. The

Egyptian flag is red, white, and green but perhaps this was a kind of patriotic shorthand.

More flags, soldiers, sailors, and paratroopers, these last quite picturesque, their camouflaged uniforms reminding us forcibly of dark spotted leopards or giraffes. They wore the paratroopers' heavy boots and passed at a jog trot, arms bent, uttering strange grunts in time to the music.

Next came the camel corps, and to me they were the stars of the proceedings. Looking haughty, and why not, they trotted by on their muffin feet, the first three in tandem, the rest four abreast. Over the first four small green burgees fluttered from the top of long wands that rose straight into the air from the backs of their saddles. They were my pets although one could scarcely sneeze at the Arabian horses, caparisoned in tasseled bibs with gleaming metal disks and wearing silver-studded saddles.

Presently the motorized troops who had been kept on ice on the bridge flowed into the parade ranks. Great red, white, and green disks were painted on the hoods of their trucks, which I should have thought would have made ideal targets for the enemy but I suppose they know what they were doing.

Glancing down into the side street at our right, I was amused to see that just like actors at a rehearsal who, having finished their own scene, will go out front to watch the rest of the play, so the companies that had fallen out, such as the paratroopers, were crowding down the street to the river front to watch the rest of the parade.

The rest consisted mostly of trucks, anti-aircraft guns, rocket launchers, and the rockets themselves in two sizes: large and the giant economy. Next we were treated to the tanks, their crews standing up inside them wearing tight black cloth helmets. It was curious to watch the tanks grinding and clattering past and to look beyond them to the pyramids on the horizon.

The heavy hardware was supplied by Russia and wave after wave of Migs roared over in formation. They flashed gleaming white against the pure blue sky and disappeared beyond the Nile.

After the military seemingly endless companies of labor and student groups passed the reviewing stand but by this time, nearly three and a half hours, we were convinced of the might of Egypt (and Russia) and mildly bored.

Wanting to pay another visit to the museum, I left our room and went down into the street. The streets and the great square —the museum is at a right angle to the hotel—were seething with people and although the gates were still closed the museum doors were open and crowds of boys were clambering like monkeys up the iron palings. When the gates were flung open the crowd poured through as though storming the Bastille. I asked a man why there was such a mob and he said, "Today no pay," but it couldn't have been only that. A good deal of it, surely, was holiday spirit, but the way the boys, in those long striped nightshirts Egyptian males wear in the street—caftans and galabias— were pouring into the building, you'd have thought they were giving away free motorbikes.

In the end, despite the tug of the museum's treasures, I chickened out, I couldn't face the mob, although for a few minutes it looked as though I might have no choice. I walked back to the hotel but there were police at every entrance and, as Nasser was still in the reviewing stand in front of the building, they were allowing no one in.

"But I'm staying here," I wailed. "I left my husband just a few minutes ago. We've been watching the parade for hours. If I was going to do anything to President Nasser I've had a golden opportunity all this time. *Please* let me in." I was a sinner at the gates, St. Peter would have none of me. Presently, however, God came along—a captain of the police force—and my honest face must have won him. He personally escorted me through the cordon and into the lobby.

Back in our room I found Norton still on the balcony and the parade still in progress. A great company of men in white was passing just as I arrived but we didn't know whether they were street cleaners or interns. We guessed the latter when they were followed by a phalanx of marching women who were obviously nurses and who were, furthermore, pretty fat.

The next batch was a group of girls in scarlet and yellow harem costumes. The oldest profession, maybe? There were still other segments of the population and then the guns boomed again, the troops snapped to attention, the colors dipped, and the party broke up. As Nasser departed thousands of people came flooding into the streets and the cacophony set up by the motor horns was deafening.

"The Egyptians love horns," Norton said, "they think that's what makes the car go."

At six o'clock that evening we left for the airport. We knew we were likely to have a long wait before the plane left for Luxor but the office feared that because of the holiday parade traffic conditions would be bad. Actually, by that time, most of the celebrating was over, so we had to wait and a hellish little interlude it was. The flies were maddening and there was no means of escaping them. We sought the refuge of the plane the instant it was called and had a good flight, an hour and a half to Luxor, where we were met by Fathi, who announced he would be our guide the next day. We drove to the hotel in a carriage and it was delightful sitting in the dark garden under the blazing stars sipping a cool nightcap. In Luxor, do not turn down any opportunity that affords coolness. That was the one place where dire predictions were almost fulfilled.

Our room, though small, was not uncomfortable but we passed a wretched night owing to the heat. The doors onto our balcony stood wide and we opened the door into the hall as well, hoping for a little cross ventilation, but despite this shrewd maneuver *and* an electric fan sleep was impossible.

We decided the Egyptian travel people knew what they were talking about when they dissuaded us from going to Aswan. That had been on our schedule originally but in summer transportation is limited and, having seen Abu Simbel, our real goal, where the great statues are—the ones that in all likelihood will be destroyed when the dam is built—we would have been stuck in Aswan for another night. "And," said the travel folk, "at this season the heat is bad." As matters turned out the unseen town gave us pleasure just the same, for we had bought a booklet about it and came upon a letter written around 2250 B.C. It was to the explorer Herkhuf from King Pepi II, who occupied the throne for ninety years, the longest reign in history. The king had heard that Herkhuf had brought home a tiny man from one of the Pygmy tribes of central Africa.

The idea so entertained him and so excited his curiosity that he wrote Herkhuf saying, "Come northward to the court at once. Thou shalt bring this dwarf with thee that thou broughtest alive, prosperous and healthy from the land of the Ghosts, for the dance of the god, to gladden and rejoice the heart of the King of Upper and Lower Egypt, Neferkare [Pepi II] who liveth forever. When he goes down with thee into the vessel, take care lest he should fall into the water. When he sleeps at night appoint excellent people to sleep beside him in his tent, inspect him ten times a night. My Majesty desires to see this dwarf more than the gifts of Sinai and of Punt. If thou arrivest at the court, bringing this dwarf with thee alive, prosperous and healthy, my Majesty will do for thee a greater thing. . . ."

What an endearing king. Since reading his letter, Neferkare is my favorite king. All those details! He is not to fall into the water . . . *excellent* people are to watch over him . . . talk about a child anticipating a new pet!

Perhaps Neferkare's enthusiasm started a new fashion, for the booklet goes on to tell us that "This letter was such an honor to Herkhuf that he had it engraved on the façade of his tomb. Dwarfs were brought into Egypt where they settled, sometimes marrying an Egyptian wife and having a family. They seem to have been occupied in dancing for the god but, sometimes, they were appointed as keepers of store houses, perhaps because they could not run away easily."

If they were reluctant little prisoners that is very sad but I prefer to think they lived happy lives married to lissome Egyptian lasses, siring normal-sized children.

After our sleepless night we were up at five-thirty, leaving the hotel at half-past six with Fathi and two American women, a mother and daughter, Mrs. and Miss Rhone of Utah. I can understand anyone from Utah traveling a great deal. I once spent two weeks in Salt Lake City.

We crossed the Nile in a small putt-putt launch but we asked the man to cut the motor so we might drift for a few minutes on the glassy surface of the water. I have never seen the light so beautiful or experienced a world so still.

Perhaps it is because the Nile *is* Egypt but we saw more river dawns in the few days we spent in the country than we had ever seen before. Whether the rising sun shines with such radiance on every river I do not know but even without its history Egypt would be worth seeing for the sublime and tranquil beauty of its mornings. In all the parts of Africa we visited the mornings were the continent's glory. It requires no effort to understand why the early Egyptians worshiped their sun as a god, the life-giving Re.

On reaching the opposite bank we stepped into a waiting car and started off. Our first sight was the Colossi of Memnon, two gigantic seated stone figures rising from the arid plain. They are somewhat eroded by time and blowing sand and although one cannot but be impressed by their size one experiences also, I am afraid, a small heretical feeling of "What of it?"

Just as people who have nothing but money to recommend them are rarely engaging companions, so the Colossi, having nothing but colossalness, are not particularly endearing. One wants to hasten on to the enchanting paintings and bas-relief sculptures—back to the human scale.

We were now in Thebes and at the temple of Queen Hatshepsut. It is built with three terraces, two of which have been restored, and work is in progress on the third. Much of the restoration has been done by Americans and Mr. J. P. Morgan built a house there, an adobe house, brown against a brown hillside. An interest in archaeology is understandable but to have been

prompted to indulge in domesticity in such baking, bare surroundings seems strange.

Queen Hatshepsut was a vigorous intelligent woman who
traveled as far as Somaliland, bringing home leopards and
giraffes and trees balled as we do it today. We know this because
they are shown on exquisite colored friezes carved on the walls
of the temple.

She married her brother, Thutmose III, but he never had much
of a whack at the throne and as Hatshepsut reigned for quite a
time his second-fiddling gnawed like a canker at his vitals. When
his wife-sister finally died, to get even, he went around defacing
her monuments. He left her body wherever it was carved but
had her face chiseled away so that she would be unrecognizable
—scotched through all eternity. He sounds a peevish one and I
think nothing of him.

Also on the walls of the temple is Hator (Hat-hor), the mother
goddess usually depicted as a cow. There is a superb statue in
the Cairo Museum, a delicately wrought animal suckling one
young king as she protects another who stands under her neck.

Anubis was another of the animal gods, the jackal-headed god
of death. The jackal feeds on carrion and by raising him to god-
hood and bringing him offerings of food and drink the Egyptians
hoped to placate him so he would leave the dead in peace in the
spirit world.

There is an entrancing picture of him seated on his throne, his
long pointed jackal's nose most aristocratic, his slim human body
swathed in tasteful draperies. Beside him is a great pile of goodies: loaves of bread and fruit and jars of wine. Although this
painting is on one of the exterior walls it is under a portico and
the coloring is still lovely. How much, one wonders, did the artists
believe the legends and how much of their work was humor and
pure charm?

The porticos are supported by Doric columns and Fathi said
disdainfully, "The Greeks! We had these columns in 1488 B.C.
and they had to come and copy us for the Parthenon—not until
480 B.C. One thousand years we are ahead." He also remarked

that one monument we would be seeing was modern: A.D. 641. It seems like yesterday.

Leaving Queen Hatshepsut, we went on to the Valley of the Kings, passing laden camels on the way and blindfolded donkeys or bullocks endlessly turning the water wheels while jets flew overhead. We drove past small square houses of sun-baked brick and black-draped women bearing water jars tipped at an angle on their heads. How they stand that black drapery I do not know. I was just managing in a sleeveless shirt and linen shorts I had had made up at Ahamed's in Nairobi and a straw solar topi from Emmé in New York. It had been inappropriate for my originally intended locale, the African bush, but was perfect for the Egyptian desert.

As a rule I frown on shorts when abroad in foreign lands. They are offensive to many foreigners and it would never occur to me to wear them in a city no matter how hot the weather but I think that in July in Luxor, walking across the hot sand, scrambling in and out of tombs with not a soul in sight but one's own small party, they are permissible.

There are 480 tombs in the Valley of the Kings and nearly fifty per cent of them still remain to be excavated. The Valley flourished—if one may say so of a necropolis—between approximately 1500 and 1000 B.C. One reason they chose the spot was a bit of symbolism. Topping one of the high cliffs is a natural pyramid. It's a little rough but quite identifiable as a pyramid.

A recently built macadam road now winds between the hills bordered by electric light poles. The anachronism may seem painful but one cannot blame the Egyptians; the living cannot forever be dominated by the past, however glorious. The same thing holds true in Abu Simbel. At first the thought of a dam destroying the ancient statues seemed desecration but if one goes to Egypt in midsummer, sees the poverty and aridity, and experiences the blazing heat of noon, one's instinct is to cry, "What are we waiting for? Let us get on with it at once."

Months later, at the Cleveland Museum, I met Mr. Mohamed Abdel Kader, Chief Inspector of Antiquities of Lower Egypt, who had accompanied some of the Tutankhamen exhibits which were on tour in this country. He told me that although it was not certain there was hope—if sufficient money could be collected—that the rock itself in which the statues are carved might be cut from the face of the cliff, raised to high ground, and the statues salvaged. But he too was all in favor of the dam.

The Egyptians are thinking of experimenting with night tours in the Valley of the Kings and it might not be a bad idea, especially in the summer when the air cools a little after sundown. As far as the tombs themselves are concerned, the hour of the day makes no difference since, once inside them, it is dark and electricity is used anyway.

One of the gay tombs is that of Nakht, a noble and scribe of the XVIIIth Dynasty. He lived around 1420 B.C. and the colors in his tomb today seem as bright as they must have on the day the artist wiped his brushes and gazed with satisfaction at his handiwork. The Nakhts were rich and gay. Birds rising in flight from the papyrus reeds were doubtless startled by a hunting party which was entertained that night by the three female musicians on another wall, beguiling young ladies playing early instruments, mostly in a state of total undress.

Another spot of pure enchantment—from the art point of view —is the tomb of Menna, who was minister of agriculture in about the same period as Nakht. There is a delightful painting called *The Hunter's Daughter,* a young girl holding a brace of duck in her right hand while over her left arm drips a bunch of papyrus. There is a barge with the captain taking soundings from the prow, and while some of the oarsmen sit resting with crossed arms a more intrepid colleague hangs over the side scooping up water. There is also a painting of fish in the river, a large fish being eaten by a small crocodile.

We were particularly interested in the marines; since the Nile was as vital to survival as the air they breathed, one would have thought the Egyptians would have painted countless river scenes but this does not seem to have been the case. Also, although their daily lives are so graphically portrayed, one misses children.

Kings, queens, maids, servants, adolescents—virtually no children or babies. We asked our guide why this was and he said, "By the time the nobles could afford to have these tombs built and painted their children were grown up."

We did not know whether this was the literal truth or a happy invention but it made sense.

Inevitably the question arises: the tombs being underground or completely enclosed, how did they paint those exquisite pictures in the dark? It is thought that one way they might have managed was to place a mirror or its equivalent, perhaps a shield of bronze, at the entrance of the tomb and others, to reflect light from the original, at the angles of the corridors. Actually one sees some of the tombs that way today rather than by electricity. It was also said that they perhaps worked by the light of flaming wine instead of oil, since wine does not smoke, but in Cleveland, when I asked Mr. Abdel Kader about this, he said that all these theories are speculation; they do not really know how the artists managed. They do know, though, that when planning the bas-reliefs the outlines were first sketched in red, then refined and corrected in black, as black better reflected light. It was the black lines the artist followed when working with a chisel.

Traveler's Tip No. 24. When visiting the tombs, carry your own flashlight and flash bulbs. You are allowed to take pictures but the flashlights used by the guides are inadequate.

The tomb of Ramos, a governor of Thebes when it was the capital of Egypt, is large, enriched by a striking composition of female mourners, all in transparent white robes with long black curls and their arms raised in supplication.

The tomb of Tutankhamen is, as I have said, small and, having seen the treasures spread over an entire wing of the Cairo Museum, it seems impossible that they should have been jammed higgledy-piggledy in so confined a space. We tried to be respectful but it lends itself too easily to alliteration. Having learned in Kenya that the Swahili word for "child" is *toto,* and the king being so young, we couldn't resist Toto Tut's Tiny Tomb. That's how we think of it.

On the wall at the head of the sarcophagus in which the body lies are twelve painted baboons, representing the twelve hours of the night. By the time we had admired the eternal home of the boy king we were getting a little glassy-eyed so we walked to a small shedlike café—they are building a grander one—for beer and coffee and a few minutes' surcease from life after death.

But the bird of time was on the wing. Revictualed, we set out again. To the tomb of Ramses VI: wide long corridors, walls completely covered with hieroglyphics, and at intervals small projections of masonry jutting from the walls. They served as twelve gates to give the sun god security in his passage through the twelve hours of the night. The end chamber of the tomb is beautiful in a sophisticated and restrained way—an arched ceiling painted black with beige flowers.

One of the tombs had a long yellow and green looped serpent. The serpent appears frequently, for his job was to swim ahead, clearing the way for the barge of the dead.

The tomb of Amenophis II has a very large lower chamber, the roof upheld by painted square pillars. They have an unfinished air about them and with reason. The king died before the work was completed and everything had to stop. Norton said it was small wonder. Having spent all that thought, money, and preparation on the tomb, he probably couldn't wait to get into it.

Medinet Habu, the tomb of Ramses III, was one of the most extraordinary we saw. It was built in the Assyrian style with a marvelous courtyard. Rows of columns carved like open papyrus flowers and a gigantic square archway. Egyptian arches were always square. The rounded came with the Byzantine Era and pointed with the Gothic.

Leaving Mr. Ramses and a camel grazing outside the walls of his eternal abode, we drove back to Luxor and to luncheon at the hotel. The thermometer stood at ninety-four in the shade but it was dry with a little breeze and despite the heat we wolfed down the good and big steaks that were served at luncheon. Absorbing culture is hungry work. Later we set off for the temples of Karnak and Luxor, about a mile apart, this time driving in a carriage. There is a charm to carriage driving not to be derived from even the sleekest of automobiles. One has time to savor the countryside, one is closer to it.

There used to be a delightful French song with the refrain "*En admirant le paysage, dans mon temps,*" in which a nostalgic gentleman sings that in his day life was lived at a more leisurely tempo in all its aspects. One drove in a carriage, admiring the scenery along the way . . . one undressed a pretty woman, admiring the scenery along the way . . . a song in praise of dalliance.

Today the span of life has been greatly prolonged and yet no one has any time. When the average life anticipation was much shorter, people had time for everything, including enjoyment.

The Egyptians had time not only to enjoy themselves in this world but to see to it that their gay ways were prolonged throughout eternity.

The chief thing I remembered about Karnak from my schoolbooks was its brilliant coloring. Today the massive columns still stand in rows in the courtyard but the roof they once supported is gone and now they rise like trees into the sky, the tallest of them 72 feet, the lowest 55, and, except in certain sheltered sections, the sun has drained the colors to a soft sandy beige. The carvings and bas-reliefs have better endured and one may see scratched into the stone—high up now but before the great sand drifts had been cleared away almost at ground level—the unexpected legend, République Française. It was carved there by Napoleon's soldiers in the campaign of 1798–99.

Karnak was built to the glory of Amon-re, the sun god, but the Egyptians had a trinity too. Nut was Amon's wife, the earth goddess, and their son was Chunsu, the moon god. The temple covers about sixty acres and was at one time joined to the Nile by a canal but today the most impressive vista is the avenue of sphinxes, with rams' heads and lions' bodies. An imposing bas-relief is the huge one of the king holding a group of his enemies by the hair of their heads before the god Osiris. This shows he vanquished them and he doubtless is saying, "Look, God, what I did with my little hatchet."

As the afternoon wore on the heat became more and more intense and I grew very tired. Left to my own devices, I think I would have slipped up on Luxor but Fathi was conscientious. We were going to get our money's worth.

"Come, we will not be long and you need only remember one thing: at Luxor three cultures are represented: Egyptian, Christian, and Islamic." He was quite right, there were traces of all three. Wars and conquests accounted for them. The columns of Luxor are marvelously graceful, capitals of lotus blossoms opened and closed. There are a pair of seated colossi at the gates and the twin of the obelisk that is in the Place de la Concorde in Paris.

Fathi was a good guide, infinitely better than his Cairo counterpart, and wanted badly to accept an offer he had had to lecture on Egypt in Frankfurt. He apparently spoke pretty fair German and the trip would have meant a lot to him in both experience and money but he had to have permission from the government to go and his chances, he felt, were not good. That, to me, would be one of the most oppressive aspects of a dictatorship: curtailment of personal freedom, of physical movement.

We had learned before setting out for our afternoon's sightseeing that our five o'clock plane back to Cairo was delayed and actually it was ten-thirty before we left and nearly one by the time we reached the hotel. This normally would not have mattered but it was an inconvenience in this instance as we were scheduled to take the train to Alexandria at 8 A.M. the next morning and had a good deal of packing to do.

The doctor took the situation in hand and announced that we would get a decent night's sleep and drive to Alexandria. Even at that hour he was able to arrange with Freddy, our chum at the American Express office, to have a car pick us up shortly after ten.

We were going to Alexandria for five reasons, four of which were Lawrence Durrell: *Justine, Balthazar, Mountolive, and Clea.* The fifth was the holiday weekend and *everybody* was going to Alexandria. The prospect of good bathing might have tempted the doctor but it was the Alexandria Quartet that had sold both of us even before we left home. We had been fascinated by Mr. Durrell's baroque tales and longed to see the shimmering city where such bizarre shenanigans transpired.

Accordingly, having paid one last visit to the fabulous museum, we set off. Things began to look pretty good right away. While still within the Cairo city limits we passed a train of loaded camels, an authentic caravan, and a little farther along we saw a man sitting on the curb washing his hair. He had worked up quite a lather and we concluded he must be planning to rinse off in the river only a few yards away.

A paved four-lane highway connects Cairo and Alexandria and runs through fertile country green with maize, sugar cane, rice, and cotton. There are road checks every few miles—they are keeping tabs on the citizens but pay little attention to tourists. We assumed they knew the license numbers of rented cars and let them go through. One of the trains that passed us had a prison car with bars at the windows and men in striped galabias and pajamas reached through the bars and waved. We waved back in an effort at cheer. Quite possibly each and every one was a villain but I would not care to be in an Egyptian prison. I don't suppose Sing Sing is any picnic either but somehow an Egyptian one . . . I've always thought French jails might not be *too* awful; good bread probably, and a little wine.

A sight and plight I found even more distressing than the prisoners' was that of the donkeys. Crowded onto big flat wagons would be literally twelve, thirteen, fourteen people all with bulky bundles being pulled by *one* small donkey. I yearned to pile fourteen donkeys with their bales of hay onto a wagon and have them pulled by one person. After twenty-five miles of this haulage he would be popped into his Egyptian jail. The mere thought perked me up and I was able to look with appreciation at the picturesque roadside scenes: a small mud village on the edge of a canal with children and bullocks in swimming, donkeys, camels, and sheep drinking, and black-robed women gossiping in the shade of the trees along the towpath.

We arrived in Alexandria in just under three and a half hours. Through our perusal of Mr. Durrell we knew exactly what Alexandria looked like. It was a little Paris on the Mediterranean with palms instead of chestnut trees and everywhere cafés with gaily striped awnings. Behind the waterfront, beyond the tree-filled gardens, was a maze of dark crooked alleys and houses of child prostitution.

Would you like to know what Alexandria is really like? It is like Miami Beach combined with Atlantic City, salted with Coney Island. The city is flung in a great arc, a superb crescent around the bay, that stretches for something like seventeen miles. It is beautiful but, if you have in mind the Quartet and an exotic atmosphere, curiously disappointing.

Amexco had tried to book reservations for us at the San Stefano Hotel, which they thought we would enjoy, but because of the Independence Day holiday and a four-day weekend were unable to get anything. The Cecil, they said, was also crowded but we would find the Windsor Palace very pleasant.

When we arrived, however, and saw it was right in town, despite the frantic gesturing of a waiting dragoman who had, rightly, spotted us as his prey, we told our chauffeur to drive on to the San Stefano. On we drove and on and on. We were tired and we were hungry and the San Stefano was about twelve kilometers beyond the town. Still, it was directly on the beach. It looked attractive and we hoped that on the spot we might be able to wangle something. We could not. As Amexco had said they had said, they were sold out. We retraced our weary way, falling finally into the arms of our dragoman, who was to pilot us around the town and who received us with irritated satisfaction. "I *knew* it was you, I waved you to stop here the first time round."

We nodded. "We know, we know too. Just let us get some lunch." Luncheon was quite good but we had to ask for and pay extra for butter. Afterward we went upstairs to unpack and found our room comfortable and the view magnificent. We stood on our balcony looking out at the Mediterranean and up and down the great crescent, reveling in the air and sunshine. The climate of Alexandria is a summer dream come true. Dry, comfortably hot, with a little breeze and the sparkling Mediterranean to bathe in.

As soon as we had unpacked a bit we went to do just that but the beach was a disappointment: crowded, dirty, and noisy. Nothing could spoil the water. The bathhouses were a mess, sloppy little cubicles looked after by a slattern. Right next to our little Nasty was a stretch of shore that looked ever so much more attractive. It was clean, there were few people, and the bathhouses were very trim.

"What about that one?" we asked. "Is it a club or may anybody go?"

"Oh no," Ibrahim said. "It is not a club, anyone can go. We will go next time."

"Why didn't we go this time?" He shrugged. We suspected he was guiding us to the places where he got a rake-off. "Let's come tomorrow."

"No, no," he said quickly, "tomorrow you won't like it. Too crowded."

When we got back to the hotel I asked to speak to the owner, Mr. Mimi, a vigorous-looking man with a vigorous beard. Was there not, I wondered, a yacht club? Would it perhaps be possible to get a guest card? Should Mr. Mimi ever come to the United States, our pleasure in returning the courtesy would be profound. I refrained from adding that though our own yacht club is attractive the bathing is nil. Members swim from their own beaches or from their boats.

Mr. Mimi graciously played into my hand. There was a yacht club, he and his wife belonged, a card would be immediately arranged. When I told Norton about this he shook his head.

"But aren't you pleased?"

"Yes," he said, "it sounds very pleasant. It's just that I wouldn't have done it in a thousand years."

"Why not? We're perfectly nice people. We're not going to disgrace him."

"Women are wonderful," was all he said. I think men are very, very conservative.

As we were having tea in the lounge that afternoon who should we bump into but old Hollywood acquaintances: Stanley Schurer, who had been the assistant director on the last movie I had been in, and Bernard Freericks and Hal Lombard. The latter were sound men and were in Alexandria with a second unit filming some final shots for *Cleopatra*. They had been away from home for eleven months and they had had Rome, they had had Egypt, and they had *had Cleopatra*. That night the Messrs. Freericks and Lombard were leaving, flying all the way from Alexandria to Los Angeles without layovers, only the time to change planes at the airports. "But you'll be dead," I said.

"But we'll be home."

They told us that in Egypt their letters, both inward and outward bound, had been censored. The censors' marks were on them. Norton and I experienced nothing of the sort but we were minnows. Picture People were something else again.

Richard Burton was in Alexandria too but not Elizabeth Taylor. He had been cautioned not to telephone her in Rome while he was there but love triumphed; he called and the next morning the papers ran an exact transcript of the conversation.

It must be hard being a dictator. You have to have such snapping eyes, not to mention flapping ears, to be sure nothing is put over on you. Barney had sent a cable to his wife and had been told he must sign his full name.

"But it's to my wife," he said.

"Makes no difference. Full name."

"I felt a fool," he said, "putting down, 'Love, Bernard Freericks.' My wife must have thought I was nuts."

Later that night we took Stanley to dinner with us and as we were wandering back to the hotel we saw two little boys asleep on a low dirty step in thin striped pajamas, a white puppy curled up under their legs. They looked so forlorn and deserted, my heart ached for them. Among all the millions of people nobody came to claim them. The nearer we returned to the esplanade the more crowded grew the streets in pre-celebration of the parade.

Whenever we walked in Egypt we were struck by the number of men sitting at café tables drinking nothing but coffee or iced water, sometimes playing cards, occasionally smoking a narghile —a water pipe—and always unaccompanied by the female sex. The togetherness philosophy so ardently espoused at home has not yet percolated to the Near East or the Orient; there they have a decent respect for apartness.

The next morning, leaning on our elbows over our balcony railing, we watched the parade in the street below. It was a nice parade but no match for the splendor of Cairo. Nasser, however, did appear, riding by in the gleaming Cadillac, a reasonably heroic gesture since he was once shot at in Alexandria and is not popular there but, as we all know, bullet dodging is the occupational hazard of those in high places.

As we waited for the parade to begin we had been watching a performance in the water just in front of us: a group of men seining for fish. The older I grow the more astonished I am to have survived as long as I have knowing nothing of the rudiments of living. Take fishing. There was my Lake Rudolf experience and maybe, before that, five times in my life when I have had a pole in my hand with a string trailing down from it, yet I enjoy eating fish and must, by now, have devoured countless bushels.

Anyway, this simple activity, a way of life followed for thousands of years before Jesus gathered the fishermen of Galilee, was unfolding before my fascinated eyes.

There were nine men in a big broad rowboat, six manning the two oars, big ones, while the other three trailed an enormous net with cork floats in the water behind them. The rowers keep navigating on a curve until they have formed a huge circle, when they head in again toward the jetty where they disembark and start hauling in the net. It narrows until the bobbing corks eventually outline a long tear-shaped enclosure. When the proportions are to their liking a couple of men holding a small net between them slip into the water and, keeping within the corks, beat their way down to the full end of the tear, driving the fish before them. Once at the end, their net and the original big one form a cage from which the fish cannot escape. Gradually the men on shore pull the lines closer and when almost against the jetty the two who have been swimming float off over the top of the net. The catch is then pulled up onto the stones, the fish in their death throes leaping and glittering in the sunlight. The men drop them, according to size, into deep baskets. We left the scene before learning whether or not they toss back the little ones.

The spectacle served to sharpen the doctor's fishing appetite already whetted at Lake Rudolf so, as we had arranged the day before, shortly after ten we started off with Ibrahim for Aboukir, a seacoast village about thirteen miles from Alexandria. Aboukir is famous for the defeat of the French fleet by Nelson in 1798 and for the defeat of the Browns by the commandant in 1962.

Ibrahim had assured us the procedure was simple; we would hire a rowboat, we would fish. We would, eh? Not so fast, my man—one or two details needed to be attended to first.

Aboukir is a picturesque cluster of little houses set on yellow sand overlooking the small harbor, anchorage of fishing boats and dhows, but as it is a military zone we would have to get permission from the commandant before we started out. Nothing to it; formality. We pop in, we pop out again.

Following Ibrahim's lead, we are received in a small office in a small fort topping a gentle rise. The commandant is most polite and asks us to be seated.

"Coffee?"

"Thank you very much."

"Cigarette?"

"Thank you very much."

"What you want?" We explain our desire to fish. "Ah, fish!"

The commandant's eyes light up. "Lovely water, lovely day. Good fishing."

Norton and I glance at each other and smile. It's in the bag! The doctor indeed is so pleased at the prospect, he becomes quite chatty, describing my prowess at Lake Rudolf and ending up with a fond flourish, "She pulled in a 68-pounder."

The commandant looks at me with admiration. "Sixty-eight pounds!" he says. "Felicitations. Here you will get not sixty-eight but maybe twenty."

"Oh, that would be wonderful." There is a pause. We are about to rise when the commandant says:

"May I see your passports?"

It was as though a filter had dropped over the radiant day. "Our passports?" The commandant smiled. I had not noticed before how many teeth he had and how sharp.

Actually we had discussed bringing our passports but, thinking that in a rowboat they would only be a nuisance and, if dropped overboard, irretrievably lost, we had left them at the hotel. We explain our reasoning.

"That," says the commandant, "is too bad." Have we any identification? From the recesses of my bag I draw out an American Express Credit Card and hand it to him. He studies the front, he turns it over and studies the back. A rare butterfly, a curiously wrought jewel, could not have provoked closer attention. Finally he looks up, we smile tentatively.

"It won't do," he says.

Still, as he does not dismiss us, we linger. He asks Norton what he does, the doctor gives a pungent little essay on American medicine. We discern no crack in the armor but still we hope. Possibly we will be inspired to do or say just the right thing, *then* we will be allowed to fish. We comment on the beauty of the Mediterranean, how dreary is New York in comparison. The commandant is interested.

"What is it like in winter, in New York?" Our description is vivid: the cold, the snow and ice, the dreadful dirty slush in the streets. No warmth, no sunshine, no fish. Another pause. "What you like to do?"

"Fish."

The commandant looks surprised. "Fish? But there are no fish here."

"But you said . . ." Thinking of the 20-pounder my voice trailed off. What was the use? Again we explain why our passports are not on our persons.

"You should *always* have them," the commandant says severely.

"But we thought we were driving to the country, to the *beach*." Norton is still trying logic.

The commandant rises. "I am deeply sorry, good day." We leave the office and we leave Aboukir.

Ibrahim is very upset. "Never mind, Ibrahim," we say, "the commandant was quite funny. We'll make a story of it."

"Yes," he says bitterly, "a funny story to tell back home."

Returning to Alexandria from abortive Aboukir, we took advantage of the guest card so kindly supplied by Mr. Mimi and went for a swim and luncheon at the yacht club. It was pretty and gay and the basin was full of small boats. I am dubious about swimming where boats are anchored but Norton said, "Don't be a sissy, they have no heads, come on." This nautical term I have always found curious but it is correct. I went but there were bigger boats beyond the little boats and beyond them two old American destroyers which now belong to the Egyptian navy. They have heads, one may assume? The swimming was pleasant, however, and after lunch Mr. and Mrs. Mimi came along with a party of friends and asked us to go out in their boat for some water skiing. We are not skiers but, watching our hostess, the doctor observed that he sincerely hoped the Mimis would one day come to America so we could return their kindness.

I couldn't imagine why. Mrs. Mimi is young and slim, with pale gold hair, pale gold skin, dark-lashed gray eyes, and in that bikini on those water skis fleet and graceful as Diana. What did *she* have, for heaven's sake?

Among the passengers was her enchanting two-year-old son Paul and an attractive English child who was working in *Cleopatra* and who was going home the next day.

We returned to the dock after an hour or two and later, back at the hotel, watched a parachute drop from the lounge window. A plane flying over released groups of men who floated gracefully downward, their shining white parachutes flowering against the blue sky. The chutists wore frogmen suits and as they plopped into the water navy speedboats scurried out like beetles to collect them. The waterfront was jammed with people, some of the men in Western clothes but the majority in caftans, striped galabias, and pajamas. Motor horns were tooting wildly as cars nosed their way through the throngs, coffee vendors clanked their metal cups to call attention to themselves, soda-pop and peanut sellers were in full cry, and horses' hoofs clattered on the pavement. The setting sun splashed over a riotous scene of color, noise, and movement against the backdrop of the sea.

We decided not to battle the crowds but to dine at the hotel where from our balcony we would have a perfect view of the fireworks. In the bar before dinner we met a curious character introduced by Mr. Mimi simply as The Professor. He was a large elderly man who stood behind the bar sipping a drink and mixing himself a cheese and tomato salad. Perched on a high stool near him sat a hunchbacked dwarf, meticulously tailored, his eyes invisible behind large shining glasses. There was something faintly sinister about the pair that reminded me of a Hitchcock movie. Had our acquaintanceship lasted longer than cocktails we would probably have discovered they were the leader of the Boy Scout troop and a writer of children's stories, but I prefer the macabre interpretation.

Dinner was indifferent but we consoled ourselves with the anticipatory delight of Paris in sixty hours. We went out onto our balcony after dinner to watch thousands of people lining the sea wall waiting for the fireworks. They burst forth in a great bombardment of sound and glitter. Dazzling branch coral, burning palms, fountains and bouquets of sparkling diamonds, rubies, emeralds, and gold. It was Armistice Night, it was New Year's Eve, it was Independence Day! Long after we went to bed and the fireworks had faded and the noise abated we heard the crowd moving restlessly through the streets under our window.

The difference in the Corniche the next morning was striking. A quiet third act opening after a second-act-curtain bacchanalia. The great crescent stretched almost empty in the sunlight, only a few stragglers to be seen and an occasional horse and victoria clip-clopping by. We watched the destroyer escorts steaming slowly out of the harbor to disappear at last over the horizon.

If one is visiting Alexandria at a time when Independence Day is not going on I should imagine that the San Stefano or one of the other hotels farther out of town might be more fun—the bathing certainly is better—but for parades and such the Windsor Palace is the fifty-yard line.

The city has a museum that we went to visit but after Cairo's it is a letdown. Graeco-Roman and much of that reproduction. Alexandria does have Pompey's column, which was brought from Aswan nineteen hundred years ago, a superb white shaft against the sky with sprawling catacombs underneath built by Caligula for thirty-nine of his relatives. The old monster himself lies in Rome. The tombs are curious because normally the bodies lie stretched full length while these are buried in a sitting position following the custom in the earliest graves ever discovered, those of six thousand years ago.

One may skip the visit to King Farouk's palace, which is huge and uninteresting, although hordes of school children came crowding in to view the doll collection, dolls of all nations, even Disneyland. The harbor on which the palace is located is an excellent one. Boats were being built, and craft from all over the world were anchored there, including four large submarines, Russian-supplied, and an aircraft carrier.

The next day we returned by train to Cairo. The Alexandria railway station is an enormous airy shed and, waiting for the train, groups of women and children sat down on the tiled platform. The management does not provide benches. Our first-class seats, while scarcely fancy, were comfortable and we enjoyed the ride. The summer weather of northern Egypt is pure perfection and the lavender water hyacinths growing in the canals were strips of glowing color under the bright sky. Unfortunately the flowers choke the canals and along the way men stood in the water uprooting them.

Our last night in Cairo we stayed in the hotel, ordering the table d'hôte dinner. It was a disaster relieved only by the view, the dark palm trees growing along the Nile silhouetted against a softly glowing pink sky.

The exquisite beauty was shattered a little later by a blaring loudspeaker in a night club across the river which made the night hideous with rock and roll and sleep impossible for several thousand people.

We were called, with small regret, at 3:15 A.M. and left for the airport accompanied by the ever faithful Freddy. We had tried to relieve him of this onerous chore but he was the sentry who never slept and was faithful to the end.

At the airport the man scanning my passport came upon "Occupation: writer." He was immediately suspicious. "Journalist?" I smiled sweetly. "Fiction." With a grunt he stamped it. I never learn. Years ago, on a trip to England, beside "Occupation:" I had written "actress." Britannia almost didn't let me in. Where was my work permit? What was I doing? Was I trying to take the bread out of the mouths of *English* actors? If you are a professional woman, never mind pride. Just write "housewife" and simplify your life.

In the plane we were able to catch up a little on our sleep before being served an excellent breakfast. I love Air France, it's such a human airline. A sweet little Siamese cat was sitting on the broad arm between the seats, his aquamarine eyes taking in everything that went on. His mistress had a collar and leash on him but he didn't have to be kept in one of those miserable containers and could enjoy the trip like everyone else.

In Paris, dear Paris, the temperature was normal, a hostile fifty on the twenty-ninth of July, and the weather cloudy; a sorry comedown from the golden air of Egypt. We drove to the Quai d'Orléans to the apartment which our friends the Geoffrey Parsons', although vacationing in St. Tropez, had generously put at our disposal and where we were to spend the night.

After we had bathed and rested a bit, we went to lunch at the Berkeley: jellied eggs in tarragon, grilled salmon, white wine, raspberries with crème d'Isigny. That night we dined at the Bouteille d'Or, a bistro we remembered from a visit in 1951. The food was delicious. Why not? The restaurant was founded in 1630, there was no reason for it to have deteriorated in a mere eleven years. The ignominy of the meals of East Africa and Egypt fell away. We rose from the tables of France, shriven.

The next morning we boarded the plane for New York and after we had been flying awhile the captain spoke. "In a few minutes," he said, "we will be leaving the French coast." My eyes filled with tears. My love affair with the country started when I was sixteen and went there for the first time and it is not a coast I care to leave. We were looking forward to home and friends but I have always thought one of the lovely lines of the English language is "Fair stood the wind for France" and any time it wafts me toward those shores I am happy.

1. Always keep your passport up to date. Who knows when opportunity may knock?

2. Make lists. People to call before leaving home: man to take down, clean, and store curtains; man to shampoo rugs; man to restore and repair hall cabinet; head off milkman; stop papers, car dead-storage; suspend auto insurance . . .

3. Aid to packing: make a list, starting at the top of the head and going to the soles of the feet; supplies to take for the care of the person. A systematic checkup at the start of the journey will save moments of suspense later on.

4. There is a cold, uncomfortable statistic it is prudent to remember. Like building a house, travel always costs more than you estimate.

5. When estimating cost of a journey do not forget to include film and charges for developing same. It can be quite an item.

6. Pack a hobby when you go. Seeing the world per se is marvelous, but I have found that one's enjoyment is greatly enhanced if it is focused, if one has a specific interest apart from what may be called the automatic sights—museums, churches, the countryside itself.

7. Take along a small, stiff nailbrush. They are invaluable for scrubbing shirt collars and cuffs.

8. Take with you Scotch Tape, labels, and manila envelopes. They are often hard to come by. The big envelopes are in-

valuable for sending home scarves, postcards, catalogues, small guidebooks, and suchlike.

9. Let each member of the family of writing age have his own pen, to fill out the countless forms handed out by officials.

10. Keep a little American money in small bills in an inner section of your billfold. You'll need it anyway when you arrive back home, and it's always negotiable in emergencies.

11. Dark glasses and a shade hat are musts, but be sure the latter will stick with you. Take bags with handles rather than envelope variety, as you will want to keep your hands free for hanging onto things and taking pictures.

12. Wear comfortable shoes. For traipsing through museums, scaling mountains, treading a promenade deck, or clambering up the Acropolis—sneakers! In Eastern countries be sure that footwear does not have laces. You may be slipping in and out of your shoes a dozen times a day.

13. There will be delays. One can suffer sad disillusion in traveling by failing to appreciate the basic meaning of the word itself. The stem is the same as "travail," meaning toil or trouble of a painful or oppressive nature. It is also like the French verb *travailler*, "to work."

14. It will be ignored, but I offer it anyhow: rest before sightseeing. Flying is fatiguing, and one needs time to recuperate. Eventually we'll be getting to Europe in a couple of hours, to the Orient in five or six. They are still a long way from home. The machines can go that fast, but the human physique can't. Time is different, food and water unaccustomed, the pace of life one to which we must become acclimated, and if arriving in a country for the first time, the emotional tension is usually high. Rest, therefore, is advisable, unless, of course, one is so taut with excitement and curiosity that trying to take a nap is tantamount to exploding. In that case, go out. *Sortez. Herausgehen.* We're a long time dead.

15. If you're not feeling well when abroad, for heaven's sake, say so. Speak up, friends, when indisposed! Don't let your

companions worry to death, fearful that this superlative, long-anticipated great adventure is a frightful frost. Colic everyone sympathizes with and forgives, and when touring there are enough hurdles little and big to be overcome—there's enough colic, too—without superimposing avoidable misunderstandings.

16. When crossing borders, draw as little attention as possible to as few pieces of luggage as possible.

17. If on a journey you see something you long for and can afford it at all, *buy it*. If you don't you'll regret it all your life.

18. Wear cotton underwear in the Orient. Nylon is too hot and sticky.

19. In the Orient stick to gin and tonic. Scotch whisky is available but costs the eyes in your head.

20. If going to Southeast Asia in the summer don't take evening clothes unless you know in advance you will positively need them for a specific occasion. Evening life is informal —a dark, lightweight suit for a man, a cocktail dress for a woman.

21. Try to hold onto a sense of values. New impressions will be flooding in upon you, strangers will be giving you facts you cannot always check. Common sense is just as valuable on a journey as at home.

22. Do not mix sedation and drinks of even low alcoholic content.

23. Carry one or two small bottles or flasks with you. Plastic ones are the lightest, but sometimes they affect the taste of liquor, yet you will need some container in which to pour the residue from a large bottle when it is too much to leave behind and not enough to make toting the parent bottle worth while.

24. When coping with letters of introduction, make a double list. On one side the names of people to whom you are

sending the letter with a covering one of your own, on the other the names of friends at home who know them and gave the letter.

25. There are bound to be slack moments, sometimes depressing ones, so never fail to have a few books handy, including a hair-raising murder or two; they will tide you over the bad spots.

26. In London always book a table in advance for Sunday night. Not many restaurants are open, and those that are are crowded.

27. When you get home you'll be tired and excited at being there. Try hard to leave twenty-four hours for readjustment; forty-eight are preferable.

BOOKS READ BEFORE GOING TO AFRICA

African Giant by Stuart Cloete
No Room in the Ark by Alan Moorehead
Serengeti Shall Not Die by Bernhard and Michael Grzimek
The Harmless People by Elizabeth Marshall Tomas (a tale of
    the bushmen of the Kalahari Desert)
Born Free by Joy Adamson
Living Free by Joy Adamson (biographies of the engaging and
    unique lioness)
Jomo Kenyatta by George Delf
African Genesis by Robert Ardrey
Africa A to Z by Robert Kane (a guidebook)
African Kaleidoscope by Pieter Lessing
African Mirage (a book published many years ago, with beauti-
    ful photographs by Hoyningen-Huene)

BOOK READ IN AFRICA

Treetops by Eric Sherbrooke Walker

BOOKS READ ON OUR RETURN FROM AFRICA

Tom Mboya by Alan Drake
Forever Free by Joy Adamson
Survival of the Free (a symposium edited by Dr. Wolfgang
    Englehardt)
Out of Africa by Isak Dinesen
Animals in Africa (photographs by Peter and Philippa Scott)
Animals of East Africa by C. A. Spinage
Simba by C. A. W. Guggisberg
Vanishing Animals by Philip Street

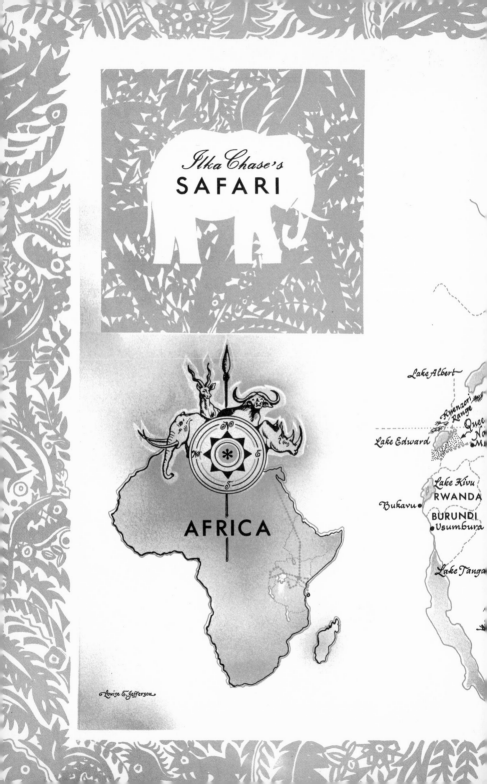

Ilka Chase's
SAFARI

AFRICA

Lake Albert

Rwenzori Range

Lake Edward

Que
No
M

Lake Kivu
RWANDA
Bukavu •
BURUNDI
• Usumbura

Lake Tanga

Louise E. Jefferson